HIGH FLYERS

ROYAL AIR FORCE MUSEUM
BRITAIN'S NATIONAL MUSEUM OF AVIATION

The Museum collects, preserves and exhibits articles and records relating to the history and tradition of the Royal Air Force, and of aviation in general. The Museum complex includes art galleries, library and archive, a cinema/lecture theatre, The Battle of Britain Experience and Bomber Command Hall.

HIGH FLYERS

30 Reminiscences to Celebrate the
75th Anniversary of the Royal Air Force

Edited by Michael Fopp
DIRECTOR
THE ROYAL AIR FORCE MUSEUM

Greenhill Books
IN ASSOCIATION WITH
The Royal Air Force
Museum

High Flyers: 30 Reminiscences to Celebrate the 75th Anniversary of the Royal Air Force first published 1993 by Greenhill Books, Lionel Leventhal Limited, Park House, 1 Russell Gardens, London NW11 9NN in association with the Royal Air Force Museum

Copyright

British Library Cataloguing in Publication Data
High Flyers: 30 Reminiscences to Celebrate the 75th Anniversary of the Royal Air Force
I. Fopp, Michael A.
358.400941

ISBN 1–85367–146–0

Library of Congress Cataloging-in-Publication Data
High Flyers: 30 reminiscences to celebrate the 75th anniversary of the Royal Air Force / edited by Michael Fopp.
p.   cm.
ISBN 1–85367–146–0
1. Great Britain.   Royal Air Force—History.   I. Fopp, Michael.
UG635.G7H48   1993
358.4'00941—dc20   92–41766
                                                CIP

Printed and bound in Great Britain by
Butler & Tanner Limited, Frome, Somerset

CONTENTS

MICHAEL FOPP

Introduction

Wᴇɴ I ᴡᴀꜱ first approached by Lionel Leventhal with the suggestion that the Royal Air Force Museum and his company, Greenhill Books, might work jointly on a book to commemorate the 75th Anniversary of the RAF, I was in two minds. There was no doubt that the Museum was keen to take part in the anniversary at all sorts of levels, but Lionel's idea was – as he put it – 'to find people who have made a mark in life after serving in the RAF'. The fact that I agreed we would join forces shows that I liked the idea; but I must now confess to having had some considerable apprehension as to whether we would ever put together anything like enough willing volunteers with the peculiar qualifications we were seeking. Nobody had done it before, so we did not know where to start and – worse still – there was no way for us to know what the response would be from those we asked to help. Were there enough people out there to make a viable book, where do we go to find them, and how do we make contact? Are they likely to respond positively, do we have any guarantee that their contributions will be adequate? All those questions remained unanswered when we agreed to go ahead with the project. All that was decided was that we would stop everything if we had not achieved a specific objective by an agreed date.

A small team at Greenhill and the Museum set about the task of tracking down potential contributors by scanning the pages of directories and reference books galore. We were a constant irritant to colleagues, friends and anyone else who might give us the name of someone famous who had once served in the RAF. I then wrote to people on the list that we had compiled and awaited their responses.

To my great delight, and some surprise, these replies came quickly and positively. Of course, there were those who could not spare the time, were out of the country, indisposed, or just too busy. One or two had to be cajoled, mainly because – as they put it – their 'careers' in the RAF had been so undistinguished. One person even refused on the grounds that he hated his time in the Service so much he did not wish to commit his memories to paper! At the same time manuscripts started coming in from some of those whose recollections follow.

What started as a germ of an idea now began to take shape for, at the earliest opportunity, it became obvious that regardless of quantity, the quality of the contributions was going to be superb. Very soon our fears over quantity would also be dashed as so many people took the time to provide recollections of their period in the Service. The process agreed between the Museum and Greenhill Books was that I would invite contributions and, because of pressures on my and my staff's time, follow-up would be undertaken by the publishers. The first few manuscripts made this simple plan inappropriate.

From the first to the last response the recollections of those that follow were riveting stuff. As each morning post arrived a queue formed to await the latest surprise, as members of the Museum staff became aware of the wealth of material that was being collected. Not only the manuscripts but also the other material supplied by the respondents engaged our curators in the work they enjoy most – reading the previously untold accounts of 'ordinary' people in the RAF. Some were generous enough to allow us to borrow their flying log books and others donated material to the Museum's collections.

Of course, those contributors who follow are far from 'ordinary' people now. All are well known and have made their mark in life. It is difficult to imagine what effect the RAF has had on their lives or to what extent their experience in the Service shaped their futures. The overwhelming bond that binds them together is their membership of one of the finest fighting services in the world. Most of them served on a relatively low rung of the seniority ladder which, in itself, gives the reader a different insight into life in the RAF. All have resolutely climbed the ladder of life to a high level and in so doing are well known by the public today. It is a testament to our armed services as a whole that these famous people come from such a variety of spheres today. The entertainment industry provides us with some of the most amusing contributions which is only to be expected; politicians of a variety of 'colours' have a common love of flying in these pages; lawyers, scientists, diplomats, authors, actors, industrialists, poets, sportsmen, cartoonists, hostages and broadcasters – all are represented here. It is this wide mix of personalities with their roots entwined in a common regard for the Royal Air Force which makes this book special.

The content of this book is arranged in alphabetical order by the author. There is, however, one very special exception. Cecil Lewis's lyrical contribution precedes the other reminiscences as befits its evocation of the very founding of the Royal Air Force and his experiences in the Royal Flying Corps. Cecil Lewis, author of the classic World War One memoir *Sagittarius Rising*, celebrates his 95th birthday a few days before the Royal Air Force celebrates its 75th.

This is a unique publishing achievement which could only have been made possible by the generosity of those contributors who follow. Commercially this book could never have been produced; it is because the RAF and its Museum have a place in the hearts of so many that we have been able to put together these recollections.

A special feature of this book is the presentation of autograph greetings from contributors. This echoes the wartime blackboards in messes and pubs.

We have in the Museum the blackout screen from the White Hart, Brasted on which pilots from nearby Biggin Hill signed their names; it is good of contributors to 'sign in' and follow that tradition in this special anniversary book.

I feel very proud to have been personally associated with this book and to have made contact with so many interesting people. Even those who were unable to contribute were unfailingly courteous and expressed their congratulations and best wishes to the Royal Air Force on its 75th Anniversary.

I am sure this book will add a unique dimension to the celebrations in the anniversary year and a splendid read for years to come. It is first and foremost a tribute to all those 'ordinary' people who served – I thank them all.

Best wishes to
all "D" Day Dodgers,

Merlyn - Rees

Nil Carburundum
Illegitimi'
Tony Benn
AC 2 1850035

Patriachal Greetings!
from one who lived thise
early days!
Cecil Parrs

Greetings & good wishes to all who have flown H.S. & MSV & their modern successors

Bernard Lovell

Having experience of all three services, I am well qualified to decide which is the best. This, however, is what I refuse to do.

C. Northcote Parkinson

In an open cockpit or a parachute at 700 feet all things are possible, and at times, absurd.

Best Ariel Wishes

William Franklyn

To those early heroes of the RAF,
who were the inspiration to all those
of us who tried to follow in your
footsteps; Many thanks!

Jim Goodson.
416 Sqdn. RCAF
43 Sqdn. RAF
133 (Eagle) Sqdn. RAF.
4th FIGHTER GP. U.S.A.A.F.

To everybody from 604.
The spirit still flies.

Martin Woodhall.

To
The long and the short and the tall —
now no doubt the stooped
and the plump and the bald!

Frederick Forsyth

To the Service
it was an honour
and pleasure to serve

Buckton

Many happy returns !!

Jackie Mann

PPORTUNITY
Heather Green Knocks

to those who had a
more serious time of it
— my respects

Gavin Lyall

The first 75 years are the worst.
Press on to the next 75.

Kenneth Wolstenholme

"Si Vis Pacem Para Bellum"

Tebbit
of Chingford + 604 Sqdn.

I, in all truth did so
little for my Country I'm
not quite sure I should
be in this book. but in
I am, and MOST PROUD
to be so.
            All good wishes

Michael Aspel

DAVID LANGDON

'Happy Anniversary'

Congratulations to the RAF on
75 splendid years of service
to the free world.

Reg Hunt

I'm flattered to be asked to
contribute to this book. After all,
I hardly merit inclusion!

With my best wishes
for a successful addition
to the list of best selling
books.

[signature]

With best wishes

[signature]

Let us not forget
those who did not survive
to contribute to this
book.

Peter Cadbury.

Press on Regardless!

Raymund Baxter

With all good wishes to the Museum
for its future.

George S Waller

With all good wishes.

R.V. Jones.

PERUDUA AD ASTRA

FROM A GREAT HEIGHT.

Michael Bentine

ACKNOWLEDGEMENTS

A N IMMENSE amount of work is necessary in the production of any book but, when there are 30 authors the work is necessarily increased proportionally. It is therefore my pleasure to draw attention to the people who have had a part to play in bringing this book to its successful publication, co-ordinating the individual contributors, the photographs and cartoons, and contributors to the blackboard.

RAF Museum staff who worked on the book include Peter Elliott, Keeper of Research and Information Services, who coordinated the project, particularly the master list of possible contributors. Vanessa Payton, my personal assistant, played a major role in collating the responses and keeping the Museum's work on track. Norman Franks cast an independent expert's eye on the draft manuscript on behalf of the Publisher, whose editorial team included Amy Myers.

Finally, my thanks to Lionel Leventhal who conceived the idea in the first place and then worked tirelessly to keep us all on schedule to meet a publication date which coincided with the anniversary. Would that all publishers stuck to schedule so tenaciously.

M.F.

THE CONTRIBUTORS

ALLISS, PETER: Served his National Service with the Royal Air Force Regiment between 1949 and 1951, spending his time in England at Catterick, and then Watchet, a small camp on the Somerset coast, where one of his contemporaries was Gordon Pirie. Already a keen golfer, Peter Alliss had become a Professional in 1946 at the age of fifteen, and a Ryder Cup player. Today a well known golf and television presenter with a number of golf books to his credit as well.

BAXTER, RAYMOND: Well known for his radio and television commentating on flying events such as the Farnborough and Biggin Hill Air Shows, he joined the RAF in 1940 shortly before his eighteenth birthday. Achieved his wish to fly fighters and served with Nos. 65, 93 and 602 Squadrons, from England, over the Mediterranean and later in Europe with the 2nd Tactical Air Force, flying Spitfires, being Mentioned in Despatches for gallantry. Began broadcasting with Forces Broadcasting while still with the RAF, later becoming a successful commentator with the BBC TV Outside Broadcasts at both flying and motoring events as well as in such programmes as *Tomorrow's World*.

BENN, RT HON TONY: Known for his political views within the ranks of the Labour Party, with which he has served as an MP from 1950 to 1960, 1963–83, and since 1984 for Chesterfield. His father was a flyer in World War I, winning the DSO and DFC, later to become Viscount Stansgate. His brother Michael was a night fighter pilot, and won the DFC before being killed in a plane crash in 1944. At eighteen, Tony Benn joined the RAFVR, gained his 'wings' just before the end of the war, and shortly afterwards transferred to the Fleet Air Arm. Succeeding to the title upon the death of his father in 1960, he later disclaimed it for life and pursued his political career, not only in parliament, but in writing and on television.

BENTINE, MICHAEL: Famous for his often off-beat humour, in World War II he had difficulty in joining the RAF as he had been born of a Peruvian father, even though his mother was British and Michael himself had been born in Watford. Finally joining the Service, he became an Intelligence officer, firstly with No. 300 (Polish) Squadron, then with 12 Squadron at RAF Wickenby during the winter of 1943–44. In the summer of 1944 he served with 350 (Belgian) Spitfire Squadron, before serving on the Continent with two Typhoon wings in 83 Group. After the war he gained fame on radio, especially as part of the early Goon Shows, by his frequent appearances on television and from his books.

BOND, MICHAEL: Born in February 1926, he joined the RAF in November 1943 with hopes of becoming aircrew but transferred to the army in February 1945. A BBC TV cameraman between 1947 and 1966, after which he became a full-time author, famous for his Paddington Bear books, which he had started in the late 1950s, and which were later adapted for children's television.

CADBURY, PETER: The son of a famous WWI Naval aviator, he was born in Yarmouth in February 1918 and educated at Cambridge (MA 1939). Flew with the Fleet Air Arm until transferred to test pilot duties with MAP in 1942. After the war he was called to the Bar, Inner Temple, practising between 1946 and 1954. Pursued various business interests, including Keith Prowse Group, Westward TV, Air Westward, Air Pegasus, Director of ITN Ltd, and currently Chairman of Preston Publications.

FORSYTH, FREDERICK: Born in August 1938 at Ashford, Kent, he attended Tonbridge School. Joined the RAF in May 1956, having obtained a flying scholarship while still at school. Trained to be a pilot, he gained his 'wings' in April 1958, shortly before completing his National Service. He joined a local newspaper, then Reuters. Now a famous author of such works as *Day of the Jackal* and *The Odessa File*.

FRANKLYN, WILLIAM: Born in London, September 1926. First appeared in a play at the Savoy Theatre at the age of 15 and after the war, continued as an actor. Has appeared in more than 50 films and has acted in or directed numerous stage plays, and is well known for his TV work. His voice too is familiar to many, as a voice-over in TV commercials, one long running commercial being a nine year period with Schweppes.

GOODSON, JAMES A.: Born in New York and educated at Toronto University as well as Harvard Business School. Was returning to the US from Europe on the SS *Athenia* in September 1939 when it was torpedoed. Surviving this, he joined the RAF, trained in Canada and the UK, and in June 1942 went to No. 416 RCAF Squadron as a sergeant pilot. Transferred to the USAAF in September 1942, he was briefly with 133 Eagle Squadron just as it became part of the US 4th Fighter Group, 8th Air Force, where he became one of their leading aces. Awarded the American DSC and DFC with eight clusters, Air Medal and Purple Heart, among other decorations. Operated as a fighter pilot until July 1944 when brought down by ground fire, ending the war as a prisoner. Post-war he held a number of top executive positions, with such companies as Goodyear and Hoover and was then vice president and group executive of ITT until his retirement.

GREEN, HUGHIE: At 23, having already worked in theatre, films and radio in both the US and the UK, Hughie Green became a Catalina pilot, flying operations over the Atlantic. He joined the RCAF at the end of 1941 and 18 months later was operational with No. 117 Squadron RCAF, from Nova Scotia. Tour-expired, he then became a pilot with No. 45 Group RAF Ferry Command, taking all manner of aircraft to all parts of the globe, even taking Catalinas to Russia, which were adventures in themselves. Discharged in October 1945, he returned to the world of entertainment, becoming a well known and well loved TV and radio presenter, especially with the show *Opportunity Knocks*.

HUNT, SIR REX: Born in June 1926 he joined the RAF in 1944 and after gaining his RAF 'wings' was sent to India where he joined No. 5 Squadron, flying Tempests during 1946–47. He then served in Germany with No. 26 Squadron, leaving the service in 1948. Between then and mid-1952 he was a Reserve Officer (RAFO), initially with the Oxford University Air Squadron, with the rank of flight lieutenant. Entered HM Overseas Civil Service in 1951, his posts including appointments in Uganda, Kuching, Brunei, Ankara, Jakarta, Saigon and Malaya (CMG). Before he retired, he was the Governor of the Falkland Islands between 1980 and 1985, at the time of the Falklands War. Hon. Air Commodore, No. 2729 (City of Lincoln) Royal Auxiliary Air Force from 1987; knighted in 1982.

JONES, REGINALD VICTOR: Born in September 1911 and educated at Oxford. Scientific officer at Air Ministry, 1936, and Air Staff, 1939, to look into German applications of science to air warfare. This was the start of scientific intelligence, which resulted in the discovery in 1940 of the Luftwaffe's system of radio beams for night bombing. He became Assistant Director of Intelligence and Science in 1941 and later Director of Intelligence (Research), Director of Scientific Intelligence 1952–53 at MoD. Best-selling book *Most Secret War,* 1978. Professor of Natural Philosophy, University of Aberdeen 1946–81, now Emeritus. Created CB 1946, CBE 1942, and became an FRS in 1965.

LANGDON, DAVID: After valiant service with the London Rescue Service between 1939 and 1941, joined the RAF and became an Intelligence officer, leaving the service in 1946 as a squadron leader. Through his ability as a cartoonist, he worked with the *RAF Journal* and the RAF's PR Department, P9. Post war he became well known as a professional cartoonist, with regular contributions to *Punch,* the *New Yorker* and *Sunday Mirror.* Made an OBE in 1988.

LEWIS, CECIL: Born in Birkenhead on 29 March 1898, he joined the Royal Flying Corps in 1915; he was twice Mentioned in Despatches and awarded the Military Cross. Postwar, he went into civil aviation, then became one of the four founders of the BBC. A career in broadcasting and writing followed, including an Academy Award for his film adaptation of Shaw's *Pygmalion.* In the Second World War he returned to the RAF, afterwards returning to the world of televison and writing. Author of the best-selling memoir of the RFC, *Sagittarius Rising.*

LOVELL, SIR BERNARD: A lecturer in physics at Manchester University when World War II began, he served with the Telecommunication Research Establishment 1939–45, which brought him into contact with many prominent men in the field of physics and radar. He helped develop airborne radar for use in Fighter, Bomber and Coastal Command aeroplanes, advising both commanders and war leaders on its uses and functions, and was awarded the OBE in 1946. Continued as a lecturer after the war (FRS 1955), and became well known for his work at Jodrell Bank, where he became director. He was knighted for his services in 1961.

LYALL, GAVIN: Born in May 1932, and educated at Cambridge (MA), then served with the RAF between 1951 and 1953 on National Service. Commissioned and gained RAF 'wings'. Worked as a journalist, writing for a number of publications, including *Picture Post* and the *Sunday Times,* before becoming a novelist. Has written more than a dozen thrillers, many with a flying theme.

MANN, JACK (JACKIE MANN): Born Northampton, in June 1914, and joined the RAFVR in April 1938 whilst an apprentice with Phillips and Powys Aircraft Co. Became a Spitfire pilot in time for the Battle of Britain, during which he shot down four Me109 fighters and was wounded twice in the air and once on the ground. Claimed a fifth 109 in 1941 but was shot down and burned in April; awarded the DFM. Became a member of the famous Guinea Pig Club at East Grinstead. After recovery he remained in the RAF till the end of the war, then became a civil pilot. Taken as a hostage in Beirut in May 1989 and was released in September 1991. Made a CBE that December.

MERLYN-REES, LORD: Born Cilfynydd, South Wales, in December 1920, completing his education at London University and joining the University of Nottingham Air Squadron. Served in the RAF between 1941 and 1946 as an operations officer in both UK and later Italy, attaining the rank of squadron leader. Teacher at Harrow Weald Grammar School until 1960 after which he became an MP. Held various senior posts, including Parliamentary Under Secretary-of-State for Defence for the RAF, between 1966 and 1968, Secretary of State for Northern Ireland 1974–76, and Home Secretary 1976–79. Became Privy Councillor in 1974 and MP for Morley and Leeds South in 1983. Created a peer in 1992.

MICHELMORE, CLIFF: Became a Halton Apprentice *Brat* in 1935, at the age of sixteen, and three years later was posted to 12 Squadron RAF. Sent to France in 1939 he witnessed the heroism of men in underpowered, underarmed bombers hurled against the enemy's blitzkrieg. Later served with HQ No. 93 Group, Bomber Command and at the Air Ministry, retiring from the Engineering Branch as a squadron leader in 1947. Today, well known as a radio and TV presenter, married to another familiar name in broadcasting, Jean Metcalfe. Made a CBE in 1969.

PARKINSON, CYRIL NORTHCOTE: Born in July 1909, educated at Cambridge and King's College, London. Master at RNC Dartmouth 1939, then commissioned as captain, Queen's Royal Regiment in 1940. Attached to RAF 1942–43, later GSO2 at the War Office as a major. Author of many books including *Parkinson's Law,* historian and journalist, and since 1970, Professor Emeritus and Hon President of Troy State University, Alabama. Contributes to the *Encyclopaedia Britannica* and a number of newspapers, including the *Economist, Guardian, New York Times* and, formerly, *Punch.*

RAYNER, LORD (DEREK GEORGE RAYNER): Born in March 1926, he did his National Service with the RAF between 1946 and 1948, in the RAF Regiment. Joined Marks and Spencer in 1953, became a Director in 1967, then Chief Executive between 1983–88. He was a special advisor to HM Government in 1970, Chief Executive of the Procurement Executive at the MoD 1971–72, and advisor to the Prime Minister on improving efficiency and eliminating waste in Government, 1979 to 1983. Created a life peer in 1983.

RIX, LORD (BRIAN RIX): Coming to fame for his comedy acting at the Whitehall

Theatre in London, he began as a stage actor in 1942, before being called up in 1944. After he joined the RAF, a question of fitness put him temporarily into the coalmines with the Bevin Boys. He became a medical orderly at RAF Cosford, then an instructor, then a corporal in charge of medical postings. Returning to acting upon demob in late 1945, he set up a theatre company in 1948 and by 1950 was working at the Whitehall. Known also for his charitable work as secretary-general of Mencap (Royal Society for Mentally Handicapped Children and Adults), he was awarded the CBE in 1977, knighted in 1986. Created a peer in 1992.

SMITH, IAN: Born Rhodesia (now Zimbabwe), on 8 April 1919, he joined the Royal Air Force from Rhodes University in 1939, serving as a fighter pilot in the Middle East, Corsica/Italy and with 2nd TAF in Europe. Later took up farming and politics, which eventually took him to serve as Prime Minister of Rhodesia, 1964–79, during which time he delivered Rhodesia's Unilateral Declaration of Independence during Harold Wilson's Labour government. Presently an MP in Zimbabwe, General Commander, Order of the Legion of Merit of Rhodesia, 1979, Independence Decoration (Rhodesia), 1970.

SUTTON, DUDLEY: Born April 1933 in East Molesey, Surrey, he joined the RAF in 1951. After his RAF service he trained at the Royal Academy of Dramatic Art in London, and went on to act in numerous stage plays and films including, most recently, Derek Jarman's *Caravaggio* and *Edward II*. His career has also involved many productions for television, and he is well known in the role of 'Tinker' in the BBC series *Lovejoy* – the first time he has worn a beret since his days in the RAF.

TEBBIT, LORD (NORMAN TEBBIT): Born 29 March 1931, and embarked on a career in journalism before joining the RAF as a national serviceman in June 1949. Trained as a pilot, and in 1951 served in the Reserve with the RAuxAF. Civil Airline pilot 1953–70. Became an MP in 1974 and has held a number of senior parliamentary positions, as well as being chairman of the Conservative Party between 1985 and 1987. Now a company director, and co-presenter with Sky TV. Companion of Honour in 1987. Created a peer in 1992.

TOMLINSON, DAVID: Born in May 1917, he was educated at Tonbridge School, served with the Grenadier Guards from 1935–6 then in World War II as a flight lieutenant pilot with the RAF. Postwar he returned to the world of entertainment (his first film had been released in 1939) and has become a well known stage and film actor, appearing in over 50 films and many stage successes.
David Tomlinson's contribution to this anthology is taken from his autobiography published by Hodder and Stoughton.

WALLER, RT HON SIR GEORGE: Called to the Bar in 1934, he joined the RAFO in 1931; when war came, he joined the RAF, serving a tour as a pilot with Coastal Command during the Battle of the Atlantic. In 1942 he was a staff officer at 19 Group HQ and by the following year was a wing commander at Coastal Command HQ, being number two in the Training Branch. Was made an OBE in 1945. Returning to law in September 1945, he became a Judge of the High Court in 1965. From 1976 to 1984 was a Lord Justice of Appeal.

WOLSTENHOLME, KENNETH: Joined the RAFVR in 1938 when he was eighteen, trained as a pilot, then flew light bombers with 2 Group RAF. Operating with 107 Squadron in near suicidal ops in Blenheims, he later became a Mosquito Pathfinder pilot with 105 Squadron of No. 8 PFF Group. Completed 100 operational sorties and won the DFC and bar. After the war made a career in journalism, broadcasting and became well known as a sports commentator on both radio and television.

WOOLLARD, WILLIAM: Born in London, August 1939, he entered the RAF after Oxford. He then worked in Social Science before joining the BBC, producing and then presenting TV films and programmes, including the popular *Tomorrow's World* and *Top Gear.* Now runs his own production company.

ZUCKERMAN, LORD (SOLLY ZUCKERMAN): Born in Cape Town in 1904, he was a lecturer at Oxford in 1939, when asked to become an advisor to the Research and Development Department of the Ministry of Home Security (FRS, in 1943). Later became Scientific Advisor to Combined Operations HQ, Allied Expeditionary Force and then Supreme Headquarters, AEF. Performed his duties with the honorary rank of group captain both in the UK and in the Middle East. Knighted in 1956 he became a life peer in 1971. He had received the KCB in 1964 and the Order of Merit in 1968. Became President of the British Industrial Biological Research Association in 1974.

LIST OF ILLUSTRATIONS

Cartoons by David Langdon.

1

CECIL LEWIS

At the Beginning

CELEBRATION IS a jubilant word and the right one to mark the foundation of the Royal Air Force in 1918, older brother of the Royal Flying Corps (all but forgotten now except to the few who still remain) which had itself been hived off from the Army six years before.

But how to celebrate the beginning of such things, the feel of those earliest days when just to 'take off' was a marvel and a mystery, and we who did it wore the paper crown of heroes?

Today it is a sort of secret, unique to all who flew the undiscovered air and now it whispers to us like the echo in a singing glass, evoking the memory of ... a ritual, almost forgotten ...

Back before dawn in the gloom of old Bessonneau hangars, mythical creatures are stabled. Stabled under roofs of dark brown canvas, flapping heavy in the dawn, roofs sloping crazily from iron poles held by ropes and tent-pegs tugging at the sullen grass. Stabled there like ghostly spirits haunting the damp without life or seemingly the remotest hope of motion, crouch awkward creatures, knocked up by children imitating insects, bits of linen, twisted wires, bicycle wheels, all sweating out the rancid breath of castor oil.

Along the hedge a row of these drab tentings stable each a pair of man-made miracles, the latest wonder of the age, an aeroplane. Around them young lads, like stable boys, are readying them for action, wheeling them out into the sunrise air. Lifting their tails high on their shoulders and slowly, carefully, pushing them out, so slim, so weightless – can this home-made toy of spruce and linen lift two young gods three miles high up into the infinite blue? – pushing them out so easily, tenderly, white wings swaying over the uneven grass, shiny cowlings catching the morning sun, to set them down in a line ready for the day's work.

Now the lads stand idle, worshiping their gawky dragons. Until late the night before they have been cosseting them by lantern light, trueing up fuselages, laboriously tightening turnbuckles, anxiously setting and re-setting tappets, polishing copper intake pipes, attending to their thousand and one imperious demands and needs. It is their pride and duty that these young strutters should be perfect in every detail, ready for the heroes who will whirl them away into the dawn.

Remember now! Recall those fearful days. Horizon haze hiding the battlefield. At hand French farmland, rolling, rich and easy, hedges of scented hawthorn, poplars lining the roads, river smells, a huge pale sky – but, under it, the dull thud thudding of ten thousand guns.

Romantic? Now, but not then. Then the dizzy catchbreath of expectancy, the wonder and the challenge of the days. What is coming? What awaits us? What is it fills the air? It is something escaping words, the dancing thrill of being alive, there, at that moment, the tumbril in the blood, life on a knife-edge, lived on the lip of nothing.

We are no gods, we young men of those days. Only the past gilds us in the eye of those who follow, gilds the stark simplicity of lonely death, gilds us with hero-gallantry and magic skill.

In life we are a scruffy casual lot. Fur-lined boots reach up almost to our thighs. Worn, tatty leather jackets flap about us as we walk. Fur-lined helmets, goggles and gauntlet gloves complete the shabby silhouette. So, strolling thoughtless, everyday, taking all adulation as routine, we shuffle over to our mounts, swing a leg over the cockpit and drop into our seats, turn on the petrol, set the altimeter and we are ready for take-off.

But not quite. First another ritual. Tension rises now. A hundred horse-power jerked into life by a pair of strong young arms. The pilot stretches for the switch, outside, screwed to the body, in reach of his left hand and clearly visible. Mind. Down for OFF, up for ON. Careful. Make no mistake. A backfire can decapitate a man.

'Switch off. Petrol on. Suck in.'

Slowly the big heavy blades are pulled round backwards, priming the cylinders. Satisfied, the boy settles one blade high above his head and reaches up for it.

'Contact!' he calls.

Flipping the switch up, 'Contact!' the pilot echoes.

With all his strength the boy heaves on the blade, pulling it down. With luck – for it does not always happen – the engine catches with a roar and cloud of blue smoke. The pilot throttles back, runs it for a little to warm it up, then opens up testing his mags, and throttles down again.

Now this home-made toy, this gawky Pegasus, begins to pant hot breath and trembles, trembles all over with suppressed desire, trembles to be free, eager to be off, shakes with frustration, pawing against the chocks that hold the wheels, demanding to show his strength, his power, his speed. It is a moment full of wonder, never to be forgotten, the end of all earthbound waiting and the way to heaven!

The pilot waves his arm from side to side. Chocks are pulled from wheels, an impatient run across the grass to face the wind, the engine opens up –

And then!

A blur of grass, a rush of wind and Earth is gone! We are rising. Rising above the map-flat plate of Earth, up, up, up, into the everlasting emptiness of God! And, sitting there, holding my breath, hardly daring to believe, it is I who am here, master of power and speed and movement, I alone, lord of my purring Pegasus! The lightest touch, left, right, up, down. He swings, soars, sweeps, servant to my command, and free! Free of all bounds, all limitations, vouchsafed the miracle of liberty, sent forth a newborn god, a child, to bounce about the blue, turn somersaults in sapphire . . .

We did not often have much time or opportunity to indulge these heady arabesques. The daily two-hour stints above the front line Somme (at 500 feet) had the knack of marvellously concentrating the attention. It was a game to guess how many shots could puncture a machine without affecting it. Twenty to fifty was the usual count (the rigger carefully patching each with a neat square of irish linen, pasted on). Shots came up through the floor, knocked the joystick out of the hand, but never (hardly ever) the one that cut the vital wires.

So, oblivious of the risks, we drifted there above it all, free of the horror, noting impartially the daily, dreary, deadly, drawn-out dance of death – and somehow uninvolved. Indeed I write it now with pain, remorse: it touched us not at all. We were anaesthetized. Better so. Could we have faced it, witness to mass murder, done our jobs? No. We turned away, lit a cigarette, shrugged it all off. 'The old Hun's fairly going through it.' Don't look. Don't see what you are seeing. Carry on.

Such was our daily flying in those 1916 days until the odd machine gun bullet or a passing shell brought down some luckless lad – another three-week hero, unknown, unsung, who died for King and Country.

2

PETER ALLISS

'I've Become a Gunner'

As IT happened, my great friend Guy Wolstenholme joined the RAF on the same day as I did; in fact he was only three or four ahead of me in the queue. We both signed our names on the dreaded paper and met. 'Well, where are we off to?' he said. 'I've become a gunner,' said I. 'You've become what?' 'A gunner.' Well, he likened the RAF Regiment (with his limited knowledge) to a cross between the convicts sent to Australia in the last century and the pioneer corps. I liked to think of them something akin to the SAS and Marine Commandos – but that's another story! Suffice to say, he went off to Cranwell, became a wireless operator and played golf four days a week. I went off to West Kirby on the Wirral and was introduced to the delights of squarebashing by a French Canadian NCO who frightened the life out of everybody. But somehow we got through it all. I think we were up at 3 a.m. on the first morning of official business; how on earth we were going to get the toe caps on the boots to shine like a mirror was totally beyond me. How we were going to learn to fold the blankets and sheets was another mystery that amazingly unfolded fairly smartly! Then after all the to-ing and fro-ing and bashing about we all clubbed together and bought the dreaded corporal a going-away present!

I was then sent on a small arms course at RAF Training Depot at Catterick. Ah, Catterick, nestling on the A1 north of Leeds – I remember it well. Father had been the professional at the Temple Newsam Golf Club for a few years before the war and my brother had gone to Roundhay School, a well-known teaching establishment in the Great City of Leeds. I thought at last I will be able to have a game of golf and I did manage one or two but it was still a battle. It was now October 1949 and October/November can be damned cold if you're wading through the river Swale with some idiot lobbing thunderflashes into the water just to give you an idea of what it would be like if you were under combat conditions. I did quite well and was asked if I would like to stay and take an NCO's course. But, I had had enough of Warrant Officer Danny Gordi. He was, in his own way, wonderful but as it was now coming up to Christmas I resisted the temptation and waited for a posting.

There were one or two skirmishes going on overseas and it was nip and tuck whether I might be posted to the Middle East, Germany, or out to Malaysia. Well, none of those came along. I was, at the end of the day, sent to RAF Watchet on the north coast of Somerset just east of Minehead. There were only about twenty-five or thirty permanent staff; it was a training centre for Anti-Aircraft gunners who came in for a six to eight week course and then moved on to greener pastures. It was here I met Flight Sergeant Denver-Fedder, a huge barrel-chested man who'd been fighting in Aden; what stories he had to tell. I also met Gordon Pirie, known then as Douglas. He was being hailed as one of the most promising athletes England had ever produced. He certainly did train a lot and on many occasions I used to accompany him... yes, I know you may find that hard to believe but accompany him I did! How well I remember jogging out of camp... then, out of sight some 100 yards around the corner, I would duck behind a friendly haystack and wait for Gordon (Douglas) to return. He'd do about 12 miles, I'd do about 600 yards! We'd jog back in through the gates with the guards looking on absolutely amazed that Alliss could be in such pristine condition and Pirie, if not on the verge of exhaustion, certainly looking as if he'd sweated up a bit. They never found out.

It was here I thought my luck had changed. The CO was a flight lieutenant (you could see it was a small camp) and a golf fanatic. He'd heard of my golfing reputation and off we went to play golf at Minehead. He intimated we would get three or four games a week, and when there were no customers in he saw no reason why we shouldn't, if weather permitted and we felt so inclined, go most days! He lasted a week. He was posted to some far-flung corner of the Empire and the next CO was a rugby fanatic who thought anyone who even picked up a golf club was a 'poof'. Thank goodness my brother was the professional at the Weston-super-mare Club only 40 or 50 miles away and by hook or by crook I managed to get there once a month for a bit of golf and to learn the delights of one or two local maidens!

The camp dispatch rider was one Bill Harris, a mad Brummy, who fancied himself as one of the world's great archers. He'd been brought up on a diet of Robin Hood books and was a devoted fan of Errol Flynn. He did the most alarming things with a bow and arrow. Once he loosed off a bolt down the length of the billet and just as the bolt was about to touch the target, the door opened, and the bolt just missed the orderly officer who I think had had a couple of 'Vera Lynns' and failed to notice his near demise!

The village of Watchet was great fun. How often we used to go to the London Inn and have a pint or two. Bill Gates was the corporal in charge of transport, and Bill Beaumont from Sheffield got married to a local girl in the village. We celebrated for goodness knows how long – was it days, weeks or months? It was in many ways a wonderful learning period and although I can look back and say it was wasted as far as a professional golfer's life was concerned, it wasn't as far as learning about life. Then, with six weeks left, another crisis loomed and another six months were put on our time. Would we be posted at the end of the day? No, we were left to wheel out the Bofors guns and wait for the old Anson plane to pull the drogue across the bay to let these new up and coming lads fire away in the vain hope they would hit it. I'm not sure they ever did in the eighteen months I was there; perhaps once or twice but it was not a regular occurrence.

Eventually, my time came to leave and suddenly I was quite sad getting my stuff together and collecting my railway pass. In those days trains ran everywhere. I got on at Watchet, on to Crewkerne, changing at Bridport, changing at Dorchester and then getting the final train to Bournemouth Central where my brother picked me up. It was 15th June 1951. It was the final day of the Festival of Britain Golf Tournament which was being played at the Queen's Park Golf Club in Bournemouth and brother Alec asked if I'd like to see the final stages of the Event. I said yes I would. We parked the car and went up onto the veranda of the old club house which is now no longer, looked down on the eighteenth green, which is now a roundabout on the Bournemouth ring road, and saw Peter Thomson, the great Australian, just finishing up. At that moment with the crowds round and my swing rusty I knew that golf would for ever be my life.

3

RAYMOND BAXTER

First Flights

THE DIFFERENCE between a modern fighting aeroplane and its counterpart of fifty years ago is that between chalk and cheese. Even the quantum leap between the Gladiator at the outbreak of World War II and the Meteor at its end is dwarfed by that between the RAF's first operational jet and the contemporary Tornado.

Yet one critical factor remains unchanged. The front-line pilot flying with the Royal Air Force today enjoys the same human capabilities and characteristics as his father and grandfather before him. And having had the good fortune to fly on more than one occasion with the Red Arrows and enjoy their company on the ground, I know that they, and other squadron pilots with whom I have flown, are precisely the same kind of chap as those with whom I flew Spitfires in a bygone age. To my taste they are the salt of the earth.

But here again there is a difference. Neither my son nor my grandson can remember his first flight. I do not mean first solo or even first touch of the controls. I mean the first time they got into an aeroplane and left the ground. This is scarcely surprising. My son was two years old at the time and, to be strictly accurate, my grandson had yet to be born.

Of course there is nothing remarkable about that. It is probably true of the vast majority of pilots flying today. And so it occurs to me that those of us who flew in the Second World War were the last generation for whom one's 'first ride in an aeroplane' was unforgettable.

For me, that is certainly the case. For as long as I can remember I have been in love with aeroplanes. A favourite uncle, with whom I was spending a weekend, took me as a very little boy to Croydon Aerodrome. It must have been in the late '20s. London's airport, together with the Lyceum Pantomime, were the most exciting things that had ever happened to me. It was dusk when we arrived and to this day I can see the silhouettes of the great biplane airliners trundling across the grass towards the control towers to disembark their elegant passengers, while men in smart blue uniforms saluted. The very name Imperial Airways made my tummy tingle inexplicably.

One of the major traumatic experiences of my childhood was missing the school excursion to the Hendon Air Display of 1932. I was rushed to hospital with appendicitis and nearly died of disappointment.

33

Later, as thirteen-year-olds, my best friend and I cycled from my paternal grandmother's birthplace, the Essex village of Little Chesterford, to the RAF airfield at Duxford. There we watched spellbound the beautiful Gauntlets and Gladiators, and secretly I knew that what I wanted most in the world was to fly aeroplanes like that.

My father was a man of remarkable perception and from him I learned as early as 1936 that another war with Germany was inevitable. In that year Alan Cobham's Flying Circus came to Fairlop, a disused First World War airfield some ten miles from our home. I took a ten shilling note and six pence from my money box and, without a word to anyone, cycled off alone to meet my destiny.

'You're sixteen of course, aren't you, lad?' said the man in the pay-box.

'Yes sir,' I lied, as I handed him nearly three months' pocket-money.

The ten or fifteen minutes which followed could have been as many years or seconds. They have assumed the dream-like quality of a great symphony. I remember looking down vertically at the earth below. Did the god-like figure in the leather flying coat and helmet loop me on my first flight? I shall never know.

As we skimmed over the hedge to land – so unbelievably fast and so close to the ground – I remember thinking: 'Can I really make myself clever and brave enough to do this?'

I cycled home still in my dream and, in response to my parent's casual enquiry, 'And where have you been, may I ask?' I said, 'I've been flying, Father. And when the war comes that's what I'm going to do.' He turned away for a moment, and then he put his arm across my shoulders and he said, 'Then I can only wish you luck, my son – but I hope to Heaven you may never have to do it.' At that moment I am sure he knew, and I knew, that I would.

So, at seventeen-and-three-quarters, as soon as I was old enough, I signed the forms and in due course achieved my ultimate ambition – not merely to become a pilot, but to become a fighter pilot, although not in time for the Battle of Britain.

Needless to say, there were other memorable 'firsts' which stand like milestones along that self-appointed path. My first solo, for example, took me totally by surprise. I had only 5 hours 41 minutes in my log-book when my instructor astonished me by climbing out of his cockpit at the completion of what I had considered by no means my 'best-ever' landing. Above the noise of the still running engine, he shouted at me to remember the change of trim and rate of climb with only one person aboard, told me to do one landing and taxi in, and, almost as an after-thought, stuck up a thumb to wish me luck. I am still proud that I was the first of my course to solo, although others of my contemporaries went on to achieve far greater distinction.

Any Spitfire pilot will never, I am sure, forget his first experience of R. J. Mitchell's masterpiece. It was not only the airframe which constituted the challenge, it was also the engine, the aptly named and legendary Rolls-Royce Merlin.

34

It was for the would-be fighter pilot a milestone of his experience; the culmination of a boyhood dream; the reward of months of demanding training – inadequate though that may appear by contemporary standards. It was also the final test. This was the aeroplane on which he must graduate in order to join a squadron, or suffer the humiliation of assignment to what seemed to him a lesser role. And if today those words read like *Boys' Own Paper* jingoism, those were my feelings at the time, and they were shared unanimously by those about me.

The Great Day dawned very soon after arrival at an OTU (Operational Training Unit), the last phase of formal preparation for being shot at. Here even the instructors were different. Almost all had at least one tour of operations behind them, and were officially 'on rest', most of them impatient to rejoin the fray. Much later, when I too became one of them, and shared with three others the final three weeks of training course after course of fledglings, I enjoyed just about the happiest six months of my life. All the fun of operational flying and the responsibility of leadership without having the enemy around.

For virtually all of us, our initial experience of a Merlin was the most powerful engine we had encountered. I had come from an AFU (Advanced Flying Unit) equipped with Miles Masters, the all wooden two-seat trainer powered by Rolls-Royce Kestrels or Bristol or Pratt & Whitney radials. It was a short course of a mere 17 hours, but its climax and final sortie was to fly a Hurricane. In fact the syllabus required one overshoot and two observed landings 'to approved standard'. This could be achieved in one sortie if one was lucky enough to get it right. The problem was that not only was the fledgling fighter pilot presented with his first experience of 1,000 hp, but it was an airframe of which he was totally ignorant, except in theory. He had to do it all by himself from scratch without the luxury of the dual instruction which had accompanied his introduction to every previous aircraft in his log-book.

So, duly strapped into the unfamiliar Hurricane cockpit, as soon as one had the thing 'fired up', it became immediately apparent that here was something very different indeed. What to do, of course, was not sit there thinking about it but get on with the job as smoothly and quickly as possible. And, despite its awesome power, the Merlin and the Hurricane proved a docile combination as soon as the brakes were released and cautious taxying was commenced, swinging the tail from side to side in order to see ahead beyond the great whale-back nose which totally obscured forward visibility while the tail was on the ground. Once the Hurricane had arrived cross-wind for the final pre-take-off checks, a further impression of power was conveyed by the engine run-up to almost full throttle – in order to test for 'mag drop' and pitch control. Then, with pounding heart, the turn into wind, a deep breath, and the firm, smooth thrust forward of the throttle lever under the left hand.

It seemed to me that the armour-plate behind my head dealt me a smart blow between the ears as the Hurricane surged forward. But the hours of preparation for this moment paid off, and I have to say that nothing really took me by surprise. Everything happened in the way I had been told it would – only quicker. In very short order the wheels left the ground, and I was flying a Hurricane.

Then came something which was a standing joke among old hands: the 'porpoise climb', typical of everyone's first flight in a Hurricane I. The undercarriage was operated manually by a wobble pump, and in the hands of the first-timer this led to a reflection of the movement fore and aft in the other arm and hand on the spade grip of the control column. Hence a 'see-saw' climb into the sky for the first thousand feet or so until the undercarriage was safely locked up, and it became possible to relax and get 'sorted out'.

The 'drill' was then, if possible, to execute a dummy approach and landing onto a cloud-top, offering a more forgiving surface than even the grass of the airfield to which one hoped to return. I was lucky. There were wisps of stratus cloud which were tailor-made for the purpose. So, wheels and flaps down for an approach and landing at an altitude of 4,000 ft. This provided the opportunity to experience the rapidity with which the air-speed fell away as the throttle was pulled back, and the pronounced change in attitude as the flaps were lowered. After this, inevitably came the business of pumping the damned wheels up again!

The requisite observed two landings and overshoot were completed to the satisfaction of my instructor, and my log book tells me that my Merlin baptism was all over in half-an-hour. To my regret now, I never flew a Hurricane again.

So off to OTU at Hawarden in Cheshire, now occupied by British Aerospace. Thereafter seven sorties on Master Is and a map-reading and navigation exercise on a DH 86, all in six days. And then, at last, I flew a Spitfire.

And on that occasion when I 'opened the tap' for the first time, a single exclamation shot through my brain if not my lips. Though perhaps blasphemous, it was a cry of pure and simple ecstasy. By dusk next day I had five Spitfire hours in my log-book and I was flying in formation the following day. So it couldn't have been that difficult. Could it?

4

TONY BENN

First Solo

Southern Rhodesia, June 1944

I WENT ALONG to dispersal this morning at six and Crownshaw told me to
get into 322 straight away, a PT-26A Cornell trainer. I apologised to him
for boobing the check yesterday and he remarked that they were really only
nominal things and that they didn't really matter. I thought that he was just
being kind and I liked him for it but all the same I was pretty depressed as I
got in and we took off. We decided to keep to RAF Guinea Fowl and not go
to Senale but conditions weren't good. In the first place the 'T' was straight
into the sun and that blinded everyone taking off and landing, and in the
second place there were an enormous number of kites flying round this
morning, and in the hour and thirty-five minutes we were up we were nearly
killed twice by one of them (whose pilot forgot to close his throttle when he
touched down on an engine-assisted approach, thus taking off and landing
three or four times before banging it right open and going round again) and
came very near to an accident while landing when two aircraft were converging
on us from behind.

We did about five full circuits – or rather I did them – and I almost
entirely eliminated the tendency to overshoot by shortening my down-
wind leg and by re-opening my throttle to 1,800 rpm as soon as my flaps
were down and I was trimmed for a glide. Another improvement was
starting my gliding turn earlier, which made certain that I didn't go beyond
my selected landing path and which enabled me, because of this early
action, to turn very gently without losing too much height. I did three or
four safe landings, but I also did one simply tremendous bounce, so I
slammed open the throttle and went round again. This, I was convinced,
was an off-day and that landing I felt sure would see me scrubbed. However
the last landing I did was as near perfect as anything I've done yet and
there wasn't even a judder.

We taxied on to the tarmac and I got out and walked back with Crownshaw.
He said we'd just have a cigarette and then go up again. I was very surprised,
but put it down to a desire on his part to finish me off ready for another
check tomorrow. However we took off, did a circuit or maybe two, and then
as we taxied up to the take-off point, he said to me: 'Well, how do you feel

about your landings?' I replied: 'Well, that's really for you to say, sir.' He chuckled. 'I think you can manage one solo,' he said. 'I'm going to get out now and I'll wait here for you,' he went on.

So this was it, I thought. The moment I had been waiting for came all of a sudden just like that. 'OK, sir,' I replied. 'And don't forget that you've got a throttle,' he said. 'Don't be frightened to go round again – okay? And by the way,' he added – he finished locking the rear harness and closing the hood, then came up to me, leant over and shouted, in my ear – 'you do know the new trimming for taking off?' 'Yes, sir,' I replied, and he jumped off the wing and walked over to the boundary with his 'chute.

I was not all that excited, I certainly wasn't frightened and I hope I wasn't over-confident but I just had to adjust my mirror so that I could really see that there was no one behind me. Sure enough it was empty and I was alone. I did my vital actions very deliberately and carefully, I looked round and paused, then opening the throttle slightly I swung into wind until my directional gyro read '0' for I had set it on the last circuit. Then I opened up to full throttle as smoothly and yet as quickly as I could. I pushed the stick forward and connecting the swing which developed with my rudder I loomed across the 'drome, swaying rather from side to side, but keeping her under control and well into wind.

The 'drome at Guinea Fowl is bad and we bounced about like a wheelbarrow but gradually I felt the pressure come off the stick and as the airspeed read 70 mph I applied a gentle pressure and we rose off the ground. I took my left hand off the throttle where I always keep it during take-off and placed it on the trimming lever which I juggled with until I could climb 'hands off' at 75 mph. I tried to sing but I couldn't hear myself very well and I still couldn't believe that I was alone. I glanced behind me quickly to re-assure myself and I felt as happy as a schoolboy.

Then I remembered my brother Mike's words: 'Whatever you do don't get over-confident; it is that that kills most people and I only survived the initial stages through being excessively cautious.' So I brought my mind back to the job, checked the instruments, looked all round and when we had reached 500 ft I began a gentle climbing turn. It was very bumpy and the wind got under my starboard wing and tried to keel me over, but I checked it with my stick and straightened out when my gyro compass read 270°. Then I climbed to 900, looked all round and turned again onto the down-wind leg. By the time I'd finished that turn we were at 1,000 ft, so I throttled back, re-trimmed, got dead on 180 and I felt pretty good about things.

There isn't much to do on the downwind leg and I was tempted to put my elbow on the side of the cockpit and look professional, but once again Mike's words were in my ears and I thought that on a first solo a fellow has enough to do without wanting to look professional. I noticed that the circuit was almost empty of other kites – perhaps that one down there was going to take off, and there, I could see one turning out of wind after landing. By this time I was – if anything – a little too far, so I silently cursed myself for letting my mind wander off the job on hand. This, too, of all things! I mused the question of undershooting.

However, I turned in and then began the step which requires judgement. I left it fairly late, knowing my weakness and then closed the throttle and let down the flaps. They didn't quite catch, and as I was trimming I heard them slip up again and sure enough the handle had moved back to its original position. I grasped it firmly and pulled right up – then I didn't let go until I heard it click-locked and by this time my airspeed needed checking – it was falling off slightly.

I opened up on the turn which I started very gently in good time to about 1,400 revs and we came in just opposite the path I had selected. I always thought that I would feel a sense of panic when I saw the ground coming up at me on my first solo, but strangely enough I didn't feel anything but exhilaration at the approach which had turned out so well. No need to use so much engine, I reflected, so I made the final adjustment to the trimmer and then rested my hand on the throttle for the first moment. I thought I was a little high as I crossed the boundary so I eased back to 800 rpm, and as I passed over, I distinctly saw Crownshaw standing watching where I had left him. Now we were coming in beautifully and I eased the stick and throttle back. A quick glance at the ground below showed me to be a little high, so I left the stick as it was, gave a tiny burst of engine and as we floated down I brought both back fully. We settled, juddered and settled again for a fair three-pointer.

I was as happy as could be. Remembering not to use the brakes too heavily, I applied them as we came towards the opposite boundary for I had touched down a little late if anything, but that's a small fault compared with under-shooting. I turned out of wind, hauled my flaps up and trimmed fully tail heavy; then I swung round on to the perimeter and, defeating the devil of over-confidence for the last time, I taxied slowly round to where Crownshaw stood. With him was another instructor from our Flight whose pupil, judging by the intense look on his face, was the one coming at that moment over the boundary. I saw him strain eagerly forward, his hands twisting the handker-chief he held this way and that. His pupil made a good three-pointer, but I shan't forget that man's taut expression and his shoulders thrown forward in an effort to see how it went. He relaxed as the fellow slowed down and smiled weakly to Crownshaw.

I taxied up, stopped and braked. Try as I did, I couldn't restrain the broad grin which gripped me from ear to ear and Crownshaw, seeing it, leant over before he got in and said ironically with a smile, 'Happy now?' I was more than happy, I was deliriously carefree, and as he taxied her back I thought about it all and I realised that the success of my first solo was entirely due to the fine instruction I had received; it was a tribute to that instruction that I never felt nervous once, and all the time had imagined what my instructor would be saying, so used had I got to doing everything with him behind me. We climbed out, and attempting to restrain my happiness I listened while he told me where and what to sign. Then I wandered back to my billets and one of the greatest experiences of my life was behind me. The lectures were pretty ordinary, and it being my free afternoon I had a bit of lemonade in the canteen and then wrote this which took me over an hour and a quarter. I saw *They Flew Alone*. 'Twas good.

5

MICHAEL BENTINE

When Yesterday Was Young

I HAD GREAT difficulty in joining the Royal Air Force. The problem was that my father was Peruvian. During the First World War he had been a pioneer aerodynamicist and an early member of the AID (Aeronautical Inspection Department). Despite this and the fact that my mother was British and that I was born in Watford, my dual nationality became the major stumbling block to my being accepted by the RAF for aircrew training.

From 1939 onwards my repeated applications to join the RAF as an aircrew cadet were received by various recruiting boards with deep suspicion. I was told that volunteers of non-European descent were not acceptable to the RAF.

In 1941, astonishingly, I was *called up* with my age group. When I eagerly reported for my medical examination the same old snag arose. I was informed that the matter of my dual nationality would have to be thoroughly investigated, and I was put on 'Deferred Service'. By 1942, I had given up hope of ever being accepted for aircrew and had become an actor with Robert Atkins, the famous Shakespearean actor-manager. I even had my name billed outside the Westminster Theatre, where I was playing the juvenile-lead, 'Lorenzo', in *The Merchant of Venice*.

One night, to everyone's amazement, I was arrested by the RAF Service Police, and wrongfully charged with being a deserter. I was carted away, still wearing my Shakespearean doublet and hose, and put behind bars at the Deputy Assistant Provost Marshal's office in Exhibition Road; the first British serviceman to appear on Defaulters' Parade in that garb for over 300 years.

Infuriated by this high-handed treatment I demanded the presence of the Peruvian ambassador, who also happened to be my godfather. The great man duly arrived and tore a resounding strip off the RAF Service Police for daring to arrest a Peruvian citizen. After many handsome apologies for the monumental cock-up, the RAF finally accepted me as an Anglo-Peruvian volunteer for aircrew training. But it was not to be.

After a close brush with death, due to a faulty inoculation of ATTTAB serum, which turned out to be the *untreated* cultures, I was desperately ill, and about to be invalided out of the service. However, at the last moment I managed to persuade my sympathetic commanding officer, Group Captain A. H. Gilligan (the famous cricketer), to recommend a transfer for me from

General Duties to Intelligence, on the grounds of my dual nationality and my knowledge of languages.

I was commissioned, in August 1943, at RAF Cosford, and graduated from the RAF Intelligence School at Highgate, where my fluent French earned me an immediate posting to No. 300 Squadron, with the *Poles*. I happily served with those gallant Polish aircrews for some months, and was then posted to Nos 626 and 12 Squadrons, at Wickenby near Lincoln, just in time for the murderous winter air-battles of 1943/44.

On the way to Wickenby and my new posting to a Lancaster bomber wing, I visited Lincoln cathedral. I felt the need for prayer. I was sad to leave my friends in the splendid Polish 300 Squadron, and as this was my second posting within Bomber Command, I wanted to do my best for the new wing as well. Hence my quiet word with the Almighty.

By the winter of 1943, our bomber losses were mounting dramatically. This was owing to the increasing power of the RAF's night offensive on Germany. Raids of more than 500 aircraft at a time over each target area were a common occurrence. The first devastating 1,000 Bomber raid on Cologne, in May 1942, had signalled the start of Air Marshal Sir Arthur Harris's all-out night offensive against the industrial heart of the Third Reich.

Not only the huge manufacturing complex of the Ruhr, but all Germany's major cities were now considered to be legitimate targets. By day, the US Eighth Air Force pounded the same or similar targets with hundreds of their heavily-armed, high-altitude B17 Flying Fortresses, and B24 Liberator bombers. By night, the RAF took over the offensive. It was wholesale slaughter, on the ground and in the air.

This was the start of that dreadful winter of 1943/44, when the RAF and the US Eighth Air Force were to lose thousands of their aircrews in this round-the-clock air war. Mainly, at this time, against Berlin.

The sky on operational nights was filled with the thunder of our aircraft, as the Halifaxes, Lancasters, Mosquitos, and Stirlings rendezvoused over the East Coast before setting course for Germany. Nobody who heard it will ever forget the sound of that muted roar reverberating like thunder across the twilight sky, as hundreds of four-engined aircraft, preceded by the faster, twin-engined Mosquito Pathfinders, climbed out of their bases and headed east towards the enemy coast.

I came out of the cathedral filled with a new resolve. Thirty minutes later, I reported to the guard room at RAF Station, Wickenby. In the operations building I handed over my orders to the Senior Intelligence Officer, Squadron Leader Williams, a gaunt, grey-haired First World War pilot. Among his medal ribbons I noted the Military Cross.

'Glad to have you with us. We are at full stretch here. Your experience with the Poles will come in handy. Just sling your kit into your hut, and then come straight back. We've got a long day ahead of us.'

There wasn't even time for me to unpack.

The target that night was to be the Ruhr. At dawn, the Top Secret 'Y' Form with all the relevant information for the night's operation had come through on the teleprinter. The arrival of this document immediately followed the 'scrambled' telephone land-link, between the Intelligence officers of each of No. 1 Group's numerous Lincolnshire bomber stations and Group HQ.

The form contained everything that the air and ground crews would need to know regarding the operation that night. It described the target in detail, under its code name, which was always that of a species of fish, and listed all the necessary requirements for the bomb-load, both high-explosive and incendiary.

The long teleprinter document also gave the mandatory route into and out of the target area, plus all the latest information on the known positions of the formidable array of enemy flak, which by 1943 had over 20,000 heavy anti-aircraft guns defending Germany. The carefully selected route passed over comparatively lightly defended enemy airspace for hundreds of miles, but it was only about *two* miles wide. It was tailored to fit each individual operation, weaving its way to bypass the heaviest concentrations of enemy guns and searchlights.

To follow the route required pinpoint navigation by the aircrews. Their lives would depend on the ability of the pilots and navigators to follow the track exactly. This was the only way to avoid passing over the predicted barrages of high-explosives. Once they left that narrow airway, they would be caught in the cones of webs of searchlights and immediately surrounded by scores of bursting shells.

Their survival depended on the skill of their pilots and a lot of luck. Those who experienced that 'coning' in the blinding glare of the searchlights, and the shattering barrage of exploding shells that immediately followed it, and lived to fly once more over Germany never forgot the experience.

In addition to the constant hazard of the heavy concentrations of enemy flak, there was another deadly obstacle lying in wait for Allied aircrew. This was the Luftwaffe's night-fighter system, the extensive 'Kammhuber Line', named after the German General Josef Kammhuber who had engineered this well-conceived interlocking network of radar-directed fighter aircraft.

The line of defences was set out like an enormous chess-board, made up of hundred-mile square boxes of enemy airspace, within which the radar-directed enemy fighters operated. These night-fighters were kept airborne in relays, orbiting beacons until they were vectored by their ground controllers onto the Allied bomber-stream. The system stretched from Denmark to the Dutch border.

Many of our planes were shot down by these skilled German night-fighter crews, most of whose faster and much more heavily armed aircraft were fitted with airborne radar, as well as being expertly directed onto their targets by the efficient ground controllers. At this stage of the air war over Europe both sides were playing for very high stakes, with the cards heavily stacked on the side of the experienced Luftwaffe fighter pilots. As many as 121 Allied night-bombers destroyed were credited to Major Heinz-Wolfgang Schnaufer, the Luftwaffe's top-scoring night-fighter ace.

The reason for the Allies' murderous losses, both by day and by night, was that many of our young aircrews of necessity had not received much more than the bare minimum of multi-engined training before being flung into the battle; whereas the Luftwaffe still had many experienced, battle-hardened fighter-pilots to meet the growing bomber threat. It was only months later when fast Allied long-range Beaufighters and Mosquitos, equipped with 'Serrate' AI, became available to infiltrate and protect part of the RAF night-bomber stream, that the enemy fighters became less effective.

What manner of men and women made up the air and ground crews of these RAF bomber stations? In essence, the aircrews were much the same as those I had met previously at Air Crew Reception Centre, in Regent's Park. But, now there was a noticeable difference in their attitudes. This was because many of them had seen their comrades killed in air accidents during training, while others had watched their mates die horribly in the nightly holocaust over Europe.

These aircrew were intent on survival and their faces showed the strain of the air battle. The eagerness of youth and the excitement of flight had taken second place to a dogged determination to make it through their first tour of 30 operations. If they did so, their prospects of survival were much greater, for after completing that first tour they would be posted to a safer job as instructors, until they were needed for their second tour, some six months later. My friend the late Group Captain Lord Cheshire vc, went on to complete a third, and even a fourth tour of operations, winning his Victoria Cross for having completed over *one hundred* operational sorties over Europe.

Considering the odds against aircrew getting through their first thirty operations over enemy territory, which were largely determined by aircrew giving 100% concentrated effort throughout their whole tour, you realize how much appalling stress these young men faced. Lack of concentration on the part of any member of the crew could spell death for them all. The survival rate was depressingly low.

There is no doubt in my mind that luck played a big part in these operations, but morale was another factor that determined the odds. Most of all, it was sheer skill that played the vitally important role in the grim business of survival. An experienced, gifted pilot, a first-class navigator, a well-trained flight engineer, each with a cool head in an emergency, were all essential ingredients in surviving those thirty operations. Alert and straight-shooting gunners, and a good wireless operator generated excellent morale, and an efficient bomb-aimer made each and every operation worthwhile. Such a crew usually made it back from the hell over Europe. But not always. They still needed luck on their side.

Apart from the perils of enemy flak and fighters, there was always the danger of mid-air collision. This was because hundreds of our aircraft were rendezvousing without navigation-lights in very restricted airspace, and then flying on to the target area in that long narrow bomber-stream. To me it is astonishing that more bombers, at night and often flying in bad visibility, did not suffer from this sort of accident, which usually proved fatal to both the crews involved.

In the crowded airspace over the target-area there was also the danger of being hit by bombs and showers of incendiaries dropped by their comrades above them. Many of our planes suffered from this extra target hazard. That is where luck played an all-important role.

The laws of chance had yet another important function. The weather could change dramatically. It was extremely difficult to predict the overall conditions accurately without the vital meteorological information needed for efficient weather forecasting over Europe. Maintaining radio silence, in order to lessen the risk of early enemy detection, often precluded in-flight information regarding unexpected changes in the weather pattern being passed back to base, and being re-broadcast to the bomber-stream.

Bad weather brought down many of our aircraft, especially on their return to Britain, when the pilots were near exhaustion after over seven hours of tense operational flying. Heavy casualties were often the result. On the night of 16th/17th December 1943, after a raid on Berlin, in addition to many casualties over Germany, the RAF lost 28 Lancasters. These were mainly due to mid-air collision while approaching their bases, or by aircraft flying into high-ground during the unexpected fog and heavy low cloud. There were pathetically few survivors. One of our aircraft from No. 12 Squadron crashed within sight of Wickenby, with the loss of all seven of the crew.

Only the bomber crews knew how lucky they were to return safely from those terrible winter operations of 1943/44 over Europe. Bomber Command alone suffered more than *55,000 killed*, during the six years of war, many of them during this long and exhausting winter air battle.

Each four-engined aircraft, whether it was a Lancaster, Halifax, or Stirling, normally carried a crew of seven, sometimes eight if a signals specialist was aboard or a second pilot was included, while the fast, twin-engined Mosquitos were flown by a crew of two, the pilot and navigator/bomb-aimer.

The aircrew of a Lancaster consisted of, upfront, the bomb-aimer, who operated the complex bomb sight while lying belly-down on the floor of the aircraft, aiming his 16,000 lb of high-explosive and incendiary bombs through an optically corrected Plexiglass window in the aircraft's nose. He would also help the navigator with visual sightings and map reading to and from the target.

Behind them, the pilot was seated on the left side of the aircraft, while the flight engineer sat behind, or stood beside him while they monitored the throttles and pitch controls of the four 130 hp supercharged Merlin engines. In addition the engineer was responsible for the fuel systems, and raised and lowered the wheels and wing flaps as required.

At a small chart-table further down the aircraft, the navigator continually worked out their position, while nearby sat the radio operator, during the long period of radio silence only transmitting when the aircraft was approaching base on its return, and needed a directional-radio positional 'fix', or, in a dire emergency, sending out their last estimated position before the pilot ditched the badly-damaged plane in the sea.

Two-thirds of the way along the fuselage, the mid-upper gun turret, armed with two more rifle calibre machine-guns, was operated by the second air gunner. Lastly, set in the end of the aircraft, between the graceful elliptical twin tail-fins, was the rear gunner, cramped into his turret, which carried four more .303 Brownings. As I have already pointed out, these light machine guns only offered an adequate defensive fire *if* an enemy aircraft attacked from close range.

The German night-fighters, armed with multiple cannon, and much heavier machine guns, could stalk their quarry while keeping well out of range of the Allied .303 inch weapons. They would then pick off the bomber's air gunners, before closing in for the kill often from below, using upwards firing guns which would smash into the bomber's engines and wing fuel tanks. Only when visibility was restricted would an enemy night-fighter come in closer and afford the Allied gunners a killable target. God alone knows why this appalling situation should have continued for almost the entire war at such a terrible cost in aircrew. Despite continual protests from Air Chief Marshal Sir Arthur Harris, and other concerned Bomber commanders, they only succeeded in obtaining a limited amount of heavier .5 inch M/G armament for some of Bomber Command's four-engined aircraft during the last six months of the war.

Undoubtedly, the Lancaster was the best British heavy-bomber of the war, especially in its night-bombing role. During the few operations that the Lancs performed in daylight, such as the Augsburg low-level raid in April 1942, it was found that they were very vulnerable to daytime fighter attack, and the percentage of aircraft lost was far too high.

But, at night, the Lancaster Mark III was supreme, carrying a far heavier bomb load per operation than either of the comparable American four-engined heavy bombers, the Flying Fortress, or the Liberator. However, the Americans' massive armament of 13 x .5 inch *heavy* machine-guns per aircraft could hit the Luftwaffe fighters much harder, and at longer range, in their daylight offensive than the British night-bombers.

Our aircraft were well serviced, and by 1943 many of these dedicated ground crews were made up of WAAF personnel. Without their skills and the care that they took in their expert trades, in all weathers and under all conditions, which were often appalling, the whole RAF bomber offensive would have ground to a halt. It was an extraordinary example of group-effort and application, in which both air and ground crews felt themselves part of a unified team, with one aim: Winning the air war.

This extraordinary team-effort continued right through to the end of the war, without any need to bolster it artificially with the usual melodramatic propaganda. These 'maximum efforts' were created and maintained entirely by the over-riding need for their existence, and this sense of team unity was reinforced by the stress and tensions of war.

It was nowhere more evident than in the parachute-packing sections of each RAF bomber station, where the lives of each member of the aircrews literally depended on the concentration of these expert packers, most of whom were WAAF. Part of their motto, which summed up their philosophy, was: 'My heart is with you at the jump.'

There were very few cases of parachutes failing to open properly and these accidents were usually associated with battle damage to the canopy, or shroud lines, or caused by jumping at too low an altitude. Among the many other wartime jobs performed so expertly by women, this was an outstanding example of the devoted efficiency of the 'female of the species'. This very fact caused the dramatic revolution in the post-war status of women in British society.

The post-war action novel's evident fixation with the endless sexual reminiscences of wartime aircrew was largely a myth. In battle there were other priorities. Survival became the strongest instinct. We had to win the war or perish. When you are fighting for your very existence, this tends to obscure lesser self-interests, even sex.

To give you some idea of how concentrated these survival efforts became, especially for aircrew, here is a brief summary of what preparing for a night-time bomber operation would be like.

By dawn, the airfield was already hard at work in response to the demands of the all important 'Y' form. Security was further tightened on these operational days, and the airfield was hermetically sealed to all but absolutely essential traffic. No one was allowed to telephone or communicate with anyone outside the confines of each operational airfield engaged in the preparation of that night's raid on Germany.

The Wing Commander Operations and the Navigation Leader were busy poring over the charts covering the whole of the Operations Room wall. This extensive mosaic was made up of a series of maps covering the British Isles, and the entire Continent of Europe from Poland to Yugoslavia, including the Mediterranean and part of North Africa.

It was part of my job in Intelligence to mark the route to and from the target area with red tape, and to display as much of the detailed target information as we possessed. Any other urgent, relevant information would arrive by despatch riders before briefing took place that evening.

Meanwhile, the whole bomber station was busy fulfilling all the necessary requirements that would make the night's operation as effective as possible.

The armourers were loading the 128 rifle calibre machine guns mounted in the various turrets of the sixteen Lancasters usually available from each squadron; an average total of 256 guns for both squadrons at Wickenby. This entailed the careful selection of ammunition, which was a mixture of HE (high explosive), tracer, and armour-piercing bullets, making them up into the long machine-gun belts, and feeding them into the steel ammo-tanks which fed the 1,200 rounds-a-minute appetite of each of the Lancasters' 8 x .303 inch Brownings.

That was only half of the busy armourers' tasks. The other part of their job was considerably more dangerous. This was the selection of the requisite bombs listed in the current 'Y' form, and the arming of each massive airborne weapon with the necessary fuses and detonators. Some fuses were set for explosion on impact, and others had built-in delays which would explode the bombs, sometimes hours after they had been dropped. This was a difficult task which required absolute concentration, for obvious reasons. The long metal canisters filled with incendiary bombs also had to be made up and loaded into the aircraft.

Before re-fuelling the aircraft with high-octane petrol, all the engines were given a final, thorough check. Meanwhile, the 'instrument bashers', the specialists who serviced the Lancasters' all-important blind-flying panels, tested their precision instruments. These dials and gauges were the only means by which the big aircraft could be safely controlled in adverse weather conditions, especially once it had entered thick, turbulent cloud, or heavy ground mist. This sort of demanding blind-flying provided additional hazards for the already highly-taxed skills of the young pilots, whose average age was twenty-two years.

At the same time, the electrical-engineers rechecked all the aircraft's radio, navigational and ground-scanning radar aids with which the Lancaster was equipped. The Top-Secret H_2S ground-scanning radar with which the Mark III Lancasters were fitted was contained in a streamlined plastic dome, set underneath the after part of the fuselage. This radar instrument could show the actual progress of the aircraft over the ground below, in the form of an amber-coloured map-like silhouette. It also could pick out the target area in outline, thereby enabling the bomb-aimers to drop their weapons, even though thick cloud often obscured their normal vision.

After all these checks had been carried out, the Lancs were 'swung' round 360° on their hard-standings, to check for any magnetic compass errors, and appropriate deviation cards were made out for the use of the pilot and navigator.

All through the day, the whole station buckled down to their various tasks. Whether the job entailed the demanding parachute-packing, the checking of special equipment, or just making up the special aircrew rations, it was done efficiently and with enthusiasm. This was because each member of the ground crews and other maintenance staff knew that they all played an important part in the night's operation. If they failed to do their job properly only the aircrew would suffer, in a major or minor way. It was an astonishing demonstration of the power of the group-mind at work, under extreme pressure. It was virtually 'maximum effort' on everybody's part.

By noon, the tempo of the whole operation was increasing. The bombs on their long, low trolleys were moved from the distant bomb-dump and loaded into each of the widely dispersed aircraft. These sinister-looking weapons ranged from the large 4,000 lb 'Cookies', or the even larger 8,000 lb version of these thin-skinned metal landmines, which were designed for maximum blast-effect, to the 1,000 lb, 500 lb, and 250 lb, streamlined bombs, used for deeper penetration before exploding.

The bomb-trolleys also carried the long steel canisters, filled with small incendiary bombs. All this complex, deadly, and sensitive weaponry had to be loaded, as required, into the bomb-bays of the serviceable Lancasters, which made up the whole bomber wing's 'maximum effort' for that night.

The exact number of fully operational bombers was variable and was determined by the state of 'aircraft serviceability'. Some of the Wickenby Wing 'Lancs' were still being repaired, due to damage sustained in the previous night's operation. Others had been sent to maintenance units, for more extensive repairs than could be carried out by the bomber station's ground crews.

Sometimes for three operational nights in a row, these ground crews with their teams of fitters, worked round the clock on the airframes, engines, fuel tanks, instruments, radio, airborne radar, armament and other equipment. Moreover, by some miracle, they produced a serviceability rate of around 75/80% of the aircraft involved, somehow managing to make the words 'maximum effort' mean exactly that. Out of the twenty-plus Lancasters that were on charge to each squadron at that time, they usually managed to provide the wing with thirty-two or more serviceable aircraft ready to undertake the night's gruelling, long-distance operation.

By some equally miraculous effort there were also sufficient crews in a fit enough state to fly them. But to those with eyes to see the strain and stress factors on aircrew showed all too clearly. Squadron Leader 'Willy' Williams, my senior intelligence officer, who had flown fighters and bomber aircraft in the First World War, remarked:

'How the hell these youngsters stand for it, I will never know. Aircrews' chances get slimmer with every operation. It's anyone's guess how many of them will get through those first thirty trips. They are really only schoolboys. It was just the bloody same in the First World War.'

By the time darkness fell, the Lancs were ready, bombed-up, armed and refuelled, all of them having been air-tested by the crews and passed fit for operational flying. Strangely, even with mass-produced aircraft, of the same mark and type, and powered by the same make of engines, there was a marked difference in the handling characteristics of each aeroplane, just as there are differences in the case of identical twins. It was up to the dedicated ground crews to see that each aircraft had, at least, an acceptable performance. But, undeniably, through no fault of the ground crews some Lancasters were much better than others.

As the evening wore on the strain of 'sweating out' the night's operation began to show. Until the briefing, none of the aircrew, apart from the wing commander operations, station commander, squadron commanders, navigation leader, intelligence, armament and engineering officers, knew the target for that night, and the degree of difficulty and danger of the operation would only become apparent once that was known. Therefore, speculation was rife and naturally those with the liveliest imaginations were under the most stress. Until the actual target was revealed at the operational briefing, these members of aircrew tended to fear the worst.

The operational briefings were straightforward, information-packed sessions, which we all kept as short, and as uncomplicated as possible.

The wing commander operations first described the target, and outlined the reason for the attack. The navigation leader detailed the route, emphasising the least dangerous crossing points in and out of the enemy coast, as well as the vital turning-points en route, and giving clear reasons why that particular, narrow track had been chosen.

My job, as intelligence officer, was to give as much relevant information as the aircrew could absorb without confusion, such as the target-marking techniques which would be employed by the Pathfinder Force. I also had to make sure that everyone had their escape aids, and knew how to use them, for maximum effect. I also taught aircrew the latest techniques to help them evade capture if they were unlucky enough to have to bail out, or were shot down over enemy territory.

The armament officer detailed the respective bomb-loads, and gave the best heading on which to release them, over target, and finally, the meteorological officer described the expected weather pattern, giving as accurate a forecast of conditions as possible, on the route into Germany, over target, and on their return, according to the latest 'Met' information.

That concluded the briefing, which finished with the final order: 'Synchronize your watches!'

Usually, take-off was timed for 2100 hrs, or later depending on the time of year or target. That meant that 'Press Tit Time', for starting the engines, would be at 2045 hrs, to give sufficient time to run up the 'Packard-Merlins' to check that there were no 'Mag Drops', (faulty magnetos), and for the thirty or more aircraft of the combined squadrons to taxi out from their hardstandings. This would put the first of them on the end of the runway, ready for take-off, at precisely 2100 hrs. Barring a cancellation from Command, nothing now could stop the operation from proceeding.

Each aircraft had a definite personality of its own, partly imprinted on its metal structure by its builders, and the aircrew that flew in it, and partly by the intense care and concentration with which the ground crews serviced the plane. Many others have told me the same, particularly members of the WAAF ground crews, who felt especially close to their aircrews, and their individual aircraft. The Lancs had captured the affection and respect of both ground and aircrews, and each aircraft was distinctly different. Just like people, some were better than others.

By 2000 hrs, the aircrews were fully kitted-out in their electrically-heated, waterproof, Sidcot flying overalls, or, alternatively, they wore fur-lined leather

Irvin jackets, known as 'Bum-freezers', some of them also wearing heavy lambskin trousers tucked into their flying boots.

Under these garments they all wore longjohns, one-piece lambswool combination-underwear, and heavy, white, polo-neck pullovers. But, despite all this outer and underwear, they could still feel the freezing cold of minus 20° Fahrenheit, at their cruising height of 20,000 feet plus altitude, throughout the long hours of operations during that dreadful winter. There were heating systems built into these unpressurised aircraft, but these often went wrong, especially with battle damage, leaving the crews vulnerable to the icy rush of of high-altitude air.

Over their flying suits they put on 'Mae West' flotation waistcoats, and their parachute-harnesses. The parachutes were carried separately, to be stowed inside the Lancaster, ready to be hooked onto the chest-clips of the harness, or, in the case of the pilot and front and rear gunners, clipped-on at the back, and sat upon throughout the whole flight. Chest-packs were too bulky for these members of the crew, who normally remained seated during the entire operation. Therefore, only navigators, bomb-aimers, flight engineers, and wireless-operators, who moved around the aircraft in flight, habitually used the chest-harness. They would have to clip on their parachutes at the last moment, just before bailing out.

At 2020 hrs, the aircrew buses and trucks, generally driven by WAAFs, collected the crews and delivered them to their waiting aircraft at the widely dispersed hard-standings.

Fifteen minutes later, all the crews were settled into their Lancasters, and were checking out their controls, instruments, radios, radar and guns, according to their specialities. The closed R/T, radio-telephone link, by which the aircrew communicated to each other above the roar of the engines, and on which their survival would depend, was also thoroughly checked out. Each aircrew member answered the skipper and navigator in turn. This procedure had certain mandatory rules, rigidly adhered to. For example, each aircrew member had to identify his position in the aircraft before giving his message.

It was vitally important that the pilot, bomb-aimer, navigator, wireless-operator, and air gunners all knew exactly who was speaking, in order to exchange information, such as changes of course, and, above all, to pass instant warnings of enemy fighters, and give instructions for the appropriate evasive manoeuvres. Hence the strict procedure, which seemed strangely formal for such closely-knit teams of aircrew, who were all on first-name terms:

'Rear gunner to skipper . . . Skipper to rear gunner . . . Navigator to pilot . . . pilot to navigator . . . pilot to wireless-operator . . . pilot to mid-upper gunner . . . Bomb-aimer to pilot . . .' etc, was the odd-sounding but absolutely *imperative* method, by which these crews communicated, under the savage stress of the average six-hour-long operation, much of the time being under fire.

All checks having been completed, the crews sat silently in their aircraft, while the last few minutes ticked by. From now on absolute *radio silence* would be maintained. Only the aircraft's intercommunication systems would be used, until they returned. In those remaining minutes before the engines were started, the crews looked at their watches and waited impatiently for 'Press Tit Time'.

When the luminous hands finally ticked round to 2045 hrs, the flight engineers leaned forward, flipped the covers off the starter-switches, and pressed the red buttons beneath. One by one, watched closely by the ground crews, who were standing tensely beside the aircraft armed with fire-extinguishers, each powerful 1300 hp supercharged Packard-Merlin engine whined, sputtered, coughed, and then finally roared into life, as the wind-milling three-bladed propellers picked up speed, and settled down into whirl-ing silver disks.

As soon as the engines had been run-up into a steady rhythm, and short bursts of throttle had taken them to full power, the watching aircrews saw a green rocket flare shoot upwards from the aircraft controller's bell-mouthed Verey pistol. The throttles were advanced and the aircraft taxied out onto the winding asphalt perimeter tracks that led the Lancasters onto the end of the runway in use.

Just as I had done with the Poles, each and every night that we were engaged on operations, I waited outside the control caravan, in order to see each aircraft fly off into the darkness. I didn't even notice the bitter chill of the freezing night as, one by one, the heavily-laden aircraft of Nos 12 and 626 Squadrons trundled along past me in line-astern, their outlines seen dimly against the cloudy night sky, until they turned onto the end of the runway, and paused there for a final check.

Above us, I could hear the muted roar as hundreds of other aircraft, mainly Lancasters, took off from the surrounding airfields of No. 1 Bomber Group, and climbed laboriously towards their rendezvous point over the tiny coastal town of Mablethorpe.

At last the green light shone from the Aldis lamp in the control caravan. The pilot and flight engineer advanced the throttles, and each Lancaster in turn lumbered forward along the glistening tarmac surface until it was thundering down the runway; the pilot as a safety measure left it to the last possible moment before becoming airborne.

As the last of the powerful Lancs heaved itself into the air, I watched the throbbing glimmer of its shrouded exhausts disappear into the darkness and the grey murk of the low cloud, which usually hung over the Lincolnshire wolds.

Ahead of my aircrews lay hours of challenging operational flying, usually under savage conditions. For me, it would be the start of a long vigil, when I sat alone in the Intelligence Room. Until they returned just before dawn, in my mind I followed the whole operation from start to finish, and every time I did so I felt that part of me flew with them.

That was nearly fifty years ago when yesterday was young, but the details are etched as clearly in my memory as the days and the nights on which they happened. I am not alone in this. I know that most other members of that hard-pressed bomber wing felt exactly the same. That mystical sense of unity that most of us experienced is what we mean when recalling our cherished years of comradeship in the Royal Air Force.

6

MICHAEL BOND

From Aircraftman to Aircraftman

I VOLUNTEERED FOR the RAF the day I was eligible. It was the summer of 1943 and I was seventeen and a quarter. When I got back home and told my mother she had palpitations. She was convinced she would never see me again.

Looking back on it, and mindful of the stories then rife that the average life-expectancy of a rear gunner was around three weeks, I can understand why. Perhaps I should have talked it over with my parents first, but I come from a family who have always served their country in time of trouble, and it didn't occur to me that there was anything to discuss.

With a teenager's lack of finer feelings I consoled her with the news that I was going to be a fighter pilot and that anyway the minimum calling-up age was eighteen, so I had at least another nine months of freedom.

In the event, I was summoned to the ACRC (Air Crew Reception Centre) at Abbey Lodge in London, much earlier than that. In theory it was so that I could attend a pre-service mathematics course in Cambridge, but along with the rest of the intake I took what to me seemed an incredibly easy exam and was exempted. There were those amongst us who thought it was a trick to get people in under age. I suppose it might have been, for I never met anyone who actually went on a course, but at the time I didn't mind that at all for I was anxious to get cracking.

Having been inducted, numbered, inoculated, uniformed, shorn of hair (contrary to popular belief, the silver coin slipped into the barber's hand before I sat in his chair hadn't made any noticeable difference to its ultimate length – nor had it to anyone else's), shouted at by people the likes of whom I hadn't previously encountered, arms aching from scrubbing wooden floors worn thin through having already been scrubbed countless thousands of times by previous inmates – on the simple premise that 'it 'elped make the jabs circulate' – we set off that evening in ragged fashion towards the Regent's Park Zoo in order to be fed and watered. Clearly singled out for early promotion, I brought up the rear of the column holding a red lantern. Halfway there the light went out and I was shouted at once again.

Queuing up at the counter with my plate, I eyed some lumpy, grey-looking mashed potato and asked a WAAF who was wielding an ice-cream scoop if she would mind only giving me one portion, not two. She told me 'I would get what I was fucking given' and I retired to the nearest table in a state of shock. I had never before heard a woman swear, and as I sat gazing out of the window, it struck me that the regular inmates of the zoo – the few that were left – were faring rather better than I was. At least their keepers probably treated them with respect. As an only child, who until that moment had always been perfectly happy with his own company, I realised for the first time the intense loneliness one can feel as an anonymous person in a crowd of complete strangers.

A posting to Scarborough meant a winter doing press-ups on a cold, wet beach, watched over by unhappy looking seagulls who had seen it all before; learning to swim by numbers on one's back in an equally freezing pool, which before the war had been condemned and was now in an even worse state; drilling, marching, being given an enthusiasm for mathematics by an elderly master from Eton who had been called up as an instructor, and who turned what had until then been an extremely dull subject into one which had elegance and precision and above all was not to be feared. The juke box in the local amusement arcade played the Mills Brothers' version of 'Paper Doll', Wills' Capstan cigarettes were 9d for ten, 'Active Service' packs of Brylcream one shilling, and on 8th January 1944 it was revealed that a new type of propellerless plane had been invented. It was powered by something called a 'jet' engine.

Letters home mostly boiled down to requests for jars of peanut butter, which I ate in vast quantities, but despite that – and the large amount of beer I consumed – when I arrived in Scotland to begin my flying training proper and to be assessed as either a potential pilot, navigator or bomb-aimer, I felt fitter than I had ever been before – or since.

At long last the great day, the day for which I'd been waiting, had arrived.

Clad in wool-lined flying boots, sheepskin flying jacket and leather-rimmed goggles, I swung the prop of a Tiger Moth and climbed into the cockpit. Fastening the safety belt, I responded confidently to a thumbs-up signal from my instructor as we prepared for take-off.

The great thing, of course, was that I knew a lot about flying. My interest had been triggered off one morning shortly before the war when I heard a strange noise in the sky over our house and rushed outside just in time to see a 'Flying Flea' pass over. It was a strange, skeletal object, completely open to the elements and powered by a single motor-cycle engine. It could be built at home for under a hundred pounds and had a short but happy life before being declared unsafe and banned; much to my father's relief, for I had been trying to persuade him to invest in a kit. Nevertheless, the sight of it excited my imagination as nothing had before, sowing the seeds of a desire to indulge in powered flight as soon as I possibly could; a desire which was further whetted by my Uncle Ernest, a rather romantic figure in my eyes, for he had lost a leg as a fighter pilot in the First World War. Uncle Ernest showed me round the Miles aircraft factory where he was then working, and at his instigation I touched the fuselage of a Magister aircraft in the making and came away with my fingers smelling strongly of dope. It was like a drug; the equivalent of today's glue sniffing.

I had even, a few months before entering the RAF, seen a German Heinkel bomber close to, seconds before it dropped a string of bombs across Reading whilst fleeing for home at roof level. I was looking out of a top floor window at the time and it was heading straight towards me. It was very nearly the last thing I saw, but clearly I wasn't meant to go that way and it didn't put me off wanting to fly.

From an early age my school exercise books had always been liberally decorated with drawings of Sopwith Camels; I could do them with my eyes shut. The Biggles books featured largely in my early reading and I had seen *Dawn Patrol* with Basil Rathbone and Errol Flynn several times. I rather fancied myself in the Errol Flynn part... 'There's no chance for a flight to get through, but one man – flying low, hedgehopping – might make it!'

Most of my practical flying had been done in a Reading Corporation double-decker bus. Whenever possible I used to bag the front seat on the top deck and practise doing landings as it hurtled downhill towards the town. On bad days when some oaf stopped it halfway down, I had to surreptitiously make up some excuse to the other passengers over the intercom; either that or convert the whole operation into 'circuits and bumps'. But on good days it was non-stop all the way. The lights would be green at the bottom, and I could execute a left turn at the end of the runway and taxi gently to a halt outside the hangar in St Mary's Butts. Being English, the other passengers never applauded when I got off, but I could tell they were impressed.

Or, to put it another way, until that moment I had never actually flown before.

Some years earlier, when we had been on a family holiday at Southsea, my father had wanted to take me on a five-shilling joy ride he'd seen advertised, but my grandfather, who was living with us at the time, put his foot firmly down on the promenade by West Parade pier, saying that if man had been meant to fly God would have given him wings, and that if we did any such thing he would leave home, so I didn't go.

Trundling along the runway at Scone airport, clutching the side of the cockpit, I realised the wisdom of grandfather's words. My instructor tapped me on the shoulder, probably intending to give another of his ghastly thumbs-up signs. His eyes, or the little I could see of them through our respective goggles, registered total disbelief as I leant over the side of the cockpit in order to be sick. I don't think he'd seen it happen before.

Several barrel rolls and one or two loops later, found me wishing I was dead. Each time the plane turned upside-down – that moment when you fall a few inches before the safety belt takes up the strain – I gazed at the ground far below and felt tempted to undo the buckle. At least the parachute would get me down quicker. Only the thought that I would undoubtedly be put on a charge after I hit *terra firma* kept me from doing it.

It was a depressing discovery; Errol Flynn would not have been pleased, and Basil Rathbone's lips would have been compressed beyond all medical aid. As for Biggles . . . he would have been lost for words. Even more dispiriting was the realisation that the RAF was not disposed to take immediate action. So unconvinced were they of the need to do any such thing, after the inevitable long wait at Heaton Park in Manchester, they sent me to Canada to continue my flying training.

It was not a good time for crossing the Atlantic in a crowded troopship. The weather was foul and the German U-boat campaign was still being fought. Squatting gloomily alongside a watertight door in the bowels of the *Aquitania*, knowing that if we were torpedoed I might have to shut myself in on the wrong side and die a quick but horrible death – although since I could still only swim on my back that could be preferable to diving over the side – I added chronic sea-sickness to my growing list of unhappinesses.

I was destined to attend a navigator's course at a place called Rivers, a small prairie town east of Winnipeg. 'Winnipeg,' according to a sergeant who greeted us with uncalled-for glee, 'was the arsehole of Canada, and Rivers was two hundred miles up it.' Certainly as far as the latter part of it was concerned, I saw no reason to argue with his summing-up during the time I was there.

From my point of view, being a navigator was an even worse fate than being a pilot in those pre-radar days. Dead-reckoning navigation was the order of the day, and trying to work out the aircraft's position on a chart, whilst every movement of the plane was transmitted via the pencil point was not good news. Admirable though I'm sure it was in its day, the Avro Anson lacked both the stability of a modern jumbo jet and its ability to fly above the weather. Sometimes the upward pressure was so great the point of the pencil broke, sometimes the reverse was true and it floated in mid-air.

Some months and a good many flying hours later, having finally convinced the powers-that-be that a navigator whose sole ambition in life was to get back down to earth again as quickly as possible was not ideal material, I left Rivers, Manitoba, for the last time, en route for England.

Sad in some ways, relieved in others, I found myself one bitterly cold December morning several weeks later huddled over a coke stove in a Nissen hut on the Isle of Sheppey, discussing with a group of others which of two options to accept; a transfer to the Army (by then Montgomery was calling for reinforcements in Europe) or a job as a coal miner. I chose the former and was sent to Edinburgh where I exchanged my blue uniform for one of khaki, my sheets for blankets, and encountered for the first time the uncivilised habit of employing a tame bugler to sound reveille; but that was the start of another story.

Having been taught to march and drill and to salute anything that moved, I had immediate cause to be grateful to the RAF, for those of us who had been in it were sent home on leave while the rest of the intake caught up.

So what did it all add up to? My contribution to the war effort at that stage had been a negative one, a total write-off as far as the RAF was concerned, but looking back I wouldn't have missed the experience. It taught me many things which might otherwise have taken years to learn; it was my university of life. It taught me discipline – sadly lacking today; self-reliance, tidiness, and many other things.

Nowadays, thankfully cured of airsickness, when I fly places in comparative comfort at 30,000 feet, idly doing a crossword or sipping a drink, I sometimes look out of the window and think in awe of what went on in the skies night after night; of what it must have been like to have anti-aircraft shells bursting all around, or to see your engines on fire; of the courage it must have taken, and of those who didn't make it back.

I wonder if others around me are thinking similar thoughts? A few, perhaps; but in the nature of things probably not very many. Most people are taken up with their own problems and it all happened a long time ago. One or two may even be feeling queasy. Poor things – they have my deepest sympathy.

I have an inkling, a very small one, of what it must have been like, because I grew up with and flew alongside many who went on to do it for real. I had the good fortune to share their lives for a brief while and I count that as a privilege; a totally undeserved bonus from my time in the RAF.

7

PETER CADBURY

Test Pilot

I REMEMBER THE RAF as a service with which I seem to have been associated all my life, although I was never a pilot in the Air Force itself. My father (Sir Egbert Cadbury, DSC, DFC) was a distinguished pilot in the RNAS and personally shot down two Zeppelins in the First World War. They were the bravest of the brave, going out over the North Sea in tiny Camels with no parachute or radio and with none of the sophisticated instruments that we take for granted to-day. He took off and landed at night on a small field outside Great Yarmouth and when I was born in 1918 he was at 18,000 feet somewhere off the coast of Norfolk in appalling weather that was cold enough to freeze his guns. From a very early age I met many of his ex-colleagues, who continued in the Service, which in April 1918 was amalgamated with the RFC and became the RAF. At the outbreak of WW2 he was made an honorary air commodore and many of his Air Force friends used to come to the house.

My father taught me to fly at the Bristol Flying Club at Whitchurch, so that when I was seventeen in 1935, I needed only a few lessons with the Chief Flying Instructor, Lin Slade (in a Moth and then the B.A. Swallow) before I passed the test to gain my 'A' Licence (No. 8356). My passion for flying was born in those days and by the time war was declared in 1939 I had nearly 200 hours in my log book (at £2 an hour!).

Following in my father's footsteps, I volunteered at once for the Fleet Air Arm, rather than the Air Force, but it was not until 1940 that I joined the Navy as an air cadet. By the time my training was finished a number of aircraft carriers had been sunk and there was little prospect of going to sea, so, along with most of my course, I went to shore-based establishments where we were held in reserve. At Lee-on-Solent one day I took off in a Swordfish and the engine stopped at 200 feet giving me no alternative but to land in the town. Fortunately I ended up in the garden of the WRNS quarters and came round to find myself surrounded by pretty girls – I thought I had gone to heaven. Apart from dislocating my neck, however, I suffered no serious injury and soon returned to flying.

I was posted to RNAS Yeovilton, where I was given the job of flight testing various types of aircraft after they had been in the workshops, including a Blenheim on which both engines failed, again just after take-off, and I came down through a barbed wire fence and ended up in a wood. I was lucky in having a rear gunner who was catapulted through a bulkhead, but was conscious and alert enough to free me from my harness and get me away before the Blenheim caught fire, as I was unconscious. Apart from lacerations from the barbed wire and a few broken bones, I was not seriously injured, but I spent some time in hospital. My father came to see me in hospital and walked past my bed, as I was unrecognisable to him, swathed in bandages, with one leg suspended from an overhead sling. Looking at pictures of the wreckage, it was a miracle that I survived, although at the time I knew nothing more than the terror of seeing the ground coming up and, I thought, taking me to join the Grim Reaper.

After my training later as a civilian test pilot, I realised how comparatively ignorant I had been in those days about the pre-flight checking and my failure to explain the reason for the engine failures, but it was a lesson painfully learned. It was a month or more before I was passed fit enough to fly again, but rather like people who are thrown off horses, by going back and getting into another aeroplane as quickly as possible, one tends not to have any fear of flying.

In 1942 when I was at Yeovilton, I was summoned to the Captain's office, where I was introduced to John Grierson, who told me that the Ministry of Aircraft Production would like me to leave the Navy and join him and other test pilots at the Gloster Aircraft Company to help with the production and development testing of Typhoons. Apparently someone very senior in the MAP had suggested my name as a replacement for Gerry Sayer, who had been killed in an accident over the sea, which was never explained, although bits of the Typhoon he was flying were washed up on the beach off Amble. I accepted immediately and was released from the Navy to take up this appointment at Brockworth.

When my release was confirmed, I drove up to Brockworth near Cheltenham to meet my new colleagues. John Grierson introduced me to the other pilots, John Crosby-Warren, Maxwell Williams, Philip Stanbury DFC, who had been seconded from the RAF, and Michael Daunt, the Chief Test Pilot, who had taken over from Gerry Sayer. I was shown the Typhoon, which was then in production, and which I would be flying. But, before I could do any test flying, I was sent to Langley for a full conversion course on the Hurricane. This I found to be not just flying and handling the aeroplane, which I had already flown at Yeovilton, but a comprehensive course of instruction on all the parts of the airframe and the engine, as it was explained to me that I had to know every part of the aeroplane by name, its function and the possible malfunctions that I was likely to experience when testing the aircraft in flight. As the Chief Designer, George Carter, told me, 'It is no good coming down and telling us that there is a fault – it will be your job to identify it, so that it can be corrected. To do that you will have to know this aeroplane inside out.'

I also had to take a series of flying tests, which included stalling, spinning, inverted flying and various aerobatic manoeuvres under the eagle eye of

Bill Humble, Chief Production Pilot at Hawkers. After a month of this concentrated instruction I was judged to be competent enough to return to Glosters at Brockworth. At Langley I was impressed by the attention to detail and the professionalism of the pilots and the design staff, and the bond of mutual respect they all had for each other.

Michael Daunt, the Chief Test Pilot, was a delightful Irishman, whose constant good humour was reflected in the whole atmosphere in the pilots' office, and his attention to detail was typical of the professionalism that was immediately obvious in all departments connected with the flying side of the company, and in great contrast to the apparent carefree attitude off duty. We all knew that a strictly professional approach to the testing of aircraft was an important safety factor, and any carelessness could be fatal. As each Typhoon came off the production line it was thoroughly tested by the WID and AID ground staff before being handed over to the pilots. But we all knew that each machine, as it was wheeled out, was about to take to the air for the first time, and even the most experienced fitters could make mistakes in connecting up the flying controls, and the final test would be ours.

John Crosby-Warren was 6 ft $9\frac{1}{2}$ in tall, and to get in the cockpit of a Typhoon he had to abandon the cushion under his parachute. Even so, there was very little clearance between his head and the canopy, which in those early days, before the introduction of the sliding hood, had to be closed and locked from the outside. Very claustrophobic for any pilot, but it must have been worse for him. John was a gregarious character and I lived with him and his wife for a time, while I looked for a place of my own. He had a very small Fiat, which he drove with his head and shoulders sticking out of the sunshine roof, and walking along beside him made anyone of average height feel like a small boy.

Like all my new colleagues, he was a very fine professional pilot, with many years of experience on all types of aircraft. He, John Grierson and Michael Daunt were spending a lot of time at Cranwell, where on 14 May 1941 a revolutionary aeroplane, the E.28/39, had made the first jet-propelled flight. It had been an historic moment for everyone concerned, not least for the pioneer of jet propulsion, Frank Whittle, who, an experienced pilot himself, had been allowed to do some of the taxiing trials, and it had been very thoroughly tested before Gerry Sayer actually took the aircraft off the ground for a short circuit. In spite of all the prophets of doom, this flight was comparatively uneventful and lasted 17 minutes.

There are available many accounts of this historic flight, covering all the technical details of the rpm (16,500), the 'thrust' (860 lb), take-off run (600 yards) and speeds for getting airborne and landing. But perhaps it is pertinent in this context to point out that Gerry Sayer had little knowledge of what might be in store for him when he took the Pioneer off the runway. He had been warned that the aircraft could fly 'like a rocket', that the jet could burn off his tail unit and that it might be impossible to throttle back sufficiently to reduce speed to a safe level for landing. In fact the aircraft handled well and over the following two weeks was flown for ten hours, including a climb to 25,000 feet, when it was in the air for 56 minutes, starting with full tanks. Apart from normal checks and refuelling, with minor trim changes, no major adjustments were necessary to the engine or airframe, which was a remarkable tribute to the design staff.

Back at Brockworth we knew something of the research and development of this revolutionary form of flight, but, such was the secrecy surrounding the whole project that we had only a sketchy idea of what they were doing. It was nearly two years later, on 5th March 1943, that the first Meteor prototype was flown at Cranwell by Michael Daunt. This was another occasion when the pilot could only guess at the possibilities of this maiden flight in an aircraft that had been put together from designs on a drawing board with engines that were revolutionary and never before tested in flight. When Mike and John flew back to Brockworth, they could not hide their jubilation over this remarkable achievement, and although the details were secret, they could tell us enough to allow us to join in their excitement. This was the birth of the 'jet' age, and we were privileged to be a part of the organisation that had made a dream a reality. Test pilots since the first days of the aeroplane have made similar initial proving flights on every type, but there was something special in flying the first jet, which in my lifetime has now become the standard form of flying all over the world.

Gerry Sayer had been a very accomplished pilot and he had also had the ability to make clear and concise reports of his flights, which were invaluable to the design staff, whose job was to correct any faults or problems that manifested themselves in the air and which could not be predicted in the workshops. In his report on the pioneer flight Gerry commented on the fore and aft instability which he said was 'due to the over-sensitive elevators'. He also found that he needed 'a lot of right rudder', which he put down to the jet-pipe being 'slightly out of alignment'. This identification of the problems enabled the designers to correct the problems, so that they were cured before the next flight. These and other comments were the hallmark of the experienced test pilot who was able, not only to report the problems, but also to identify the probable reasons for the malfunction, which would have been outside the scope of other first class pilots who had not the detailed knowledge of the airframe and flying controls.

The art and science of test flying has been handed down by generations of test pilots and I was fortunate in being trained by experts, such as Michael Daunt, John Grierson and John Crosby-Warren, who in turn had learned their trade from the previous generation of pilots. Not only should a test pilot be above average in flying skill, but he must have an analytical mind and the capacity for small detail. In addition he should have a sound, practical knowledge of aerodynamics and the components of airframes, engines, hydraulics and other working parts in order to be able to identify or make an intelligent guess as to the reasons for any control or engine failure or malfunction.

It was to acquire this knowledge that I had to spend many hours on the factory floor, before I could be trusted to take an aircraft on a test flight. The best way to learn about the analysis of faults was to sit in at all meetings and discussions with my experienced colleagues, where the measures to be taken to correct the faults in the air and also on the ground were debated. At these meetings there was never a suggestion that the pilots were an élite group of men who could not accept advice from designers or ground staff, and in a similar spirit of democracy, the designers were always happy to hear comments on their work from the pilots. Co-operation and understanding between all members of the team was essential, although a suggestion that a second seat should be fitted for the designer to 'see for himself' was turned down with the comment that 'flying is for the birds and crazy men like you'! Quite often a pilot would climb out of the cockpit after a forced or difficult landing with the comment 'Back to the drawing board', which was a suggestion readily accepted by the designer in the spirit of camaraderie that existed among all the group.

We had little to do with the directors or management of the company, who seldom appeared on the airfield. One night I had a call from Security to say that they had a man in their cell who claimed to be the managing director, and asked if I would go and identify him. When I got there, I found Frank McKenna, who actually was the managing director, looking out through the bars. It seems that when little Mac was stopped walking his dog round the airfield and said who he was, the security man replied, 'Oh yes, and I am Head of the Combined Operations. You just come along with me.'

The flying, development and maintenance sides of the company were all together and some distance from the main offices, from where the top echelons seldom ventured and so were unknown to the security guards, who, because of the link with the jet propulsion unit, were extremely vigilant and would arrest anyone they did not know on sight and ask questions later. Mac was not pleased by the indignity of being thrown in a cell and freed only on the word of a comparatively junior member of the organisation. But they all turned up on occasions such as visiting royalty or Winston Churchill, who was a frequent visitor, especially after we had the Meteor in production. It is reported that when he went to see the E.28/39 fly at Hatfield, as Mike Daunt went past at 400 mph, he turned his head so fast that his cigar fell out of his mouth. Queen Mary was living near Cheltenham and she often came to see a display, which she watched from the back of her Rolls, which had a roof that folded to allow her to stand up. In those years we had a number of distinguished visitors, none of whom had ever seen a jet-propelled aeroplane before, because there was none before the Meteor.

While my senior colleagues were testing and developing the Meteor at Cranwell and then at Barford St John, I was learning my trade at Brockworth on the airframe and working parts of the Typhoon, having done my basic training at Langley on the Hurricane. When I was considered sufficiently competent I was strapped into a Typhoon that had already had its first flight, and told to check whether the faults already reported had been corrected and to do a routine test flight. This involved flying at various heights and speeds, and recording all the pressures and other readings on the instruments on a specially designed kneepad, with a stopwatch held in the stainless steel frame. The paper was in a strip that could be rolled on and backwards to check previous notes, on which all the figures had to be written as well as comments on the controls, the cockpit fittings and the handling in flight. I was also required to do some basic aerobatics over the airfield to show that I was fully in control of the machine. When I landed, my notes were compared with those made on the previous flight by John Crosby-Warren, which was a worrying moment for me; but John seemed satisfied and I was told I could then take up another aircraft and, if satisfied with all aspects of its performance, I could 'sign it off' as being ready for collection by the Air Transport Auxiliary for delivery to an RAF squadron. So, at long last I could count myself among the official test pilots and 'start being of some use' to the company, rather than a spectator.

I did not resent in any way this period of instruction and it was to prove invaluable over the following years, when I was more competent to detect and analyse a malfunction and take steps to avoid a possible disaster. However carefully an aircraft was tested on the ground, it was seldom without a snag of some kind when in the air, which had to be put right before being sent off to the RAF. Vibrations in the propeller were common faults, which usually meant a change of prop, and invariably the trim tabs had to be adjusted to correct a tendency to fly one wing low. Sometimes there were more serious problems, such as the time when I found I could not reduce the engine power and had to land by switching on and off the ignition. It was found that the nut securing the throttle had fallen off, so making the throttle lever inoperative. Sometimes it was impossible to change the pitch of the propeller, which made landing rather hazardous, but the more common faults were with the Sabre engines, which at that time were notoriously unreliable, to the extent that the ATA would allow only their most experienced pilots to deliver them to the RAF.

The Typhoon was designed as a high speed fighter but it failed in this but became instead a low level fighter-bomber. It was a comparatively heavy, substantial aircraft and to be effective needed the most powerful engine that could be housed in the airframe, which was the Napier Sabre. Everything possible had been done to increase its power and performance, with the result that most of its working parts were at maximum stress levels. Compared with the Rolls-Royce Merlin which had been flown and developed for some years in Hurricanes, Spitfires, Lancasters and other operational types, it was a new design. The inevitable result was that its development and the correction of faults became the responsibility of the Gloster test pilots up to and after the introduction of the Typhoon into active service with the RAF.

Brockworth was not an ideal airfield for experimental or development flying, with one short runway, heading south-west into a row of hills, and having a line of hangars at the north-eastern end. In a strong cross-wind it was possible to land to the west on the grass, but the run was insufficient for safely going round again, as there was a row of buildings on the eastern perimeter. Obviously it had been adequate for the Gladiator and similar Gloster aircraft, but it was marginal for Typhoons in bad weather.

Michael Daunt had recently had an engine failure but managed to get down in a field between two trees, which removed both his wings. Other pilots had been forced to land through engine failure and it was with some apprehension that I made my first official test flight in an aircraft that had just been wheeled out of the workshops. However, all went well and, apart from a few adjustments, followed by a second test, I passed it fit for delivery. Over the next year or so I was to have several frightening experiences, a common fault being the failure of the glycol cooling system, which produced an almost impenetrable cloud of blue smoke over the engine cowlings, so making landing extremely difficult. Once the engine caught fire and I considered baling out, but this was a much more terrifying prospect than chancing my luck in getting down with the aeroplane. The controls were often seriously unbalanced causing the aircraft to fly one wing low or yaw to one side or the other at high speeds. Occasionally the green lights to show the undercarriage was down would fail to light, which meant flying past the pilots' office low and slowly in the hope in the hope that someone could tell me that the wheels were down and it was an electrical fault. Instruments sometimes gave inaccurate readings or failed completely, which meant a quick return to base, in case they were correct!

By this time there were several Typhoon squadrons on active service and we sometimes had messages to say that they were having problems. When this happened, one of us would fly up to the squadron concerned, check the nature of the complaint and hopefully suggest a way in which it could be cured. Often this was a case of engine failure, and we had no alternative but to fly the aircraft concerned, if it were serviceable, give it a comprehensive flight check, write a report for the engineers and, before leaving, give them the inevitable aerobatic display – they always seemed to assume that test pilots could do these aerobatics better than they could, but this was not necessarily so. It was more of a public relations exercise than anything, but, if the fault was serious, we would fly the suspect aircraft back to Brockworth for a thorough check in our workshops, or transport it by road, if it was not safe to fly.

Gradually the faults in the Sabre engines were cured and we had fewer problems, and they were eventually deemed safe enough for the girls in the ATA to collect them. It was always a pleasant surprise to see a trim female form step out of the ATA transport. We had one tragedy with an ATA pilot, who, against our advice, insisted on taking off on the grass. We told him it was wet and boggy, but he would not listen and he taxied to the west side of the field. When he ran up the engine, the wheels dug in and the aircraft turned over on to its back on top of the cockpit hood. With shouts of 'serve the arrogant *****r right', we ran across the field to find he had drowned in three inches of water, having had his head pushed into the bog with the aeroplane on top. It was a ghastly moment for everyone, and after that we always made sure that the visiting pilots did as they were told.

In October 1943 the runway at Moreton Valence had been extended to 2,000 yards and hangars had been built to house the workshops for the production of the Meteor. This was only a few miles from Gloucester and more convenient for the design staff and pilots than Barford St John, where the test flying had been done for some time and which was some 50 miles from Brockworth. Shortly after this I was allowed to go down and actually see and touch the revolutionary jet-propelled Meteor. Once again I was put through an intensive course of training on the airframe and also the jet engines at the factory where they were made and assembled. And I met Frank Whittle!

When Michael Daunt was satisfied that I knew enough about the Meteor to be trusted to fly it, I was put in the cockpit and he stood beside me to check that I knew what each instrument and control was designed to do. 'Line up, set the rpm at 14,000, watch the jet pipe temperature and good luck,' he said, slapped the side of the aeroplane and walked away. I did as I was told and released the brakes to make my first jet flight. It was a thrill I shall never forget, as the aircraft accelerated down the runway and, with little effort, took off. My immediate reaction was the lack of noise or vibration, especially after flying so much on Typhoons, which vibrated horribly, yawed hard to the left on take-off and were very noisy.

On the ground I had noticed the wonderful all round visibility from the cockpit, with no huge engine cowling blocking my forward view. And, being a tricycle undercarriage, the forward view was panoramic. I climbed to 2,000 feet, did a circuit of the airfield and came into land. I had been warned that the response from a jet engine was not so immediate as a propeller, so I allowed myself plenty of height for the approach and touched down to what seemed to me a perfect landing. However, my confidence evaporated slightly when the aircraft showed no signs of slowing down and I had to apply the brakes quite hard to stop before the end of the runway. Of course, there was no drag from the propeller or the tail wheel, and no flare after the nosewheel was on the surface. Anyhow, I stopped in time and taxied back to the apron to be told by Mike that 'When you have done a few hundred hours, you should be quite competent.' But he seemed pleased enough to let me take off again, with instructions to do a simulated flight test on an aircraft for which they already had the report. My report apparently coincided with his, and I was told I was qualified to do production testing.

To modern pilots it may seem strange that in those days there was no dual flying instruction. With Hurricanes, Spitfires and all single-seater aircraft, a pilot was put in the cockpit, shown the 'taps' and told to get on with it. Of course we had all been trained initially on Fairey Battles and similar two-seater aircraft and in the Fleet Air Arm I had done some flying on Blenheims.

Also I had flown Mosquitos, so I had experience on twin-engined aircraft, which would have been essential before flying the twin-engined Meteor. It can be embarrassing in a twin, if one of the engines stops, with the immediate tendency to swing towards the dead engine, and great care has to be taken, flying on one engine.

The Meteor project was Top Secret and we were told not to fly out of the Moreton Valence area and avoid having to force-land anywhere else. When we had to take an aircraft up to Farnborough or Rolls-Royce for testing or displays, we had to arrange for a 'lane' to be cleared with Fighter Command and usually we were accompanied by a Typhoon and at least one Spitfire to avoid being mistaken for a hostile unidentified aircraft and shot down. As there were no pictures available for distribution to the RAF, the Meteor was unknown and an over-zealous fighter pilot might easily have assumed we were one of the German jets, which were already on active service. During those months I learned how to be a successful spy, as I was often asked what the British were doing about finding a suitable aeroplane to take on the German Me262 and why we were so far behind. It was very tempting to say, 'We have a much superior jet in production', which I am sure would have caused me to be locked up in the Tower of London.

My current girl friend, whom I subsequently married, was driving for the American Army at Cheltenham, and on a low flying exercise I would sometimes fly over her HQ, until one day she said, 'That new aeroplane you are flying leaves a trail of black smoke, like Bobby's tractor. Does it run on paraffin?' The fuel, like everything else, was secret and I ceased these flypasts after that, in case someone else was observant enough to notice that there were no propellers either! Our aerial photography reconnaissance had picked up scorch marks round German airfields, which were identified as being made by jet engines, so we always had to run up on a tarmac surface in order to avoid giving the Germans similar information. But the cows in fields round Moreton Valence would line up in the hot air coming from the jet pipes and even worms would come out, thinking presumably that it was an unexpected hot summer's day.

Another hazard was discovered by Mike Daunt, when he was looking for a suspected fuel leak in the engine nacelle. He was picked up, as he passed the front of the engine, and sucked into the air intake. He was a very big man and was saved by his size and a big floppy Irvin jacket he was wearing, and also by the presence of mind of the pilot in shutting down the engine. He was badly bruised and shaken, but he could easily have been killed, and after that we fitted grilles on the intakes, known as 'Daunt stoppers', but these did not prevent seagulls and other birds being sucked into the engines, which was extremely dangerous and caused immediate engine failure. The first time it happened, there was no obvious explanation as to why an engine had suddenly stopped and disintegrated, until on inspection after landing the remains of a seagull were found in the compressor, 'cooked to a turn'. As this would have been particularly dangerous on take-off, someone always went to the end of the runway with a gun to scare away the birds, but on low flying tests we still collected the occasional gull or crow.

Throughout 1944 we had a series of new and more powerful engines, each of which caused new problems with the airframe, as we reached higher speeds. Our objective was eventually to reach the speed of sound, the elusive Mach 1, which at ground level was about 760 mph, decreasing with altitude to about 660 mph above 35,000 feet. The indicated airspeed at 20,000 feet of 300 mph would represent a true airspeed of about 400 mph, due to the thinner air, and so the Mach meter was introduced, which registered the speed as a percentage of the speed of sound, Mach 1. We were gradually getting up the .7 scale and then over .8 with the new W 2/700 engines, each of which were giving 2,000 lb of thrust in March 1945. But from the early days we had run into the problems of compressibility, which is when the air builds up in front of the aircraft into a cushion, which quickly causes instability and locking of the controls, in addition to severe buffeting, which is uncomfortable and dangerous, making it impossible to pull out of a dive at altitude and in some cases not before reaching 10,000 feet or even lower.

Longer engine nacelles were fitted and a variety of changes made to the airframe, all of which had to be tested at high Mach numbers, which could not be reached in level flight, and meant starting a shallow dive from at least 25,000 feet and hoping to pull out before hitting the ground. At the same time we were testing the pressurised cabin and Philip Stanbury was at 40,000 feet when a panel blew out of the windscreen, so changing the cabin pressure from 24,000 feet to 40,000 feet in a split second, which caused him to pass out in severe pain. At 28,000 feet he began to regain consciousness to find the machine in a violent spin, and he was lucky to regain enough control at 15,000 feet to straighten up the aircraft and dive out of the spin at 3,000 feet. Although he was only semi-conscious, he decided to try to land, rather than bale out, and after narrowly missing the control wagon and holding off 20 feet above the runway, he was safely down. The nervous and physical reactions from his ordeal meant his spending some weeks in hospital and a reasonable time to convalesce.

Earlier, in May 1944 we were flying an aircraft 'to the point of destruction', which meant that we all took turns to fly two hours at a time at various altitudes and speeds to check if or when the aircraft had had enough and would break up, or the engines fail. I had done my stint and had gone back to my flat in Cheltenham, when the telephone rang and the police said one of our aircraft had crashed on Minchinhampton Common. I rushed up there to find a large hole in the ground with bits of aeroplane spread over about an acre of the golf course. There was no sign of John Crosby-Warren, apart from one of his shoes, and his body must have disintegrated. Various eye-witnesses reported a 'loud explosion' before the crash, and we assumed that an engine must have blown up.

At the time John was doing the 400 mph low level part of the test and we were all very worried as to the possible cause of the crash, as there were no clues. However, all the bits were meticulously collected and taken to Farnborough, where they were spread out on the floor of the hangar and minutely examined. While this was taking place we were apprehensive about parts of the test programme, as we had no idea what had gone wrong. Eventually Farnborough told us that an aileron tab was missing and had obviously broken off, causing the wing to come up and invert the aeroplane, so that it went into the ground upside down at over 400 mph. At least we knew what had happened, but the loss of John Warren was a bitter blow, and when Philip was also put out of action later in the year, we were very short of experienced jet pilots.

In November 1944 I went to the Rolls-Royce works at Barnoldswick with John Grierson to see the new Nene engine they had developed, which they claimed would deliver 4,000 lb of thrust and could be increased to 5,000 lb. Sadly, it was too big for the Meteor, but Dr Hooker at Rolls said he thought it could be scaled down to fit into it, which he did in the following year. These engines made it possible to increase the ground speed of the Meteor to over 500 mph and then to 600 mph, so that on 7th November 1945 Group Captain Hugh Wilson broke the world's airspeed record in the Meteor IV at 606 mph.

To describe this record-breaking flight as rather a mundane event would be to disregard the research, problems and loss of life that had made it possible, not to mention the many occasions when pilots had 'got away with it'. A common problem from the early days was to find a metal that would withstand the very high temperatures for the turbine blades which were rotating at supersonic speeds and had a habit of disintegrating in flight. Main engine bearings failed and needed strengthening to accept the 'G' forces, and these mechanical failures inevitably caused bits of engine to make holes in the cowlings and so affect seriously the control of the aircraft. Compressibility had unpredictable effects and could cause the ailerons to lock, which sometimes resulted in the aircraft going violently out of control. This happened with Squadron Leader Davie, and he was hurled out through the canopy at 33,000 feet to find himself without oxygen, mask or goggles. He was lucky to have the skill and presence of mind to open his parachute and land outside Guildford, very shaken and frostbitten.

Turbine and impeller failures were common, sometimes being ejected through the engine cowlings and damaging the tail, which seriously affected the controllability of the aircraft. Davie was later killed when an engine disintegrated at 20,000 feet and many times we would find that rivets had come out all over the aeroplane, presumably when pulling out of a dive, but our main problems were the loss of control of the ailerons, when compressibility built up in the wing roots and round the engine nacelles at speeds over Mach .8.

The reports coming back from RAF squadrons were encouraging and complimentary on the general handling of the Meteor. In July 1944 we delivered two Meteor Mk Is to 616 Squadron at Manston, where they were to be employed chasing the V1 flying bombs. Flying Officer 'Dixie' Dean made history by diving to intercept a 'buzz-bomb' heading for London, and, when his guns jammed, he pulled alongside and gently lifted the wing of the V1, so that it went into a spin and crashed in a wood near Tonbridge, so possibly saving lives in London, where it was designed to fall.

With the end of hostilities I left Glosters and I was asked to stand for Parliament in the 1945 Election. I was sitting in the pilots' office one morning when I had a call from Judge Woodcock, asking me to tea. As I always intended to go to the Bar, I thought it was never too early to meet the judges and, when I got to his house, he asked me if I would like to be a parliamentary candidate. I asked him which party he had in mind, as I had little interest in politics. He said, 'The Liberal Party of course', so I said I would have a go, but could he lend me some books about Liberal policy, as I knew very little about it? I borrowed the books, read up the policies and went to the adoption meeting where I gave a speech on the information I had and then said, 'Those are my views, but if you don't like them, they can be changed'! I was duly adopted and fought the election, eventually ending up with 30% of the votes and succeeding in allowing the Labour Candidate to win, removing Bobby Perkins, who had been the Conservative Member for 15 years. I was accused of splitting the vote and was not very popular in the Stroud area, but it was a great mental exercise, which I needed to re-train my mind for the Bar Finals, which I had been unable to complete before the war. Having spent five years flying and reading only aeroplane text books and trashy novels, it was not easy to concentrate again on the law, but my short political venture certainly helped.

Looking back on my time with Glosters, I feel privileged to have been involved with the technical revolution that in only eight years from the first jet flight reached the summit of the world's speed record. It had not been achieved without many tribulations and failures, including the cost in lives of a number of my friends. Jet flight is now such an established means of mass transport, with Concorde and military aircraft flying at over twice the speed of sound, that it is strange to look back on the days when we encountered and overcame so many problems. This is not intended to be an article on the technical side of developing aircraft, but each step towards the sound barrier brought new problems. Because the wheels had to be small and light, it needed many changes in the brake linings to stop the Meteor, with its streamlined airframe. It was only by trial and error that we reduced the effect of compressibility, and every increase in thrust created new hazards. We had to test the ejection system, luckily for us, by being propelled up a pole, rather than baling out, and also the pressurisation of the cockpit, which is now extended to the cabins and taken for granted by the many thousand passengers who jet round the world, as well as the pilots of military machines.

Testing aeroplanes is not one of the safest occupations, but, when faced with a potential disaster 20,000 feet above the ground, it was comforting to know that we were unlikely to be shot at by an enemy fighter, and the dangers we faced were minimal, compared with the RAF pilots who took our Typhoons and Meteors into battle. Because I was more frightened by the prospect of baling out than I was by the chances of bringing the aircraft back to an airfield, I never abandoned an aeroplane. Nor did I suffer any serious injury in my forced landings, and, unlike many of my pilot colleagues, I am still alive to recall my long association with the RAF, before, during and after WW2. I made and still have a lot of friends in the RAF, and Douglas Bader was once my best man. It has always been a wonderful service since the early days when my father was a Camel pilot, and, if I had my time over again, I would want to repeat my flying experiences as part of the team that produced jet propulsion. Although not actually in the RAF itself, at least I worked with them and for them, and I will always remember the RAF.

8

FREDERICK FORSYTH

Per Ardua ad Acting Pilot Officer

I CANNOT RECALL exactly when I decided that one day I would fly, but it must have been quite early. Perhaps when, as a toddler in the fields of Kent, I looked up at the Spitfires and Hurricanes turning and wheeling above my head; perhaps during the Korean War, sitting in the Odeon watching the first grainy footage of the American Sabres taking on the MiG-15s. Whatever, by thirteen I was pretty determined.

For two years I read, with the voracity only the young can bring to an ambition, everything I could lay my hands on that concerned combat flying. I read the stories of the First World War aces in their Camels and Pups, Spads and Fokkers. I devoured the then-appearing memoirs of the Second World War aces, Johnnie Johnson, Bob Stanford Tuck, Douglas Bader, George 'Screwball' Beurling... By fifteen I think I could identify almost every combat fighter of the Second War and the years since. I crowded my room with models of them and persuaded a long-suffering father to take me to Farnborough every year, shocked when John Derry's DH-110 (later the Sea Vixen) broke up in mid-air, and marvelling at the sleek grace of the prototype Hawker Hunter.

My first chance came at sixteen, in an obscure paragraph in an aviation magazine. The RAF was prepared to award flying scholarships to suitable candidates. Scholarships? It meant that selected boys could learn to fly at their local flying school and the RAF would pick up the tuition fees. The total cost then (happy days!) was £120. In my best copperplate, tongue firmly gripped in teeth, I sat down and wrote to the Air Ministry. A small buff envelope, the first of many, arrived a week later. It contained a rail pass and an instruction to report to RAF Hornchurch in Essex. Fortunately I was on holiday from school, so there was no need to make excuses.

The underground train, for long firmly above ground, seemed to rattle on endlessly across the Essex flatlands until finally it stopped at what was then a quite small town and the end of the line. I handed in half my rail pass and enquired where the RAF base was situated. A five shilling taxi fare away. I walked, swinging my small fibre suitcase containing wash-kit, pyjamas and spare pants. For the course, fatigues would be provided.

The tests involved five days. First, two days of intensive medicals, everything examined from feet to follicles. The reason was simple – one did not need these tests to fly a Tiger Moth, but the RAF was looking for possible future pilots for itself. Moreover, the rest of my course was not there for a flying scholarship; these were young men heading for National Service and seeking to spend those two years as trainee pilots rather than broom-pushers.

Day Three was for aptitude tests – speed of reaction, reflexes under pressure, manual dexterity, that sort of thing. Slowly the number on the course diminished. The medics discovered flaws of which the candidates were not even aware – astigmatism, colour blindness, night blindness. We were thinned out day by day. The fourth day was for initiative exercises – building a bridge over an impossibly large chasm with impossibly short planks. The fifth morning was for interviews, personality assessment.

In my own case the latter was quite jocular. As soon as the middle-aged officers (some must have been forty or more!) discovered I was sixteen, they relaxed. Their decision after all would only involve £120 of taxpayer's money. After thirty minutes I was dismissed and returned to Ashford. Another buff envelope arrived. It instructed me that the scholarship was mine; I should attend at RAF Kenley to be issued with boots pair one, heavy socks, white pairs two, canvas flying suit one, leather helmet one and goggles pair one. After that I should arrange my own instruction with Bluebell Hill Flying Club at Rochester air strip. Wonderful. The only problem was school. The summer term of 1955 was about to begin, and Tonbridge was then a rigorous, monastic institution utterly unlikely to give exemption from sports afternoons to indulge an already rebellious youth in a personal ambition to fly a Tiger Moth.

My father rose to the occasion – he always did. He bought for me for £80 a second-hand Douglas Vespa. Mechanically unreliable and lethally unstable in the wet, it nevertheless could cover the fifteen miles from Tonbridge to Bluebell Hill in thirty minutes. I found a complaisant old gardener with an allotment in South Tonbridge who allowed me to store it in his shed.

Quite suddenly that term my superiors in the House were pleased but amazed to find that Forsyth F, who had previously loathed cross-country running, was volunteering for the Senior Cross (eight miles of misery) twice a week. With their benign agreement I would set off in running shorts, jog to the allotment shed, don the canvas flying suit, helmet and goggles (which doubled perfectly for scooter-riding) motor up to Bluebell Hill, have my flying lesson, motor back, hide the Vespa, strip down to jogging gear, and come panting home at dusk. The first delight from the House sports fanatics turned to puzzlement and then irritation. How could anyone who took four hours to cover eight miles ever win a cup for Parkside?

I loved the Tiger Moth. It was really basic flying. A silver bi-plane, open cockpit, head battered by the wind, struts and wires creaking and twanging high over Rochester and the Medway estuary – bliss on a summer's afternoon. The CFI, a world-weary ex-squadron leader, let me go solo after six hours' dual instruction, with admonitions to stick to the rules, the procedures and the set exercises. Some hope. Once aloft I could fantasise that this was not North Kent beneath me but the fields of Flanders. With a quick check to ensure that Bishop, Ball, Mannock and McCudden were strung out in formation beside me, and after a cheery wave to Garros, and Guynemer of the Cigogne Squadron, somewhere down-sun, we would all set off to find Immelmann, Boelcke and perhaps the lethal Manfred von Richthofen himself somewhere in the mists over Maidstone.

Aerobatics were a problem. The Tiger Moth had not been stressed for aerobatics and might crack a mainspar if pushed too hard. Moreover the carburetter had no inverted-flight valve and would cut out if turned upside-down – petrol supply being by gravity feed. Still, nothing ventured... After a few perfectly successful wingovers, I tried a gentle loop. I thought I would be upside-down at the top of the loop for such a short time the engine would not cut out. Wrong again. It did, and I found myself heading vertically down with nothing between me and Rochester Cathedral but a lot of fresh air getting rapidly less. But the Gypsy Queen engine was a sweet old lady and coughed back into life with enough space to save part of Britain's heritage taking a nasty dent. After that I stuck to barrel rolls where no negative-G forces are involved.

Term ended and then I could abandon the fiction of cross-country running and complete the course by motoring from Ashford to stay with an aunt in Gillingham. I was ready for the final test – the written exam had been passed – four weeks before my seventeenth birthday, but had to wait upon that date to take it. (Bureaucracy again.) I hitch-hiked to Italy and back, then reappeared at Bluebell Hill and took the test. The CFI sighed deeply and gave me a pass. By the by, he said, you have entitlement to one last hour of solo flight, pre-paid by the Air Force. Did I want it? Is the Pope Catholic? I had a score to settle.

Never having acquired a taste for the twin British educational obsessions of sodomy and the lash, I had not really 'got on' with Tonbridge, nor it with me. It was a wonderful last hour. Dipping low into the valley of hopfields beyond Le Flemings rugby field, surging up over the fence, hammering across Le Flemings and Martins, through the gap in the giant elms fringing the Head cricket pitch, across that and then the gravelled Quad. Old Big School straight ahead, the Chapel and science block on the left, the Arch's house on the right; two groundsmen raking gravel going flat face-down, a last burst from the imaginary Lewis gun straight through the windows of School House, then a hard pull up and left, the chapel roof under the wing-tip, level over Park House and my own prison Parkside, then climb hard over Tonbridge and head northwest. No. one caught the number of the plane. A week later I was back in that chapel singing 'O for the wings of a dove'.

I would have preferred to have left school that July, but my father, for once agreeing with Tonbridge, had persuaded me to stay on for the extra autumn term. For one thing my 'S' Level results did not come through until mid-August and I might have to re-sit, for another he had to give a term's notice or lose the school fees, for a third I could not get into the RAF at seventeen and a week. So I chafed and kicked my heels through the Michaelmas term, went up for an interview at Clare College, Cambridge, fluffed it fairly deliberately and was given up by the academic luminaries as a pretty poor show. Anyone who declined to go to university and told the careers officer that commuting for forty years to a stock-broker's desk in the City was a form of slow death, was an oddball and the British public school system was not in the business of producing oddballs. My ambition to fly in the Air Force was greeted with amused tolerance and the second ambition to be a journalist with stunned horror. So I slipped away from Tonbridge that December on lissom, printless toe, and went to the nearest RAF recruiting office.

The warrant officer in charge was bemused but firm. Even in January 1956 it was fairly common knowledge that National Service would soon end. If one could find a reason to avoid conscription for, say, two years one would probably be in the clear. Most of my contemporaries were developing a range of maladies from fallen arches to trick knees and defective vision. What made it worse was that National Service commissions, even for public-school boys, were already being phased out, which meant that a delicately nurtured youth destined for Daddy's team at Lloyds might have to spend two years in a barracks in Malaya with all those terrible people from the proletariat.

The warrant officer's bemusement stemmed from finding himself facing a boy pleading to get in nine months early. He patted me on the back and escorted me to the door. 'Just wait till you're eighteen, lad; perhaps it'll be over by then.' That was the problem; I didn't want it to be over.

Anyway, I went off to Spain for four months, ostensibly to study Spanish on a course Granada University ran in Malaga. I attended the first and 160th of the 160 classes. The middle 158 I spent with a bunch of Spanish youths in the bull ring learning cape-work from a gimpy old matador who had stopped one horn too many. We never faced a real bull of course; expensive creatures, fighting bulls, not to be wasted on young hopefuls. But I could understand the dreams of the Spanish boys; they wanted to walk alone onto that patch of sand in Madrid, I wanted to fly alone into that vault of blue above my head.

In April my father came down with news of a possible breakthrough. Lady Luck had shown her hand. Ashford Air Cadets had a marching band, and the band had a big drum. But the drummer had no leopard-skin. The CO had written to Dad asking if he had one. By chance he did – a magnificent skin abandoned in his vaults years earlier by someone who had never reclaimed it. He took a gamble the owner would never show up, re-cut the skin, backed it with red baize and presented it to the ecstatic cadet force. The Honorary CO, a retired air marshal, sent a letter of thanks. If there's ever anything I can do ... etc. My father wrote back; as a matter of fact, there was.

Hearing the details, the air marshal was incensed. Not prepared to take him? We'll see about that. Lady Luck again – the chief of recruiting at the Air Ministry turned out to be a group captain who years earlier had served under the air marshal. Strings were pulled, or yanked; wheels ground. When I got back from Spain there was another buff envelope. Report to Hornchurch.

Back at Hornchurch, the tests were much the same but the stakes were higher. There was no jocularity in the final interview. £120 of flying fees was one thing; £80,000 to £100,000 of training to 'wings' standard was different altogether. Even to get half way through the course before being 'chopped' would cost the taxpayer a lot of money. The screening officers wanted to make very few mistakes. After five days I was sent home again. But at least the Air Force was playing very fair; if I did not pass Hornchurch, there was no obligation to join the RAF and push a broom for two years. I could join the 'Ow-my-legs-hurts' brigade and try to stay in Civvy Street. About 1st May another buff envelope arrived. Selected for GD (general duties, the euphemism for flying branch) training; take this rail warrant and report to RAF Cardington next week.

Cardington had once been the home of the airships and then the barrage balloons. By the mid-fifties the gigantic hangars were converted into stores where millions of socks, shirts, boots, ties, belts, caps, berets, trousers and blouses were piled in rows awaiting the arrival of the tidal wave of National Servicemen. Cardington was for kitting-out. The human wave arrived by car with proud dads and weepy mums, or by bus, but mainly by train at Bedford station and thence by pale-blue coach. At Main Gate we checked in, a motley assortment of youths and young men, the long and the short and the tall; the miserable and the determinedly cheerful, the snooty, the aggressive, the languid, the apprehensive, the wimps and the wallies. Some came in dark suits, others in tweeds and flannels, the Teddy Boys in oily jeans and black leather. The maw of Main Gate, Cardington, engulfed us all.

After check-in and self-identification against a host of clipboards, the first stop was the barber. Here a row of bored clipper-drivers awaited, their ennui only relieved when they saw a Teddy Boy's shock of greasy, shoulder-length hair. Then they could really go to work, reducing the oleaginous shrubbery to a bristly stubble. My own short-back-and-sides fared better and was left more or less alone.

The next day brought kitting-out, a long straggling queue of civilians with hedgehog haircuts entering a hangar at one end to emerge at the other with an off-white kitbag bulging with standard issue gear. For many of the boys fresh from home the first night in a barracks and the mountain of webbing, Brasso, Blanco, boot polish and clothes were traumatic. Fortunately I had done it all for ten years at prep school and Tonbridge. The blue serge uniform and webbing were no problem – I had been in the Air Corps at Tonbridge also. I picked the biggest bruiser in my barrack, a semi-professional from Bermondsey, and taught him how to melt the boot polish over a match to get a decent shine on the toe-caps. My first 'oppo' and a good investment. He warned the others off me, despite my accent.

But there was another hazard. There were five of us destined for GD training, and that meant, after cadet camp, an automatic commission. To mark the difference, we five were given soft cotton/poplin shirts in the palest blue; the rest received those hairy confections which, with an admixture of body sweat would soon make the hairshirts of the Benedictines seem positively indulgent. After dressing in our new gear and handing in the civvy clothes, we were paraded again. Then the five soft, pale shirts stood out a mile. About three thousand eyes stared at us balefully. Officers – to be. It was no time to explain. The five soft-shirts, three destined for pilots and two for navigators, formed a defensive laager at one end of a barrack and survived the next three days until a stiff and disapproving corporal summoned us to Main Gate. There were more rail warrants, this time to a basic training camp for officer cadets. The destination said: RAF Kirton-in-Lindsey. Where the hell was that?

Kirton-in-Lindsey turned out to be a small former WW2 air station with a grass strip, set amid the bleak and windswept flatlands between Lincoln and Scunthorpe, just over the Humberside border. In winter the northeasters would sweep in straight from the Arctic Circle with nothing but a brace of church steeples between the base and the North Pole. Fortunately, we arrived in May and were due to leave in August.

Tumbling from the train, dressed in the itchy serge of aircraftmen second class (apart from the anomaly of the soft shirts) we were met by Corporal Davis. He was very short and wore his peaked cap in the style of the Guards, its black plastic brim a fraction above the bridge of the nose. This meant he had to walk bolt upright to see where he was going and tilt his head backwards to look up. Although I was only 5 ft 9 in at the time and still growing, he was yet shorter. On the platform he selected me, the shortest of the five new arrivals, marched up to my chest and peered up with baleful eyes.

'Do you know who I am?' he screeched in a manic yell. His voice was strangely high-pitched, as one in a permanent rage.

'No, Corporal,' I admitted.

'Well, I'm Jesus Christ, that's who I am. And from now on, that's how you'll bleeding well treat me.'

Other selected youngsters had been waiting for our arrival to constitute enough for a 'course', which we now formed, eighteen in number. The oldest was Bill Broatch, a PhD from Edinburgh at the ripe age of twenty-six. Without demur he became course leader, and we were called Red Squadron. There were six squadrons at cadet camp, each inducted once a fortnight for the three month basic training programme.

National Servicemen were not the favoured sons of the long-serving officers and NCOs. We were sloppy, we were Bolshie, meaning we had a habit of querying the wisdom of orders and systems. Marching and counter-marching was not our forte, spit and polish elicited little enthusiasm, bull earned our derision and ribald humour was our method of self-expression. Little wonder we drove our instructors to despair.

The squadron commander was Squadron Leader Miller, plump and jovial, owner of a beautiful classic sports car in which we got free rides around the base if we polished it. Flight commander was Flight Lieutenant Brown, as tall and mournful as Miller was round and cheerful.

Taken to the gym, we were introduced to Corporal 'Tiger' Thompson, tracksuit trousers and singlet, bulging muscles and a fitness freak. He started with chin-ups, hoisting ourselves by the arms to a bar above our heads. Anthony Preston, one of the other two public schoolboys, was also into physical fitness and did sixteen. Vernon Marks did a half. The rest of us managed six or seven. The corporal contemptuously did twenty-five without breaking sweat and led us on a run. This time I had no Vespa.

Flight Sergeant Isherwood was our drill instructor, a lovely man who screamed abuse at us across the parade ground then called us 'lads' when drill period was over. We nearly broke his heart. After three months we were still dreadful. The dress rehearsal for the passing out parade was a disaster. Law-rence, a navigator-to-be, got his 6 ft 3 in frame next to Tony Bostock, the shortest at 5 ft 2 in, with ludicrous results. Vernon mixed up left and right during a turning manoeuvre and was last seen striding purposefully towards the NAAFI all on his own. Mike Porter, a Winchester product, bumped into Bill Broatch and spent several seconds apologising profusely in cut-crystal accents. Someone's bayonet nearly pierced the larynx of the man behind him during a 'squad halt'. Finally Flight Sergeant Isherwood called us over. To our horror he was on the verge of tears.

'I have never,' he mumbled, misty-eyed, 'in my entire career, come across such an incompetent, hopeless, useless bunch of bastards as you lot, gen-tlemen.' (He could call us pregnant penguins, dispute our paternity, whatever, so long as he called us gentlemen at the end. After all, we were officer cadets.)

We felt genuinely touched and moved. The following day, Passing Out Parade, went like a dream. We marched as Guardsmen. The Blanco glowed, the brasses glittered. Even Vernon Marks had a gleam to his toe-caps, which was unheard-of. Anthony Preston straightened his shoulders, Tony Bostock swung his tiny arms shoulder-high, Bill Broatch swept his sword down to the saluting dais during the marchpast with the panache of a fencing master. Only Cadet Forsyth was out of step part of the time – the old problem of starting out on the wrong foot. When it was over we took Flight Sergeant Isherwood down to the World's End and got him gloriously plastered.

The question we were eager to solve was: where would we go for basic flying training? In those days some UK pilots were sent to a NATO school near Winnipeg, Canada. Our own posting turned out to be for Ternhill, Shrop-shire. We bade farewell to the six navigator candidates who would go to navigator school, and the remaining twelve of us headed across country after a brief week's leave for Shropshire.

After 'boot camp' Ternhill was the real thing. After our leave we all reunited, not as cadets with the distinctive white lapel tab but with smooth blue barathea uniforms as pilot officers, albeit only 'acting.' For the RAF the distinction was useful; if 'chopped' from the course, a substantive officer could not be reduced back to 'erk' and given a broom to push; an APO could. Still, I was glad I had got my commission while still seventeen. The trick from now on was not to flunk.

We were joined by several others, some being moved back from earlier courses and given a second chance, others already career officers who had started in 'ground' duties but had now qualified for pilot training. The National Servicemen quickly learned there were two standards: career men could make a few slips and be pardoned or re-scheduled, but already National Servicemen were quietly regarded as a waste of time and money. One slip and it was the dreaded 'chop.'

We were quickly introduced to the Hunting Percival Provost trainer, a low-wing, fixed undercarriage monoplane powered by a large propeller-driven rotary engine and with side-by-side seating. My own instructor was the wonderful Flight Lieutenant Grzybowski, known just as 'Grib', a short Pole who had been a World War II fighter pilot and shot down a number of Messerschmitts. He called us all 'boys' and pronounced it 'boyce'.

Classroom studies went alongside actual flying: meteorology, theory of flight, radio, navigation, airframe, engine, emergency procedures, aviation medicine. But the flying was what we wanted, what we were there for.

Learning that I had flown before, and convinced I would neither seize up on him nor decorate his lap with my breakfast, Grib took me aloft for aerobatics at last. He wheeled, spun, dived, rolled, looped and turned until the sky, the horizon and Shropshire merged into a kaleidoscopic blur. When he was happy that I was happy, he let me take over. The Provost was a sweet-natured beast and never did unpleasant things unless seriously insulted.

After two weeks we all went off to a grass-strip satellite airfield called Chetwynd for our first solo flights. Nothing untoward occurred as, one by one, watched by a tight-mouthed bunch of instructors, we took our Provosts off for a single circuit and back down again. Only Bill Broatch, at twenty-six the daddy of us all, caused amusement when, having got aloft, he declined to come back down again. Twelve times he drifted down the grass strip, ten feet up, gazing dourly down at the terra firma beneath him. His instructor was about to send for bird-seed when Bill finally cut the power and dropped the Provost rather bumpily onto the breast of Mother Earth.

After that came instrument-flying (with a hood over our heads to simulate dense cloud and only the instruments visible) cross-country navigation, simu-lated emergencies, aerobatics, night-flying, dog-fighting, and formation flying. Bill was a difficult man upon whom to formate, having established his reputation as the most mature and cautious among us. One would close up with him, wingtip to wingtip, he would throw a worried glance at the few feet of fresh air separating the wingtips and move skittishly away across the sky. One closed up, only to see him do it again. Progress became a crab-like gavotte across the sky. He was proud of his membership of the same-day-same-way school of formation flying.

After nine months at Ternhill we passed out, having lost three or four of our number to the dreaded 'chop'. The procedure was always the same. The instructor would become gloomy and confer with the Wing Commander Flying. Eventually the pupil would be sent for and told he seemed to be having too much difficulty with this, that or the other. There would be one last beery and morose evening at the pub with the departing pupil, then he would be gone. The rest of us just breathed a sigh of relief – it was like playing musical chairs.

But Ternhill had been a happy posting. We were all aged from eighteen to twenty-two (bar two older men), happy-go-lucky, exasperatingly irreverent, appallingly scruffy, immature and slightly drunk on the new sensations of open-topped sports cars, student nurses in the back of them, pints of beer, the throbbing rhythm of Bill Haley and his Comets and the young Elvis Presley and most of all on the sheer exhilaration of throwing a Provost around the sky. It was a carefree nine months; it would become less so at Worksop, near Sheffield, when we met the single-seat jet, the de Havilland Vampire.

The slightly gung-ho, pre-war hilarity of Ternhill and the Provost had no place at Worksop. The Vampire came in two versions: the T-11, a side-by-side seated trainer for instructional flying, and the Marks 5 and 9, single-seated and very similar. The former had been made specifically for flying training; the latter had been front-line fighters five years earlier, superseded by the Hunter and the extraordinary Lightning.

It was a strange little aircraft, comprising a tiny hull with a miniscule cockpit backed by a de Havilland Goblin engine and twin-boom tail. The wings were short and stumpy, the two pencil-thin booms jutting backwards to support the tail. It was not supersonic, its top speed being only about 540 mph at 20,000 feet, and extremely manoeuvrable.

As we were lectured upon it, a gloomy flight sergeant pointed out that while the T-11 had the Martin Baker ejector seat the Mark Five did not. Nor the Mark Nine. The cockpit was too small; it was Britain's only jet fighter not to have the ejector seat. Also, he intoned, no one had ever bailed out alive. Encumbered by dinghy pack and parachute, a pilot in trouble could not lever himself out between the steel seat and the front windscreen. So that was it; either land it or die in it.

As at Ternhill, the classroom lectures started again, teaching us more of the same, plus the characteristics of transonic flight (the reason for all that buffeting near the sound barrier) bale-out procedures (purely theoretical) and high-altitude flying (at 40,000 feet the air becomes thin and aerobatics more sensitive).

In August 1957, just before my nineteenth birthday, I waited tensely at the threshold of the runway for clearance, eased the throttle full forward, felt the Vampire crouch until the handbrakes came off, then roll and finally hurl itself down the white strip towards the chunk of Nottinghamshire called the over-shoot area. Just over 95 on the clock she lifted off; flaps up, wheels up, check for three green lights (wheels up and locked), lift the nose, register a fleeting impression of the brown fields dropping far away, ease out of the climbing turn, level at 1,000 feet and turn downwind on the first 'circuit and bump'. First solo. A huge sense of exhilaration. Done it.

We had been joined at Worksop by fresh additions to the course, including Derek Brett, a flying officer and Cranwell man on a permanent commission who had started in ground duties and tried manfully for flying duties until he finally made it. He was married with a baby daughter. I believe there were four or five other additions to keep up the numbers.

We proceeded to the usual disciplines: navigation, flying in dense cloud (as winter closed in there was plenty of this, the 'clag' made thicker by the industrial smog), high-altitude aerobatics (almost all of us managed to fall out of a loop or a roll in the thin air and plummet like a brick for several miles before recovering control), low-level and night-flying.

The latter came in January, bitter, freezing nights locked into that tiny, warm coccoon under the perspex, aware of our thin nylon flying suits and the lethal 76 degrees below zero outside the cockpit, lonely in the isolation of a tiny hull eight miles above the earth in total blackness. Later I would use the memory to try to evoke the near panic that possessed the pilot in a short story called 'The Shepherd'.

Low-level flying was gut-wrenching and wonderful. We were supposed to stay at 100 feet, but most of us went down to the deck, say, fifteen to twenty feet which at 500 mph does seem rather quick. One of our instructors Glyn Owen had a habit of sliding his wing tip into a fenland dyke (ie below ground level) and running down the field on his wingtip. He liked to make sure the pupil was on the side nearest the field and I recall once seeing a potato clamp flash past the roof of the cockpit.

The losses continued. Anthony Preston, with us from that first day at Kirton-in-Lindsey, tried a power dive from 40,000 feet with a slight head cold and blew out both eardrums. In the mid-course Derek Brett, accompanied by his instructor 'Jonah' Jones, flew into the Pennines in dense cloud. The Pennines won. Some fragments were found. A week later we stood miserably in the streaming rain in a cemetery outside Worksop and watched the pine coffin ballasted with sand slide into the weeping earth. The next morning we climbed back into the cockpits and went up again. Across the airfield the squadron with whom we shared Worksop, an outfit using Meteors to give senior officers re-familiarisation courses after years behind a desk, lost a Meteor with pilot and pupil.

In the spring of 1958 we took our final tests – flying and classroom – and prepared for passing-out parade. In late March in an empty hangar (it was sheeting rain outside) an air vice marshal took the salute and one by one pinned those coveted 'wings' on our chests just above the left breast pocket.

There were three weeks' terminal leave during which I hitched lifts from Lyneham to Malta, Cyprus and Lebanon, and then we were out. Well, half of us. The others were nine-year or twenty-year men and they stayed, hoping in vain for a flying posting.

There were few hopes of a course at Chivenor to convert to Hunters and then a fighter squadron. More and more the front-line squadrons were for Cranwell men, or long-service direct commission officers. National Servicemen signing on tended to get a desk job or transports. Anyway, I had sated my appetite and wanted to become a foreign correspondent.

Of the eighty-five in my week at Hornchurch, three had been selected; the next week, out of two hundred, none. Of the twelve pilots-select who tumbled out of the train at Kirton-in-Lindsey, there were six left. Tom Ashworth emigrated to America and became an airline pilot; Tony Bostock tragically died of cancer in his early thirties; Bill Broatch also emigrated to the States with his PhD in organic chemistry and became a scientist for a large corporation; Ian Frow joined BA and has just retired as a captain; Mike Porter became a chartered accountant and settled in North Wales. I joined a local newspaper and later Reuters.

It may be unfashionable but I loved National Service. Of course, I was doing what I wanted to do. It left me a host of memories – of friendship and camaraderie, of laughter and crazy escapades, of bright summer dawns on the flight line, of whirling propellers and howling jet engines; and also of Derek Brett's graveyard in the rain, and the hammer of the blood-pulse in the ears, bucketing down through cloud and fog to a runway that might or might not be a mile ahead.

Those two years taught me things I would not have learned elsewhere; meeting people from quite different backgrounds to my own, whom I would not have met if passing from a public school to a stockbroker's office; meeting people from different parts of our land, whom I would not have known if I had stayed in the south-east. This is not given to young men today and more's the pity.

Mostly I think the RAF took a boy of seventeen and a half and turned out a man. Not always a very sensible or mature one; but somewhere, sometime, at the controls of a Vampire, I think we all crossed that threshold.

9

WILLIAM FRANKLYN

Roger Able Baker Charlie and Friends

A s a young boy brought up in Australia, I was weaned on aviators. The word pilot was a long time coming into my vocabulary. And aviators, who were part of my mother's and father's social circle, were Scotty Allen, Amy Johnson, Jim Mollison, Charlie Ulm, H. J. (Bert) Hinkler, and Charles Kingsford-Smith (later knighted for services to aviation). I still have an autographed photo of this legend.

In 1928 Bert Hinkler flew from England to Australia covering the 12,250 miles in 15 days. Later that year Captain Kingsford-Smith and Ulm of Australia, and Lyon and Warner of America flew from Oakland, California to Sydney, 7,400 miles, stopping only at the Hawaiian Islands, Fiji and Brisbane. They flew the 'Southern Cross', a Fokker monoplane. In the early thirties the 'Southern Cross' disappeared with all its passengers, and despite a prolonged and extensive search, including Kingsford-Smith in the sister air-craft the 'Southern Cloud', it remained lost until about thirty-five years later, when it was found in the mountains between Sydney and Melbourne.

In 1930 Amy Johnson completed a 9,900 mile flight from London to Australia in $19\frac{1}{2}$ days. Amy Johnson's plane, 'Jason', was wheeled onto the stage of the Theatre Royal, Sydney with her wedged in the small metal seat in its cockpit. She was asked by my father, who was in the current production and introduced this unique event, why she was carrying a large sheath knife. 'In case I come down in the Timor Sea and meet a shark,' was her calm reply. She flew on to New Zealand quite safely.

In what was an exciting era of aviation in Australia, my own fantasies were being nourished by the biographies of Captain Albert Ball, vc, dso, Major Mick Mannock, vc, dso, mc, and Major McCudden vc, dso and Bar, mc and Bar; all First World War RFC pilots.

By the time I saw my first Hendon air show in 1937, on the very site of the Royal Air Force Museum, I could spot most of the Hawker, Fairey, Vickers and De Havilland aircraft in service. I remember vividly the Hawker Fury II with the Kestrel VI engine, the Dragon Rapide by De Havilland, the Vickers Armstrong Wellington (to continue from its inception well into the Second World War), the Gloster Gladiator, the Fairey Battle and the early Hawker Hurricane.

Many of my generation were motivated to become RAF volunteers by the deeds of the Battle of Britain fighter pilots, later by the exploits of Mosquito night fighters, and the Blenheim, Wellington and Lancaster bomber crews.

The white flash slotted in our blue forage caps, the symbol of potential aircrew above our newly pressed RAF uniforms, was worn with a fierce childlike pride. My memories of Scarborough and St John's Wood aircrew intake centres are always revived as I drive to Lord's Cricket Ground. I lived within a stone's throw of St John's Wood so naturally I was sent to Scarborough.

After initial training at Scarborough College a group of us were sent to No. 3 (Pilot) Advanced Flying Unit, an air school at South Cerney. It was to be where we got our first flight experience. The training aircraft were Avro Ansons and Airspeed Oxfords, very solid and reliable work horses of the air.

My most vivid recollections of this posting were an unusual duet. I became very air sick over Wiltshire in an Airspeed Oxford, and availed myself of an extremely large bung in the floor of the kite (period word), and having recovered some of my poise stood up to see the most amazing sight. To left and right, and below, and very soon above was the largest air armada I, the pilot and later the world was to see, if only on newsreels. Bombers, and bombers towing gliders darkened the sky in a sight so overwhelming as to seem an hallucination. The pilot's words still ring in my ears, 'Well, young Franklyn, there's a bit of a show on.' It was the beginning of the invasion of Europe.

To a young sprog (new recruit) this was his first view of Armageddon. Even without the magnifying glass of memory, there had to be at least 600 pieces of winged aviation in sight, and we were distinctly de trop. By now, I was sitting in the other side-by-side cockpit seat. The flight lieutenant pilot's face was as bemused as mine, but I suspected was camouflaging an experienced mind, which was soon evidenced. 'I think we'll just creep back to base, and maintain a discreet silence.' We low-tailed it back to South Cerney and left a sky full of Britain's youth to fly into the pages of history.

A month later we were posted to Cranage, between Holmes Chapel and Northwich – south of Manchester. It consisted of huts for about 600 aircrew trainees and their instructors, alongside a medium-sized airfield with a few hangars. It is now totally arable land except for the brick remnants of the fire engine sheds, and a couple of mounds growing over some collapsed air raid bunkers. The highlight of this posting was to have a peacetime reverberation. It was sport's day at Cranage. In the 440 yards (not metres in those days) I ran a competent second to a long-legged Jamaican. It was only competent in that third was way behind and I was 20 yards adrift of this beautiful mover.

Three years later, by which time I was coming up to demob from the Paras (more of this in a moment), I was recalled from leave to run against the Guards, and after motor-cycling through the night from Cornwall I ran out of road outside Fleet, in Hampshire, and broke my leg. My running at high level was curtailed and any 1948 Olympic dream disappeared. This was a confirmed reality when watching the '48 Olympics in London and the 440 yards line-up included that beautiful mover from RAF Cranage. Ex-

Aircraftman Arthur Wint of Jamaica was to win the Gold medal. The circle was squared.

Back at Cranage in October 1944, an Airborne major, newly survived from the Arnhem battle, arrived to give us a propaganda recruitment talk on the merits of, and need to join, the Parachute or Glider Pilot Regiment. This followed hard on a very realistic talk by our own CO on the future of potential RAF aircrew. There were, by then, far too many trainees in the pipe line for the number of aircraft and the future needs of the Royal Air Force.

The alternatives were a ground posting in an administrative capacity for a minimum of one year, re-training in a technical branch, the Army or the Navy; both forces that were looking for specialist madmen. The major from Arnhem won eight recruits from Cranage, but when we arrived for basic infantry training prior to parachute training, at Fulford Barracks, York, we had an entire company of ex-aircrew trainees from around the country.

It was sixteen weeks later that the RAF came back into our lives at Ringway (now Manchester airport). There I dropped through the hole in the floor of a Whitley and went out of the door of Dakotas.

Two memories of Ringway, which are as much RAF tales as Para ones. A Canadian ex-Mustang pilot was posted to fly us on training jumps. On my fourth qualifying jump he flew the Dakota like a Mustang and at a height of 390 feet, instead of 600 feet. We were jumping with loaded kit bags on one leg, which we released so that they dangled below us. From 390 feet and at a crazy speed the kit bag hit the deck almost as we were releasing it, and our hopefully controlled landing had the effect of a skeleton tied to a sack of potatoes hitting the ground at 45 mph. The Mustang pilot was posted to a less life-threatening job.

In historical rather than personal hindsight, some of the earliest parachute training in the desert, which consisted of being plucked off the lower wing of a Vickers Valentia by releasing your 'chute into the old bi-plane's slipstream, doesn't seem that cosy either. That was equalled by Russian parachute troops, who in the 1930s climbed out onto the wing of the monoplane Tuploev Ant-6, and indulged in freefall.

The second memory of Ringway did not concern me but I'd like to meet the man it did concern. A parachutist trainee exited from the underbelly of a Whitley and his static line (which connected the parachute to a cable in the aircraft and released the chute under the pressure of gravity) caught on the tail wheel. There he dangled in very mid-air. Every emergency alternative was thought of and acted upon. Cutting his static line, wobbling the aircraft, climbing and shallow diving were all tried – to no avail. So the Whitley approached the runway and the pilot put her down with all the gentleness that $8\frac{1}{2}$ tons of old aircraft would allow. The parachutist still had the chute strapped to his back, and by a miracle of intuition and cool-headedness he tucked his knees as far up as possible, and was dragged along the runway on his parachute pack. He survived, despite the chute thinning down to a fraction of its thickness. Although not present, we saw the pictures in the *Daily Mirror* of the time (researchers please note) so this is not one of those 'fishing tales'.

For a peaceful, sleep-inducing trip to the DZ (dropping zone) the great Lancaster was a winner. The combination of deep throbbing Merlins and acute nerves were my cure for insomnia; and the neat floor exit from the Lancaster was a perfect compromise between 'ringing the bell' (hitting your head) as you exited from the Whitley hole and waiting and looking down the long open coffin trench of the Stirling just before you stepped into eternity.

In 1982 I made a television film called *The Purple Twilight*. It was the story of an ex-bomber crew, who found and re-built, to full flying capacity, their old Lancaster bomber. They flew it on a re-run of one of the wartime Berlin raids. This part of the the story was set in the 1980s. The air lanes and radar controllers of Europe were agog at this mystery wartime ghost come to life. The wires hummed and Air Ministry archives came up with its original designation. It was a fantasy of living history.

The very realistic flying scenes were created and accepted by many as totally convincing. They were all photographed, with effects, in the Lancaster at Hendon Air Museum.

Another circle in my aviation story squared.

If you are still with me, thank you for your patience and a very Happy Anniversary.

10

JAMES A. GOODSON

A Yank in the RAF (Overpaid, Oversexed and Over Here)

I BECAME INVOLVED in WWII on the first day, 3rd September 1939, when I was on the wrong ship going back to the United States from my studies in Europe. I still don't know how Mr Hitler knew I was on that ship! She was the SS *Athenia*, the first ship of the war to be torpedoed.

I helped to rescue as many people as I could until we were picked up by a Norwegian tanker which had been at sea for some weeks and still didn't know that war had been declared. Our party included some young girl students who had been dressing for dinner when the ship sank and were mainly dressed in their underclothes. I cannot tell you the admiration I have for the seamen's gentlemanly reactions when these half-clad girls climbed into the bunks with them to get warm! Instead of doing what I would probably have done, they made us coffee!

I managed to get from Eire, where we landed, to Glasgow. My steamship ticket had small print absolving the shipping line from any responsibility for anything that happened as a result of action by 'the King's Enemies', so I decided if I couldn't get back to the States I had better help the King deal with his enemies!

I began haunting an RAF recruiting station in Sauchiehall Street, Glasgow, asking, 'Can an American join your RAF?'

It took them some time to sort out the right forms and discover I could; but even then, they said, 'And don't bother to put down that you want to be a fighter pilot!'

'Why not?' I asked. 'That's what I want to be.'

'So does everyone else – forget it!'

I think the breakthrough came when I was asked, 'Have you done any flying?'

'Yes,' I replied. 'I have a few hours.'

'Don't move!'

This news warranted a telephone call to London – not something lightly undertaken in those days.

'Sir, we've got a *pilot*!'

They did warn me that because of the US Neutrality Acts, I could lose my citizenship by swearing allegiance to the King of England.

'If the King wants my allegiance,' I brashly replied, 'he's got it!'

'There is one other thing,' the officer said diffidently. 'The question of pay – it's 7/6d a day.'

I was crestfallen. 'Sir,' I stammered, 'I've just lost everything I owned on the *Athenia*. I don't think I can afford 7/6d a day!'

'No, no,' he said hastily, 'we pay *you*!'

I remember thinking, 'You lovable fool! I'd have done it for nothing!' To be able to fly a Spitfire, *and* get paid for it? The feeling of deep gratitude to the RAF remains with me to this day.

At the time, the RAF were having difficulty training enough pilots, so I was sent to Canada for training. Long before there was any flying, there were months of frustration as they tried to make soldiers and airmen out of young civilians from all over the world. The Empire Air Training Scheme was eventually set up in Canada and became one of the most successful of all Allied undertakings.

We finally arrived at an EFTS (Elementary Flying Training School) where we were introduced to our first aeroplane, the American Fleet biplane, similar to a Tiger Moth. Most of the instructors were American civilian pilots, but they were rapidly being replaced by RAF and RCAF pilots as they became available.

From Fleets, we graduated to the ubiquitous AT-6 Harvard at the Advanced Training School. It was here that my flying career nearly came to an end. My American instructor and I didn't get on and it showed to such an extent that he recommended that I be 'washed out'. Fortunately, this decision required the agreement of the Chief Flying Instructor, who took me up for a test flight.

'Well, show me what you can do,' was all he said as we took off. I took him at his word. When we landed, he said, 'You're a fighter pilot.'

It's interesting that, some time later, the first instructor arrived in England to join my squadron in the 4th Fighter Group – at his own especial request. He said he wanted to prove himself to me! He didn't quite make it; he was killed on his first mission.

At last, I was posted to RAF Tangmere, one of the great Battle of Britain airfields in England.

Initially, I flew Hurricanes, a wonderful aeroplane, steady as a rock. It has become a great mystique that the Spitfire won the Battle of Britain, but the RAF didn't have so many Spitfires then and there were twice as many Hurricanes. The mystique of the Spitfire even extended to the Germans.

The great Peter Townsend once told me of an occasion when he was able to visit in hospital a German pilot he had shot down.

'I am glad to meet the Spitfire pilot who shot me down,' the man said.

'No, no,' said Peter, 'I was flying a Hurricane!'

The man took a lot of convincing, but finally said, 'Well, if ever you meet any of my friends, please tell them it was a Spitfire that shot me down!'

One of the great advantages of the Hurricane was that it could take a great deal of punishment and still fly back to base. A great many landed with so many cannon-holes in them and bits shot away that the ground crews couldn't understand how they ever got back.

On one return trip across the Channel, my Hurricane caught fire. I eventually decided I had better get out and climbed onto the wing. The sea looked a long way down, and very cold. At that point, the plane side-slipped and the flames went away, so I decided to get back in and was able to land it at Manston.

(There was one occasion when I told that story in an after-dinner speech at an American airbase in England. When questions from the floor were invited, the first on his feet was a New Yorker from the Bronx.

'Yes sir, Colonel sir, I have a question. I can understand someone getting out of a Hurricane that was on fire. What I can't understand is what sort of damnfool idiot would get back in!')

With No. 416 Squadron I flew Spitfires – a wonderful plane. Every pilot who flew a Spitfire had a sort of love-affair with it. It was so beautifully manoeuvrable. If I dropped my cigar lighter, I didn't grope around on the floor for it. I just turned the stick a little, the plane went over and I caught the lighter as it came down.

The Empire Air Training Scheme was producing more Canadian squadrons and American volunteers were put in them, since to the English, they spoke the same language! I was posted to 416 Squadron, RCAF, where we were immediately made to feel at home. The cosmopolitan nature of RAF Fighter Command was due to the men it absorbed from all over the world. Long before America entered the war, there were Americans flying with the RAF. Thirteen of them (not seven, as many books state) flew in the Battle of Britain.

Apart from flying missions over occupied Europe and fighting over the Channel and south-east England, we also had the same problems the civilians did. The main one for us wasn't dried egg – it was transport; or rather, the lack of it, to get from deepest Surrey to the West End to meet a girl or two. Our problem was solved for a while by a wonderful New Zealander in our squadron, John Weroheia.

He burst into the Mess one day crying, 'I've solved our transport problems! Come outside and see!'

Outside were a zebra and a small pony-trap.

'The local circus is getting rid of its animals because it can't feed them. I got him and the trap for only seven pounds!'

So four large airmen set off up the A23 in this vehicle and finally tethered the beast to a tree in Hyde Park. Returning after a lovely evening, we were horrified to discover that Stripey had slipped his halter and disappeared. We were beating the bushes calling out, 'Stripey! Stripey!' when a representative of the Law appeared.

'All right, gentlemen, you've obviously had a very good evening. Now why don't you just go home?'

'You don't understand officer – we want to go home, we're standing dawn readiness, but we can't go home until we find our zebra!'

He decided to humour us and join in the search. I can still see the look on the face of that London bobby when he came face-to-face with a zebra in the bushes. His mouth was still open when we drove away!

It makes me rather angry when RAF pilots are portrayed as neurotic, worn-out, weeping into their beer every night. I never saw any of that – what I remember is the FUN! And the comradeship, many friendships which have lasted to this day among those who are still with us.

In spite of the American Neutrality Act, many young Americans wanted to get into the fight, and Britain badly needed pilots. One man made it possible for them to do so, an American businessman living in London, Charles Sweeny. He formed the American Eagle Squadrons, American pilots who had their own squadrons in the RAF. I was asked to transfer to the Eagles, and initially I refused. I was very happy where I was.

Then one night I was ordered, not asked, to go down to Debden and re-form 133 Eagle Squadron. When we arrived, there was no-one to be seen, until one man appeared. He was Don Gentile.

'Take any room you like,' he said. 'Nobody has come back.'

Each room in the barracks was littered with half-finished letters to parents and girl-friends. Toothpaste and haircream stood on lockers amidst the photographs. Not one of the planes that had taken off that day for Morlaix had returned. The whole squadron had been lost over Cherbourg on a raid to Morlaix, owing to bad weather and strong winds. Gentile had been spare pilot and was lucky not to have gone himself.

One of the most noticeable things about the RAF in those days was that men had come from all around the world to join in the fight. Shoulder flashes read 'Canada', 'South Africa', 'Australia', 'New Zealand'.

Vic France's read 'Texas'. The day America came into the war, he started a discussion in the Mess as to whether the United States had the right to declare war on behalf of Texas, which had never acceded to the Union!

Another Texan in the Eagle Squadron – I think it was Snuffy Smith – caused consternation when King George VI came down to Debden to present some medals. The King said how glad he was that we were helping out, if ever there was anything he could do, etc. etc. Snuffy stepped forward.

'Yes, sir,' he said, 'as a matter of fact, there is something.' As a result, King's Rules & Regulations were amended to allow the wearing of Texas cowboy boots with RAF uniform – provided they were black.

After the attack on Pearl Harbor in December 1941, America had at last come into the war, and in the autumn of 1942 we were asked to transfer to become the 4th Fighter Group of the US 8th Air Force, because they were badly in need of pilots with combat experience. We were not all that keen to do so. We had enjoyed our time in the RAF, we didn't want to leave our squadrons and our Spitfires and our friends. However, we were persuaded that this was the best contribution we could make. We did, however, insist on the right to wear our RAF wings and decorations on USAAF uniforms.

This was later to cause me some trouble. I was stopped in Grosvenor Square one day by a US Army General, probably a West Pointer.

'Major!' he barked. 'You are improperly dressed. Who gave you permission to wear foreign wings and decorations on the uniform of an officer of the US Army?'

'Sir,' I replied, 'the President of the United States and King George VI of England.'

He knew when he was beaten. He was also a Southerner.

'They're mighty purty!' he said.

The Spitfires we kept for a while, but we were told to paint out the RAF roundel and replace it with the United States star. I don't know if you have ever tried to draw a 5-pointed star, but it's not easy. Dixie Alexander and I were chivvying everyone to get on with it, because we wanted to fly a low-level attack over France that day.

Eventually, my crew chief said, 'Sir, I have a star on this medallion my mother gave me. Perhaps you could copy that.'

We leapt at this idea – we didn't know one star from another anyway. But it's an interesting thought that, as a result, the first two US fighters to fly over occupied Europe were originally British – and were emblazoned with the Star of David!

I am still immensely proud to wear the RAF tie, and my British decorations, whether at a Remembrance Day service, a squadron dinner or on any other occasion. We were made to feel welcome in the RAF and by the whole of the English people. They did, of course, say that we were 'Overpaid, over-sexed and over here' – but I reckon that, after fifty years, to still have two out of the three going for me can't be bad!

11

HUGHIE GREEN

Flying Boat Captain

THERE MUST be few to visit the RAF Museum at Hendon who can with surprise, and sudden fond memories, look at an aeroplane they actually flew during their time in the service.

I am one of the lucky ones; For there in the main hall is Stranraer Flying Boat 921 which I trained on at the Royal Canadian Air Force, OTU, Patricia Bay, British Columbia in January 1943. Flying Officer Bill Brooks, my instructor, who taught me the joy and fascination of water landings and take-offs both by day and at first – hair-raisingly at night – used to say, when introducing an anxious new student to the old, multi-wired bi-plane, 'You don't know whether to fly it or play it.'

Prior to my service in Canada's air force, and thanks to a reasonably successful theatrical career, both in Britain and the United States, my income allowed me to pay for flying lessons and the 40 hours in my log book. Showing the RCAF recruiting office in Montreal, (the family home town) in 1941, 40 hours, logged, bought, paid for and certified, put a halo round your head and made you a veteran in their eyes. It was, I must say, being a young theatrical ham just out of civvy street, nice to be needed. Quickly signed and kitted out, AC2 H. Green received a ghastly two-day train journey to Regina, Sask., followed by a short indoctrination course in the prairie city.

The course completed, I was posted as a flying and instrument instructor to an Elementary Flying School at Windsor Mills, Quebec. Holding the RCAF rank of sergeant, I wore a civilian uniform that made me look like an admiral in the Swiss Navy.

I learned a lot at Windsor Mills. In particular teaching extremely strong and enthusiastic young pupils, many of whom were French-Canadian and whose English was as sparse as my French. And who, the first time I showed them a spin, crying through the voice tube, 'It's yours!' or '*Pour vous!*' with the ground spinning towards us at great speed many froze in stark terror, their strong hands gripping the control column like a vice. To save the plane, the student, and with a tinge of selfishness, me, in such an event – and they happened reasonably often – I cracked the terrified man gently over the head with a spare control column carried for that purpose in the hopes he would release his grip on the stick.

Even as an actor, I worked out such an operation was dangerous, and certainly less courageous and unattractive than fighting the common foe!

Death in those macho days was accepted as part of the job but to the home town folks, to leave the world at the hands of the Luftwaffe was more acceptable than in the strong hands of a petrified student. Worried about what the townfolk might say should my number be called in Canada, I wangled out of Elementary School.

Following my service training on Ansons, my posting to flying boats at Patricia Bay was a real dream-come-true: the realisation of my greatest ambition so far as the Air Force was concerned. Flying-boats are graceful fascinating things, using the sea, inland lakes and rivers for their alighting areas which God provides free, compared with the millions contractors charge to lay lengthy concrete runways for land planes.

Our West Coast OTU course complete, my best friend Art Teulon and I were posted early in May 1943 to 117 Catalina Flying Boat Squadron, North Sydney, Nova Scotia.

What a contrast to the theatres of Broadway and London's West End, as well as the bustling sound stages of Hollywood studios. Let me admit quite honestly the feeling of stark, insane panic that came over me on the cold bleak morning when I got off the train at the desolate station perched on the furthermost eastern tip of Canada. My friend Art Teulon and I, the two new boys on the squadron, drove in silence with our kit to the base, our eyes on the rolling grey carpet of the Atlantic stretching cold and under a storm-blackened sky. Convoys were out there plodding heavily eastward, low in the water with men and arms; the enemy U-boats were out there too.

Thoughts tumbled around madly as I tried to remember everything that had been crammed into my head in the preceding months during the excellent Commonwealth Training Programme. The raw material in the detailed text books that aimed to keep me alive, my ship in the air, and Canada free.

With Wing Commander Jack Roberts as CO, the boys of 117 were a great bunch to fight a North Atlantic war with. I was crewed as co-pilot with Flight Lieutenant George Huxford (RAF). George had joined the air force as a boy, and there was nothing he couldn't do from flying the planes to drilling the troops and drawing the rations. He taught me a lot.

On 8th June 1943 I went off on my first job with George. The 'jobs' we did were numerous, rugged and rarely uninteresting and we would find ourselves in the air for periods of up to 21 hours at a spell. Sometimes we played wet nurse to a crawling convoy hundreds of miles out at sea; sometimes we would shadow the *Queen Mary* or the *Queen Elizabeth* as they raced like greyhounds for England packed with thousands of American troops, unescorted and relying on their speed and us as their only source of protection.

Gazing down though at the great grey acres of the Atlantic for the tell-tale plume of an inquisitive enemy periscope is wearing work. A dozen times a day the tension in our boat would explode.

'Over to port. Over to port. Look!'

George would blow the klaxon for action stations and swing the big flying boat with a 108 foot wing-span suddenly onto a new course as if he was turning a Tiger Moth. Angling into a steep dive I would be priming depth-charges as fast as if I had learnt the art in the cradle, and at the same time straining for a better view past the front gunner as he blasted off a few rounds to check his charges.

And again, a dozen times a day George's voice would crackle in the headset at zero minus one: 'Hold off, hold off. Just a seagull.'

For ten minutes, 700 miles from land, George would skim the wave-tops just to make sure. Whilst in the distance, zigzagging continuously, one of the giant *Queens* with thousands of lives aboard would proceed at flank speed.

In October '43 I was given my own crew and my very first job that nearly was my last. An aircraft from another squadron had sighted a fully surfaced U-boat the previous day, believed he'd damaged it, and to me fell the job of finding it again and, if possible, destroying it.

Some 500 miles out from Sydney, Nova Scotia, maintaining strict radio silence, we searched backwards and forwards across square miles of the Atlantic for hours on end, until in the late afternoon sea fog came down and completely obscured the surface. Base was sending us weather reports constantly. The prospect was grim. The crew pleaded with hollow eyes, rimmed with red, the same unspoken question:

'When the hell do we start back?'

I had to do a good job on my first trip: 'Let's give it another thirty minutes just in case the fog lifts.'

The fog didn't lift; 'Course for base, Larry.' (Larry, a lawyer, was later to become one of Canada's chief public prosecutors.) The crew forced a laugh at my orders as Sparks, hunched over the radio, copied the latest Sydney weather. It was an early late-autumn evening as we set course for our four hour flight home. Wearily we maintained our radio silence as the minutes ticked by; slowly, agonisingly. It began to snow!

'Sydney weather' – one of the radio operators handed me the message slip. 'Heavy snow showers. Visibility less than half a mile.'

'Ask if we can divert to Newfoundland,' I ordered.

The reply came back: 'Keep coming.'

In what was now pitch blackness, we obeyed. The coffee the engineer was brewing on the galley stove smelt good.

We were fifty minutes from Sydney when the blow fell: 'Base completely down. Try Argentia, Newfoundland.'

This was great for my first trip as captain. My heart played footsie with my Adam's apple as I put the boat on its new course for the American base a full three hours away in Newfoundland. We were flying and bumping about in what had developed into a full blizzard as the engineer reminded me anxiously that we had been up for a full fifteen hours and gas was getting pretty low. The three hours dragged by with leaden feet and still no indication of a land-fall blip on our radar screen. Astro bearings were impossible, as we were flying in thick cloud. I left the first officer, against all air force instructions, to pull the power back and fly the boat slowly in a circle.

Joining Larry in the warmth and bright lights of the navigation table, I said 'Something's wrong! We've missed Newfoundland! Any suggestions?'

'Cross your fingers,' he replied. 'I've got the frequency of a brand new station for fixing aircraft positions on the east coast of Newfoundland.'

We tried it, and as luck would have it, they were about to close down after an experimental two hours on the air. The position they gave made us feel sick. We had completely missed the coast and were flying back into the black maw of the Atlantic. Nursing us back with a string of bearings we put down in Argentia harbour with fifteen minutes' fuel left and just as the weather started to close there as well.

Something had been wrong. Yes, the radar leads had been connected the wrong way round!

Late in '43 the majority of 117 were posted to Ceylon. Whilst on embarkation leave in Montreal two flying boat pilots were wanted by 45 Group RAF Ferry Command. My friend Teulon and I begged for the job, and got it. And so late that year for the first time I was under RAF control in their élite 45 Ferry Group. Thrilled out of our minds, Teulon and I were to deliver a Catalina to the UK as joint captains.

We left Montreal with three feet of snow in the clutch of winter, and we were flown as passengers to the warm sleepy southern town of Elizabeth City in North Carolina where Consolidated handed over brand new Catalina flying boats to the RAF at the US naval air station for the ferry trip of over 4,000 miles to Great Britain via Bermuda. Our trip to Bermuda was uneventful, and whilst our Cat was given a thirty-hour inspection before the ocean hop to the UK, we sat in the lounge of the luxury Belmont Manor Hotel, which the RAF part-occupied. Teulon and I listened to the three other highly experienced American veteran civilian ferry pilots who were flying an aeroplane apiece in our group. Suddenly we began to realise there was no going back and we might have bitten off a real mouthful with this one. The first thought that came into my mind was that I was the biggest fool to have volunteered in the first place. I had not just volunteered: together with Teulon I had practically pleaded on bended knees for the Ferry Command job.

In Coastal Command one rarely went over 2,000 to 3,000 feet, and here the two greenhorns were listening to the three experts talking about 8,000, 9,000, 10,000 and 11,000. An entirely different technique from our training. They were good guys, and over a number of rum and Cokes we quickly got the picture of how it should be done.

After one week's wait for the winds in this island paradise we had the required tail component that would take us from Bermuda to Largs on the River Clyde in 24 hours. This left us a reserve of three hours, on a distance of 3,277 nautical miles – the world's longest hop, then, for a twin-engine aircraft. Both Teulon and I were twenty-three, and neither of us, nor any of our four-man crew, had ever flown both up and across the Atlantic before.

Our take-off one sunny November morning with the weight of fuel and cargo in the boat took us three minutes before we bumped out of Bermuda harbour and into the Atlantic air.

At eleven o'clock that evening, in the dark at 9,000 feet, I found out with radio silence just how treacherous the unforecastable winter weather over the North Atlantic was. The temperature rose, indicating we had reached what is called an occluded front. Rain falling on an aeroplane in these conditions forms clear ice. The sudden added weight can render a machine completely unmanageable in minutes. I'm not trying to over-dramatise the situation when I tell you that a life or death choice faced us: to descend as quickly as possible, in the hope of reaching a point where the rain wouldn't freeze, or climb to a height where the temperature was minus 18 degrees centigrade and, theoretically, ice could not form.

If we went down, an altimeter error after so many hours' flying could put us in the drink. 'Hold tight, everyone,' I shouted. 'We're going up.'

We climbed to 17,000 feet before we were out of danger, but as the Catalina was not fitted with oxygen two of the crew collapsed. Before leaving Bermuda, I put a hand-operated oxygen cylinder aboard, and that saved us, passing it from mouth to mouth, one to the other. When we reached the UK, Largs was closed, and so we made our first flying boat delivery to Beaumaris on Anglesey. Yes! To celebrate that night we got very drunk in the Beaumaris Arms.

My job at RAF 45 Group Headquarters, Dorval, Montreal, was fabulously interesting. The training was tremendous, and I was, like others, brought up to scratch to fly practically any plane anywhere in the world at a moment's notice. I took VIPs to Washington, San Diego and Australia. I flew to South America, Africa and India as well as on a regular basis to the UK.

The world at twenty-three had suddenly shrunk to tennis ball size, and to prove my point I left Montreal at noon one day, delivered a Liberator to Prestwick at six in the morning and was back in Montreal for a cocktail party at six the same evening. At the age of twenty-four I could fly some thirty different types of aircraft and thanks to tough Ferry Command training had the same qualifications as a regular airline pilot in the United States.

But my most hair-raising experiences in five-and-a-half years of wartime flying were with the Russians. President Roosevelt decided in the summer of 1944 to sell Stalin 90 Catalinas at a nominal price of $3 apiece. That was a dollar for each engine and a dollar for the hull!

The US Navy, after training the Russians to fly the President's gifts, felt it was only fair the RAF should have the honour of ferrying both crews and aeroplanes back to the Soviet Union.

Art Teulon and I, together with Clyde Pangbourne – the first man to fly a single-engine aeroplane from Tokyo to Seattle – as well as a Norwegian navy flyer, soon found out why.

1. Bofors 40mm Light Anti-Aircraft gun of the type used by Peter Alliss at RAF Watchet.
(Crown Copyright, Royal Air Force Museum)

2. Peter Alliss.
(Lawrence Levy/ *Yours in Sport*)

3. Flight Lieutenant Raymond Baxter, second from the left, briefing pilots of No. 602 Squadron.
(Imperial War Museum)

4. Raymond Baxter.

5. Tony Benn with his RAF 'wings', March 1945.

6. Tony Benn.
   (Benn Archives Collection)

7. Flying Officer Michael Bentine, Intelligence Officer to No. 350 (Belgian) Squadron at Hawkinge in 1944, painting a Red Indian motif on the CO's Spitfire.

8. Michael Bentine.

9. Aircraftman 2nd Class Michael Bond, second from left, second row up from bottom, with No. 10 Initial Training Wing, Grand Hotel, Scarborough, 1944.

10. Michael Bond.

11. Peter Cadbury seated in the cockpit of a Hawker Typhoon, with Glen.

12. Peter Cadbury (left) with the legendary Douglas Bader, DSO, DFC.
(Desmond O'Neill Features)

13. *Above* Frederick Forsyth
    receiving his RAF 'wings',
    March 1958.

14. Frederick Forsyth.

15. *Right* William Franklyn.

16. *Opposite page top* James A. Goodson with, on his right breast, RAF 'wings' and on his left USAAF 'wings'.

17. James A. Goodson, USAAF.

18. *Opposite page bottom* Coastal Pilot, Flight Lieutenant Hughie Green at twenty-four years of age.

19. Hughie Green.

20. *This page* Flying Officer Hunt second from the right on the wing of a Hawker Tempest II, No. 5 Squadron, Poona, November 1946.

21. Sir Rex Hunt.

22. R. V. Jones.

23. Squadron Leader D. Langdon, RAFVR.

24. David Langdon.

25. Cecil Lewis with an SE5, No. 56
    Squadron in France, April 1917.

26. Cecil Lewis.

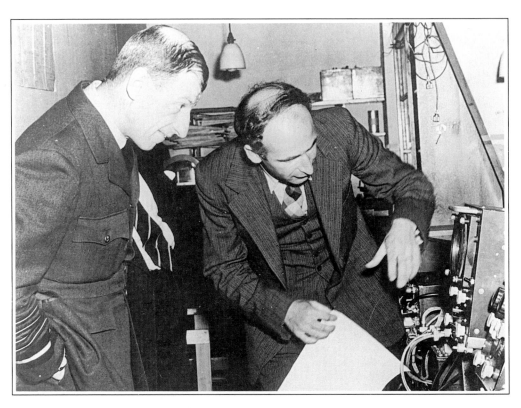

27. *Opposite page* Bernard Lovell (centre) with Marshal of the Royal Air Force Sir Charles Portal examining radar equipment, 1944.

28. Sir Bernard Lovell with Margaret Thatcher, then Secretary of State for Education and Science, during her visit to Jodrell Bank, 1975. (*Guardian*)

29. *This page* Pilot Officer Gavin Lyall with Tiger Moth, 1952.

30. Gavin Lyall.

31. Flying Officer Jack Mann, DFM, Fighter Pilot.

32. Jackie Mann, celebrating with his wife, Sunnie, on his return from captivity in Beirut.

33. Squadron Leader Cliff Michelmore with the Rt. Hon. Arthur Henderson, Secretary of State for Air, 1947.

34. Cliff Michelmore.

35. C. Northcote Parkinson: The RAF
Regiment training for war, 1943.
(Crown Copyright, Royal Air Force
Museum)

36. C. Northcote Parkinson.

37. Derek Rayner, on the right
    of the Commanding
    Officer in the centre of the
    front row, RAF Regiment
    Instructors School,
    Shallufa, Egypt, February
    1948.

38. Lord Rayner of
    Crowborough.

39. *Left* Brian Rix, at the top, appearing with Leo Franklyn and Basil Lord in one of the famous farces at the Whitehall Theatre. This was one of the great successes of the London stage in the 1950s.

42. *Opposite page* Dudley Sutton in his first professional engagement, a theatre workshop production of Macbeth (1957).

43. Dudley Sutton.

44. Norman Tebbit in flying kit at No. 604 (County of Middlesex) Squadron, North Weald, Royal Auxiliary Air Force.

45. Norman Tebbit during the 1983 General Election.

40. Spitfire XIV as flown by Ian Smith in No. 130 Squadron, 1944–5.

41. Ian Smith.

46. *This page* David Tomlinson training in Canada.

47. David Tomlinson directing Peter Sellers in *The Fiendish Plot of Doctor Fu Manchu.*

48. *Opposite page* Flying Officer G S Waller, RAFVR, Whitley Pilot, RAF Coastal Command.

49. Sir George Waller.

50. Flight Lieutenant K. Wolstenholme, DFC and Bar, second from left, in Oslo, September 1945, with Crown Prince Olav (left), Crown Princess Märtha (right) and on far right Air Chief Marshal Sir Sholto Douglas.

51. Kenneth Wolstenholme with Stanley Matthews, the great footballer.

52. William Woollard with Harvard Trainers, Canada.

53. William Woollard.

54. Solly Zuckerman in Tobruk, 1943.

55. Lord Zuckerman.

The Russian crews comprised six of the largest non-English speaking guys you've ever seen, and the RAF supplied two of us – a pilot and a radio operator – to act as overseers. None of us, of course, could speak Russian, and our only source of communication, unless on the ground with an interpreter, was through a very bad phonetic phrase book handed to us at Elizabeth City by a naturalised Ukrainian trouser-presser from Philadelphia.

Acting as an overseer, and in the hands of the two Russian pilots, I was the first of the four to take off from the Pasquotank River at Elizabeth City.

After four death defying attempts at take-off with the Russian at the controls, not only I, but also my three associates still waiting to dice with death and watching on the slipway, realised why our American naval friends gave us the honour as allies of ferrying the planes back to Russia. This, the first of many Russian trips, was one of the worst. Stalin's boys were determined from the start that we should fly our delivery quota of four Catalinas across the Atlantic in formation. It was a ridiculous suggestion. Keeping heavy flying boats in formation for fourteen hours in and out of thick cloud is not only impossible, but dangerously impossible. The Russians refused to see it our way. The British had tried it and failed, and so had the Americans, we explained, and with all due respect – negative reaction.

When the Red Starred boats finally got into the air that morning from Elizabeth City and climbed up to 5,000 feet, we kept a reasonable ragged formation – that means at one moment you could shake hands with the man in the next aeroplane and a minute later one needed a telescope to see him. Out over the Atlantic, off New York we hit thick frontal cloud. At once the three other planes vanished in the white cocoon. Next minute one of them thundered over me missing our propellers by less than ten feet. I, together with my new-found Ivan friends, was petrified.

Thankfully however, before taking off, my English-speaking colleagues and I had secretly agreed – facing the emergency we expected – systematically to break formation. The Russian captain of my plane was a hefty thick-set man, but in moments of great stress strength comes to the weakest of us. I pulled him out of his seat and grabbed the controls, making a 25 degree turn to port (left) and descending 500 feet as agreed with the others who were taking safety action of a similar nature.

Reaching Gander Lake, one of the Russian captains made such a heavy landing he knocked most of the rivets out of the hull causing his plane to be beached for repairs.

Thank God for the fame, experience and persuasiveness of that late, great gentleman flyer, Clyde Pangbourne, who at Gander, after our hazardous flight from North Carolina, in the interests of safety persuaded the Americans, and the RAF that if Commonwealth crews were to be used on this ferry mission, Commonwealth captains should be at the controls.

The change of command Pangbourne, as a revered civilian, was able to make for service crews, who had no channel of redress, was most helpful in contributing to the safe delivery of these flying boats that had to be operated by Russian and Commonwealth human beings whose chief means of communication were bad phonetic phrasebooks.

Take it from me, off the tip of Greenland if you want to get across to a friendly and grinning Russian engineer that one of the engines is about to ice up and stop if he does not pull a certain lever, your ability to read conversational titbits like: 'Is your mother well?' or 'Does your sister drink beer?' will get you nowhere except into a spiral dive. This happened to me when through lack of understanding I had to rush back from the flight deck to the engineer's compartment and switch on the carburettor heat then, panic-stricken, rush back and straighten ourselves out of a 200 mph spiral dive that broke cloud at 1,000 feet five miles south of the towering mountains of Greenland's Cape Farewell.

I made six trips with them in all – three round the North Atlantic, and three South-about. The latter took us from North Carolina to Puerto Rico, Trinidad, Brazil, Natal, the West Coast of Africa including Morocco, Gibraltar (where the CO nearly collapsed when he knew there were 'Russians on the Rock!'), Sicily, Kasfareet on the salt lake of the Suez Canal, the lake at Habbaniyah, then Britain's greatest air force base in the Middle East, and finally on to Baku on the Caspian Sea.

We were thrown together for long periods as a result and, individually, I got to like them a lot, particularly the few who began to pick up the odd word of English. But as air crew, whilst they understood the engineering aspects of the Catalina extremely well, they were from an operational point of view, way, way, below RAF standards, and they had a disconcerting way of making up for their lack of skill and horse sense with an abundance of zany courage.

For example:

One appalling night at Gander I was shaken awake at two in the morning by our interpreter, the Ukrainian trouser-presser from Philadelphia. He crouched beside the bulk of an enormous Russian colonel, three times Hero of the Soviet Union, in full uniform.

'The colonel says, according to his orders laid down in Moscow, you must take off in an hour for Iceland,' wheezed the weary interpreter.

Pulling the curtains back from the window I gazed into thick fog. The tree not even five feet from my window was invisible. 'Tell this guy,' I mumbled sleepily, 'that even the birds aren't flying tonight.'

Sheepishly, the man complied. The colonel barked aggressively. Russian is no language to get angry in at two in the morning.

'What's he say?' I asked. I was wide-awake now.

'He says,' grinned the interpreter, 'are you afraid to die?' I told him that frankly I was and went back to bed. But as an example of a man hide-bound by his orders I think it illustrates the attitude we were constantly grappling with. The Russian respect for discipline at that time was ridiculously complete.

On one occasion I allowed a Russian captain flying with me to land a Catalina in the vast area of water available at the US Navy base at Argentia,

Newfoundland. He followed his senior officer in the flying boat in front of us into the roughest bit of water in the bay in an attempt to land exactly where his superior had put his plane down. Not crediting what I was about to see, I watched with amazement. My pilot bounced his aeroplane, hit a wave, making the giant plane – after I quickly applied full power – bounce over the top of the one in front already in the water.

Finally moored up, I staggered ashore, a somewhat shattered man, and took a bearing on the nearest US Navy bar and the largest Scotch in the house. I was intercepted halfway by an American admiral. He grabbed me, shook my hand solemnly and said: 'Son, I've been flying and watching flying boats all my life – but that's the first time I've ever seen one of them play leap-frog.'

Don't get me wrong, despite the language barrier, they were great guys, who helped us win that war.

What a pity that for the next one, we won't have a great Commonwealth airforce like the last time. I was proud to have been part of it.

12

SIR REX HUNT

Tempests in India

MAKE NO mistake, the Hawker Tempest II was a superb aircraft to fly. It was a rock-steady gun platform and slow-rolled to the range and back without losing a foot of height. My first encounter with it, however, was hardly auspicious.

Having graduated in the usual way during 1944–6, from Tiger Moth to Harvard to Spitfire, followed by leave, leisurely troopship to Bombay and – typical of the RAF in India in those days – a three-day train journey on the Frontier Mail to Peshawar and a three-ton lorry to Risalpur, I joined 152 (Nizam of Hyderabad's) Squadron, only to be told that it was all a mistake and that I should have gone to 5 Squadron in Poona. So it was back on the three-ton lorry to Peshawar and a three-day return trip to Bombay. (The journey was not entirely wasted: as well as seeing a large slice of the sub-continent, I learned to play liar dice on the way up and bridge on the way down.)

RAF Poona, sixty miles east of Bombay across the Western Ghats, was where I first saw the Tempest II. I had seen photographs of it, of course, but they had given no indication of its size or power. The jump from Tiger Moth to Harvard had been quite a leap, but at least there had been an instructor in the back to ease the transition. No such luxury in the elevation from Harvard to Mitchell-designed Spitfire, but settling into a Spitfire's cockpit was like putting on one's favourite shoes. By some Mitchell magic, one immediately felt an integral part of a beautiful machine. Despite her killing power, here was the perfect lady, sweet and without vice.

The Tempest II was a different kettle of fish. I beheld it with awe and apprehension. Was I really expected to control that monster?

After local familiarisation and a few back-seat landings in the squadron Harvard, I certified that I understood the starting and stopping procedures of the 2,520 hp Bristol Centaurus V engine as fitted to the Tempest II; the fuel, oil, hydraulic, pneumatic and oxygen systems; the emergency operating of the undercarriage and cockpit hood, the procedure for ditching and landing with a burst tyre, and the vital actions before take-off and before landing. Finally, I signed a certificate to say that I had read and fully understood the Provisional Pilot's Notes for Tempest II aircraft. (Why 'Provisional'? I wondered – I never did see a definitive version.)

Climbing gingerly into Tempest OQ-R, my thoughts went back to the comfortable, shoe-horn fit of the Spitfire. This was vast by comparison. My flight commander followed me on to the wing and leant over with some memorable pearls of wisdom. Taciturn by nature, he had what can only be described as an undertaker's sense of humour.

'Make sure the throttle friction nut is tight before take-off,' he said. 'We just lost a poor sod who didn't. Throttle came back when he raised the undercart and . . . ' He finished with a violent arm movement downwards.

'And make sure your straps are tight,' he went on, 'or you'll smash your face in the gunsight.' He illustrated this by smashing his own face into his hand and making a terrible grimace. I looked at the angular gunsight and imagined the mess it could make.

'And make sure the hood's locked back. Had a silly sod who didn't and – see those two spikes? – right through the back of his head.' This was accompanied by two fingers dramatically placed on the back of his own head.

Noticing that I had my feet on the upper (anti-G) pedals, he told me to put them on the lower ones. 'Those are just for aerobatics and dogfights,' he explained.

With the parting remark, 'It doesn't swing much on take-off, but watch the bastard on landing,' he was gone and I was on my own.

It says much for the RAF system that I accepted without question that, if the RAF considered me qualified to fly a Tempest II, then fly it I could.

With a bang from the Koffman cartridge starter, the Centaurus exploded into life. The noise was far different from the cough and splutter of the Merlin. I was also relieved that it had started on the first cartridge. In the Indian heat, pilots frequently had a 'duck-shoot', firing away a dozen or more cartridges before the engine caught.

I switched on the radio and the oxygen (we used oxygen from ground level because of the exhaust fumes from the Centaurus) and waited for the engine temperatures and pressures to rise. When all were in approximately their right positions, I requested taxi clearance and released the brakes. With the seat at its highest, the view was, if anything, better than from the Spitfire's cockpit, though it was still necessary to swing the nose from side to side in order to see ahead. I remembered to check the brakes before taxying cautiously round the perimeter track to the runway in use. I ran up the engine, tested the 'mags' and checked all the instruments. Everything OK. There was no other aircraft in the circuit and a cheerful voice from Air Traffic Control told me I was clear for take-off.

It is at times like this that the RAF training bears fruit. The pre-take-off drill, etched indelibly on my brain by successive flying instructors, was automatic:

Throttle friction nut – tight
Trimmers – rudder full left, elevator two-thirds forward
Mixture – rich

Pitch – fine
Fuel – on main tank, enough for flight
Flaps – up
Gills – open
Gyros – set and uncaged
Harness – tight and locked
Hood – open and locked back.

I lined up on the runway and slowly pushed the throttle lever forward. It got to the first gate and stuck. I tried to ease it through but I'd tightened up the friction nut so much that it shot from –3 to +5 boost. The result was spectacular. The nose swung about forty-five degrees to starboard. As it began to swing, I instinctively applied more left rudder but, with my short legs and using the bottom pedals, I found I could not put it on fully. I tried to stretch forward off the seat, but I'd strapped myself in so tightly that I could not move.

Instead of accelerating serenely down the runway, I found myself careering over rough brown earth and heading straight for the control tower. All I could do was to ram the throttle through the emergency gate and haul back on the stick. I swear that, as I staggered into the air, I had a fleeting glimpse of people scattering out of the control tower in all directions.

Once airborne, I was able to raise the undercarriage, throttle back and collect my thoughts, the first of which was, 'If it swings like that on take-off, what's it going to be like on landing?' I had been authorised for a one-hour flight, one landing only, and spent much of the time getting the feel of the aircraft with wheels and flaps down and making dummy approaches on to a convenient bank of cloud at about 7,000 feet. It handled well and I felt more comfortable in the cockpit with my feet on the top pedals (which I always used thereafter) and my straps less tight. I also tried the throttle friction nut at different settings until I could make more sensitive adjustments to the throttle.

All too quickly, the time came for me to return to base. As I approached the airfield, the air traffic controller said that I was the only aircraft airborne, that I was free to land and that he was clearing out of the control tower!

I rejoined the circuit and was amazed to see what appeared to be the whole station gathered on the apron to watch me land. Obviously, news of my take-off had got round. More sinister was the sight of fire engines and ambulance at the beginning of the runway.

The Tempest's cruising speed was considerably higher than the Spitfire's, which meant that there was less time on the circuit to complete the pre-landing drill, but again the RAF's standard training paid off and it was done almost automatically while concentrating on getting the aircraft in the right position, height and speed for landing. The approach was a curving one, as in the Spitfire, in order to see over the nose, but again it was much quicker (over the threshold at 120 knots). Unlike the Spitfire, the Tempest was not designed for three-point landings, but only for tail-down wheelers, and the Pilot's Notes advised that, as the tail began to come down, it was necessary to tickle the brakes to keep the aircraft straight – rudder by itself was not enough. Indeed, pilots were instructed to make a wheels-up landing if the pneumatic system failed (i.e. no brakes).

'Tickle' was the operative word and I was very conscious of this as the main wheels touched down. I knew that there was not a lot of clearance between the four-bladed propeller and the ground, and that more than a tickle on the brake-handle was liable to tip the aircraft up on its nose. I also knew that, as it lost speed, it would tend to swing to port – the opposite to take-off. I was ready for the swing and, with my feet on the upper pedals and fingers lightly on the brake-handle, I was able to react immediately to any hint of movement of the nose to the left. The tail-wheel came down gently and I trundled to a stop along the centre of the runway.

Taxiing in, I was immensely relieved at having got the aircraft down in one piece, but apprehensive about my future. After the take-off fiasco, would I be kicked off the squadron? After all, there was a glut of pilots post-war, most of them itching to carry on flying. Fortunately, I had an understanding squadron commander, who gave me a second chance. I did not let him down: never again did I swing a Tempest, on take-off or landing.

Thus began the most fascinating and enjoyable year of my life. I feel guilty writing this now because the partition of India took place that same year, but in a way the RAF cocooned us from the tragedy that was being enacted all around us. We were observers rather than participants and savoured the twilight of the British Raj without becoming involved.

Above all, I was flying the fastest propeller-driven aircraft in squadron service in the world over some of the finest scenery in the world and enjoying the privilege of belonging to the most exclusive of clubs, an operational RAF squadron. At the age of twenty, I could not have wished for more.

After about six hours of local flying, I, as the new boy, was put in charge of a groundcrew party departing for Bangalore, whither the squadron was bound in order to demonstrate a rocket shoot for the Indian Army's Southern Command. It was thrilling to see twelve Tempests lined up on the apron and hear twelve Centaurus engines roaring in unison. As they took off in pairs and joined up in tight squadron formation, I couldn't wait to be one of them. Nevertheless, I had an interesting train journey to Bangalore and an enjoyable return via Madras, where we spent a night. It was our good fortune to be travelling back to Poona at the same time that Southern Command head-quarters were moving there from Bangalore, and they had commandeered all the passenger seats on the direct route.

On our return, I was delighted to hear that the squadron was moving to – of all places – Risalpur. With independence approaching, the Nizam of Hyderabad's squadron (No. 152 which I so nearly joined) was being disbanded and we were to take its place on the North West Frontier. Even better, Poona was to remain our base for major servicing, so we should have plenty of flying back and forth.

By this time, I was deemed to be sufficiently experienced on type to fly in formation and, on 14th December 1946, I took off from Poona with the rest of the squadron. Instead of the $3\frac{1}{2}$ days that it had taken me by train and lorry, we reached Risalpur in $4\frac{1}{2}$ hours' flying time (plus a short stop at Palam to refuel). We had left Poona in shorts and shirt and climbed out of our cockpits in Risalpur to a bitingly cold wind and a frosty nip in the air. That night it was grand to have a fire in the mess and to wear ordinary uniforms again (albeit badly creased, since the only space to pack our kit in the Tempest was in the wing ammunition bays).

Within a week, two of us were on our way back to Poona with aircraft due for their 500 hour service. As my senior colleague was an old Indian hand, he had a girl friend in Agra and arranged that we should refuel there, whereupon his aircraft conveniently went unserviceable for three days, so I saw the Taj Mahal by moonlight. We reached Poona (where we both had girl friends) via Bhopal on 23rd December and had a wonderful Christmas and New Year before heading north again, this time via Salawas, Agra and Lahore. The weather clamped in on our final leg to Risalpur and we had to turn back from Jhelum, which gave us the opportunity to spend a night in Lahore.

Towards the end of January 1947, the squadron moved again, from Risalpur to Peshawar, and we got down to some serious rocket and cannon firing on the range at Jamrud. On my first run-in, I had lined up on the target and was about to press the firing button when I saw figures popping up from behind the butts. I hurriedly turned the button to safe and aborted the attack. The range officer called me up and asked what was wrong. I told him that there were people on the range. 'Take no notice of them,' he said, 'We can't keep the beggars off – they're after any bit of metal they can find.' On my second run-in, there they were again. I fired a short burst, desperately hoping that my aim was true and, as I pulled out of the dive, I could see them scrambling for my spent shells. Amazingly, according to the Range Officer, there had never been any casualties.

In February, a few of us had an interesting trip, ferrying Tempests to No. 8 Royal Indian Air Force Squadron in Kolar, near Bangalore. We stopped off at Agra and Poona on the way, returning by Douglas Dakota via Santa Cruz (Bombay) in 10 hours compared with 6 hours by Tempest.

At the beginning of March, 5 Squadron was instructed to detach a flight to Miram Shah and I was lucky enough to be chosen as adjutant to the flight commander. This was undoubtedly the highlight of my year in India. For the next three months I lived in the world of Rudyard Kipling.

Miram Shah consisted of two runways (one long, one short), a fort and a civil sarai, where passing caravans spent a night or two. On such occasions the place mushroomed into a bustling tent town, with camels, goats, sheep and wonderful Bokhara carpets. The RAF shared the fort with the Tochi Scouts, a fine body of Pathans officered by British volunteers in the great tradition of Nicholson, Hodson and Lumsden. In one corner of the fort lived the political agent and his two assistants; mysterious, romantic fellows who came and went we knew not where but appeared to be in charge of our stretch of the North West Frontier.

I think it was at Miram Shah that the seed was sown for my subsequent career in the Colonial and Diplomatic Services. For the first time, I began to envy somebody else his job. For the present, however, I was blissfully happy looking after our small detachment and flying over some of the most rugged terrain in the world.

One of our routine tasks was to fly round the military outposts in North and South Waziristan and check by radio that all was well. I shall never forget the magic of those names: Spinwam, Datta Khel, Wana, Sarwekai, Dosalli, Jandola, Parachinar, Bichekaskai...

On the Road Open Days (RODs), one of us used to fly along the road from Miram Shah to Bannu and then back to Razmak to check for road-blocks and ambushes before the supply convoy set out. I once saw a road-block near the notorious Isha Corner and flew up to Razmak to report it. For some reason, I could not raise anyone on the radio and had to drop a message on the football field. The Tempest was not designed for dropping messages from the cockpit, particularly when surrounded by mountains up to 10,000 feet. It was a mad rush to lose height, lower flaps and undercarriage, reduce speed, open the hood, hurl out the bag, pile on the power, close hood, raise undercarriage and flaps and turn to avoid the mountainside.

Most exciting of all were the emergency calls – code sign XX – for air support from the Tochi Scouts. The Tochis went out on lengthy *gashts* (patrols) and sometimes encountered hostile tribesmen. The local enemy warlord was a man with the unlikely name of the Fakir of Ipi. He had been fighting a holy war against the British since 1938 and rumour had it that, with an independent Pakistan about to be created, he intended to declare an independent Ipistan. Whatever his intentions, he was a formidable foe, with arms allegedly supplied by the Germans during the war. To my regret, I never saw any of his men.

We always kept one aircraft on five-minute standby, with a duty pilot ready to scramble whenever the Tochi Scouts sent us an XX call. We had to find them by map reference because there was no direct radio link between us. In any event, once we found them, they had a simple way of communicating the enemy's position to us by laying out a big white 'V' pointing in the enemy's direction, followed by a number of white dots, each of which represented 200 yards. The closest I got was four dots, 800 yards. I flew as low as I dared but still could not see anyone or anything to shoot at. Later, the Tochi platoon commander told me that he had been shot up by over fifty hostiles and that they were still in the area that I had flown over. How they merged into that rocky background I shall never know.

Seasoned Tochi hands always insisted that the best air support they had was from the old Wapiti. Pride of place at their mess table went to a beautiful silver model of that aircraft, which 5 Squadron had presented to them in 1936. (In return, pride of place at our mess table went to an equally beautiful silver model of a Tochi Scout.) The Wapiti was well armed and armoured and could fly slowly and low enough to spot the tribesmen. It could also land on dirt strips and pick up the wounded or sick. I could see why the Tochis preferred it to the Tempest.

All too soon, our detachment to Miram Shah came to an end. I flew my last sortie to Parachinar and the other North Waziristan posts, our four Tempests flew back to Peshawar and I was left with a small groundcrew party to pack up 5 Squadron's equipment and get it safely back by road.

We were the last RAF unit to be based at Miram Shah and I believe that I was the last RAF officer to set foot there. An Indian (shortly to be a Pakistani) squadron from Risalpur took over, but after we had left. It was strange to be travelling along the Bannu road, past Isha Corner and all the other places that had become so familiar to me from the air.

Back in Peshawar, I found that we were sharing the airfield with No. 1 Royal Indian Air Force Squadron and engaged in converting their pilots from Spitfire XIVs to Tempests. There was mounting confusion over partition, with many of their pilots and groundcrew agonising over whether to stay or go south. It was a mixed squadron of Hindus, Moslems, Sikhs and Anglo-Indians, well led and with an excellent spirit, and we were sad to see it disintegrate in front of our eyes.

No matter that the sub-continent was breaking up around us, RAF procedures had to be followed. An Indian Air Force Spitfire had crashed on a flight from Peshawar to Karachi, and a Court of Inquiry was convened to ascertain the cause. I was detailed to be a member and the chairman was a Pathan flight lieutenant of the Indian (shortly to be Pakistan) Air Force, a Burma veteran known as 'Cobber' Khan. The two of us caught the last Dakota into Lahore before the rampaging Sikhs closed the airport. We were stuck in Stiffle's hotel for my twenty-first birthday, eventually leaving by train for Shikarpur, the scene of the crash. I shall pass over the horrors of the Punjab and the panic in the rest of the places we visited: Karachi (where the pilot was in hospital); Poona (fitter's evidence) and Secunderabad (rigger's evidence). We eventually returned to Peshawar firm friends, chastened by our experiences and with a report that nobody ever read.

I did not fly again in 5 Squadron. My last task was to pack the squadron silver. I hoped that in the mounting chaos it would arrive safely in England. No. 5 Squadron had been in India since 1920 (and Burma during the war) and during that time had amassed a splendid collection.

Now, the squadron was being disbanded. My most poignant memory is of our last day in Peshawar. As we boarded the Dakota to fly us to Karachi, then Bombay and the troopship home, the Pakistanis-to-be were spraying the green star and crescent over the RAF roundels and obliterating the squadron letters of our Tempests, soon to be reborn as No. 1 Pakistan Air Force Squadron.

13

R. V. JONES

Tunic and Gown

A MONG THOSE characteristics that differentiated the Royal Air Force from its sister Services I would at once point to its attitude towards the universities, where in my experience it paid much greater attention to the University Air Squadrons than did the Army to the OTCs, even though these long preceded the Air Squadrons; the Royal Navy had no university units at all until 1965 when Aberdeen University revived its earlier suggestion to the Navy that such a unit should be formed.

One reason why the Air Force had originally valued the universities, or so I was told in the Second World War, was that three of the most distinguished air officers in the war were university graduates: Sir Leslie Gossage and Sir Arthur Tedder (Cambridge) and Sir Charles Portal (Oxford). The Army, of course, could have cited its own example in Lord Haig, who had been at Oxford before proceeding to Sandhurst, but his precedent does not seem to have enthused the Army into taking as much interest in the OTCs as the Air Force did in the UASs. An additional factor in the latter case was that flying demanded much from both science and engineering if its problems were to be solved, as well as the personal skills required for handling and navigating an aircraft.

These requirements were all brought together in the First World War, and particularly at Farnborough where a galaxy of scientific talent was assembled. Among its most distinguished members was the physicist F. A. Lindemann (later Lord Cherwell) whose pupil I afterwards became. It was he who first worked out the aerodynamics of a spinning aircraft, and who learned to fly so that he could test the drill for recovery that he had accordingly devised.

A sidelight on the relations between scientists and the serving officers of the time was thrown by Lindemann's engineer friend W. R. (later Sir William) Farren, who learned to fly in 1916 along with him and Keith Lucas. Farren afterwards wrote:

> I doubt whether anything about him impressed me quite so much as his complete indifference to the difficulties of arriving at an RFC Station in a bowler hat and carrying an umbrella. Lucas and I were in khaki, and therefore relatively inconspicuous, for which we were thankful. Lindemann was unperturbed, and, to

our surprise, so was the RFC. Their instructions were to teach us to fly, and presumably did not extend to what particular kind of clothes we wore.

At much the same time Henry Tizard (later Sir Henry) also became a test pilot, and with such examples it is easy to understand the empathy that grew up between the airmen and university scientists.

In the early twenties the newly created Royal Air Force therefore suggested to Oxford and Cambridge that they should form university air squadrons, but Cambridge, at least, was not originally enthusiastic. In October 1925, though, both the Oxford and Cambridge squadrons were started, Cambridge being earlier by a few days. In 1935 the London University Squadron (600) was formed; one of its earliest members was a nineteen-year-old electrical engineer, Robert Hanbury Brown, who was promptly recruited by Henry Tizard to join the radar effort at Bawdsey, where his engineering and flying experiences contributed vitally to the development of AI Mark IV, the radar for the nightfighting Beaufighter.

At the outbreak of war in 1939 the UASs were 'stood down' but they were revived in 1941, when new squadrons were now created at other universities to a total of twenty-one in all, for it was by then evident what a tremendous contribution the pre-war Cambridge and Oxford squadrons had made to the cadre of officers in the front line air force.

I myself tried to join the Oxford squadron in 1937, but I was already a graduate of five years' standing and was therefore disbarred by regulations which envisaged only undergraduates as cadets. These regulations must have been revised by the end of the war, for one of the former Oxford cadets, Rupert Cecil, had in the meantime joined me in 1943 in Scientific Intelligence as a bomber wing commander with the DFC and bar. I heard that on returning to Oxford after the war he was, although already a graduate, the first candidate to be interviewed by the selection board for admission to the Air Squadron, which he wished to rejoin to maintain his flying experience.

From 1946 onwards I was myself at Aberdeen University, where I quickly became involved with its Air Squadron and participated regularly in the selection boards. These were usually presided over by a visiting regular officer, with the object of deciding whether a candidate for admission had, besides the necessary physical and mental abilities, the potential to make a good RAF officer. Most of our students were drawn from north-east Scotland, and often came from country backgrounds which led them to be reserved in the presence of senior company. Actually it was interesting to watch how such a student might be 'brought out' as he gained confidence during his years in the squadron, once he had been accepted; but it was not always easy for the visiting officer, especially if he were accustomed to the more 'forthcoming' students of the south, to discern the sterling qualities that might lie under the shyness of a typical 'Buchan loon' at the interview.

One year, the presiding officer was a very gallant and extrovert wing commander with the DFC and two bars, whose abruptly direct questions caused most of the candidates to close up like clams. To test a candidate's interest in the Air Force, the wing commander would thrust out his arm with the three rings on his sleeve and ask sharply: 'What's my rank?' And for family background he would ask: 'What does your father do?' If the candidate's answers were satisfactory, the wing commander would then test him by embarrassment, asking: 'Do you have a girlfriend?', followed by: 'What's your sex life like?' – Remember this was the mid-fifties when such questions were far beyond polite expectation.

The wing commander explained to those of us on the board that his questions were intended to catch the candidate off-balance and see how he reacted. The result, though, was such devastation that after two days of interviews he had rejected nearly all the candidates, even though we ourselves knew that if they had overcome their shyness several would have shown up well.

We had a break from the interviews over the weekend, and on the Saturday night one of my colleagues and I had dinner with the commanding officer of the squadron and the wing commander, whom we led on to tell us of his years in the Service. It turned out that one of his early postings had been to RAF Kinloss as a flight lieutenant, and this gave me an idea by which we might turn the tables on him at the interviews which would follow after the weekend.

I will not give the wing commander's real name, but for the purposes of this account let us call him 'Matthews'. In the meantime my idea was to offer him a bogus candidate who would be well provided with suitable answers to the battery of questions. It happened that the adjutant of the squadron was a bright young National Service officer who had already been accepted for a regular commission, and in civilian clothes he could well pass for a first-year student. When the candidate was brought in, the usual questions followed, with the candidate giving increasingly wild answers. Challenged by the three rings, for example, his reply was something like, 'I think that you must be an air vice captain, sir.' When it came to 'What does your father do?' the candidate answered, 'I don't know, sir. You see, I never knew my father. To tell the truth, sir, my mother was never married. All that she would tell me, sir, was that she thought my father was a Flight Lieutenant Matthews from Kinloss'; and the candidate's papers showed that he was born near Elgin at about the time when the wing commander would have been a flight lieutenant at Kinloss. It took several paralytic seconds for the wing commander to recover his equilibrium enough to realise that he had been 'set up' and he then concluded his report on the candidate with the comment: 'Whoever put this man up for the Air Force ought to have his head examined!'

Some years later, in 1964, when I had been appointed by the Ministry of Defence to conduct an enquiry into requirements for the air defence of British interests in the decade 1975–1985, I had been invited by the Commander-in-Chief Fighter Command, Sir Douglas 'Zulu' Morris to address his annual conference at the Central Fighter Establishment at RAF Binbrook. It started with a pre-conference dinner, where I discovered that 'Zulu' was one of those senior officers, of whom more later, who would stay to the last in the bar afterwards, and I did my best to keep alcoholic pace with him. But I had to 'strike my flag' at 2 a.m. because I was the first speaker in the morning and still had part of my talk to prepare. So around 3 a.m. I was still working in bed when I heard 'noises off' in the corridor outside my room. After various bumps and fiddlings with the knob of my door, I heard a voice saying, 'This must be it!' and in came Wing Commander Matthews in a gait somewhere between a lurch and a stagger and an air commodore who turned out to be Micky Martin of Dambuster fame. Swaying triumphantly, the wing commander had realised his determination to introduce us, and although it was a singularly inconvenient hour I was delighted.

Indeed I drew on that introduction another seventeen years later, when I was giving the Christmas Lectures at the Royal Institution in 1981, and I invited Micky to explain to the enthusiastic audience how the principles of triangulation and similar triangles had been used by the Dambusters in May 1943 to establish their height above the water surface by looking for the coincidence of intersecting spotlights, and the correct distance from the dam at which to release their bouncing bombs.

One point that came out from the discussion between Micky and me in front of the audience and the TV cameras was that when a bomb exploded at the dam such waves were created on the water that it took three minutes for the surface to settle down sufficiently for the next aircraft to establish its height, and also for the spray to disperse enough for the towers on the dam to be seen clearly. I had previously known that Micky and Guy Gibson had stayed 'on target' after dropping their own bombs on the Möhne dam and had then flown on either side of the next aircraft to drop in order to draw the flak away from it, but I had imagined that this was only a matter of a minute or two. The need, though, for three-minute intervals between attacks resulted in Guy and Micky flying repeatedly for nearly half-an-hour into the teeth of the defences – after which Gibson then went on to bomb the Eder dam. I myself only realised this fact as we were talking in front of the most appreciative audience of about 400 schoolchildren that anyone could imagine. Their cheers endorsed my dazed admiration.

The fact that Micky and I had first met after a late session in the mess was entirely in keeping with RAF tradition. I was repeatedly impressed by the readiness of air marshals to fly up to Aberdeen for an Air Squadron dinner – sometimes two or even three of them would go, while it was unusual for even a single rear admiral to appear at the Naval Unit dinner, and the OTC hardly ever had as senior officer as a brigadier come to its dinner. Moreover, it was usual for the air marshals to stay on in the bar afterwards to meet as many cadets as possible, well into the small hours. I can recall Chiefs of Air Staff, Commanders-in-Chief, and Air Members all staying on in this way.

An outstanding example was Air Chief Marshal the Earl of (Paddy) Bandon, one of the most legendary of officers. Some of my friends served under him, and more than one told me that he was the best C-in-C they ever worked for.

One of them was Walter Pretty, later himself an air marshal and C-in-C of Signals Command, who had been my exact contemporary at school. At one point he was either AOA or SASO to Paddy when the latter commanded the 2nd Tactical Air Force in Germany. At one Staff meeting, the question arose about the need to extend the runway at, I think, Wahn, which Walter reckoned would be too expensive to cover from 2nd TAF resources. 'Couldn't we get the Germans to pay for it?' asked Paddy. 'I don't think they'd like the cost,' demurred Walter. Paddy replied, 'It's their commitment, and they damned well ought to pay. Look, Walter, you have been bullshitting me for the past eighteen months – now you go and bullshit them.' Which, Walter told me, he then proceeded to do, and so successfully that not only did the Germans pay, but they later thanked the C-in-C for the privilege of being allowed to do so.

I also knew another of Paddy's SASOs, when he was C-in-C of the Far East Air Force with its headquarters in, I believe, Singapore. One of Paddy's duties which he relished was to visit his stations, and his tired SASO told me his typical routine. After the formal inspection there would be a dinner in the mess and then a drink in the bar with the officers. Paddy would then move on to the sergeants' mess, the corporals' mess and the airmen's mess, which he would reach in the small hours. In this way he picked up details that otherwise would not have come to his notice. Bright as a daisy in the morning he would say to his SASO, 'By the way, John, when I was in the corporals' mess one of them told me . . . ' and then would follow an account of something that needed to be done. 'There may be nothing in it but you'd better look into it' – and enquiry often showed that there was.

Paddy was a remarkable character who could truly 'walk with kings nor lose the common touch' and I admired the way in which he could drink at any level and to any extent without forfeiting the slightest shred of respect. How can some men do it, and others not? I could not help recalling this some years later when I was guest of honour at a Command dinner of one of the USAF Commands in America. It was at the the height of the US hostage crisis in Iran, and the commanding general, who was in the chair and my host, asked me to excuse him when an urgent message had been received that required his action. One of his colonels then took over as host and at the end of the dinner asked me, 'Would you mind coming into the bar and meeting some of the junior officers?' I, of course, replied with alacrity because this was the routine that was normal in an RAF mess.

The subsequent party went so well that one of the junior officers was afterwards picked up by the police for being over the alcoholic limit. I was told that the general was shocked, not so much by the misfortune of the officer, but that his staff had taken their British visitor into the bar. It appeared that it was by no means usual for senior officers to mix in with their juniors in the way that ours did. The colonel was therefore about to be 'on the carpet' in front of his general; but fortunately I heard of the prospect in time enough to thank the general most profusely for the dinner, saying that I had particularly enjoyed the session in the bar afterwards and the opportunity to meet the junior officers because this was what I was absolutely used to with our own air force.

Paddy Bandon, of course, started with the advantage of being an earl, but his character was such that this probably made little difference. Somehow he instinctively knew where to 'draw the line' as I later saw when he and I were advisers to one of our friends running an industrial company. He disapproved of any doubtful practice such as birthday parties being given at the firm's expense. It was refreshing to know someone like Paddy who could so command the affection and respect of his staff at all levels, while being able to mix with them on equal terms.

I thought particularly of his example when a few years later I was lecturing on problems of command, and the need for a commander to know at first hand what was going on at any level. I was at the time in correspondence with Marshal of the Royal Air Force Sir John Slessor, a colleague of 1940 and one of the most philosophical of our air commanders, and I cited this gift of Paddy's for being able to mix and drink without losing dignity. I still have Jack Slessor's reply, part of which ran, 'Of course, Paddy was a law unto himself and could get away with that sort of thing. I was staying with him when he was C-in-C FEAF at Christmastime (Jack Slessor himself, incidentally, was then Chief of Air Staff). On the day we all went to serve in the garrison church, after which Paddy went off for his usual round of messes. He came back to the C-in-C's residence very late in the afternoon, minus his gold hat, medals and badges of rank, but with an Australian flight sergeant's stripes up! But I don't know anyone else who could have got away with it'.

Thoughts of Paddy and other commanders may seem far from the subject of University Air Squadrons, but time after time their presence at dinners testified to the extent to which the squadrons were, and still are, valued. There was a challenge, presumably from the Treasury, in 1967 which sought to abolish the squadrons on the grounds of expense; indeed, a similar challenge had led to the abolition of the Auxiliary Squadrons a year or two earlier, and it looked as though the UASs might be the next. It happened, though, that the AOC 25 Group, which administered the squadrons, was Air Vice Marshal H. J. Kirkpatrick, who had served in Fighter, Bomber and Transport Commands, and who had himself been in the Oxford Squadron in 1929–1932. He fought valiantly for the survival of the squadrons, and produced a report which argued that the squadrons more than paid for themselves, because a cadet who subsequently took up a regular commission had been so well trained that he required so much less further training than a new entrant when he became a regular officer.

There were, of course, several other arguments in favour of the squadrons, one being that their object was not so much to produce regular officers as to ensure that there was a body of opinion among those leaving the universities for civil life that was sensitive to the objectives, requirements and ethos of the Royal Air Force. I can recall the example of a chemistry graduate who subsequently worked with ICI, when one of his first jobs was to design starter cartridges for propeller aircraft. He told me that he tackled the work all the more thoroughly because he knew from experience how much depended on a reliable cartridge.

Besides such arguments and others admirably presented in the AOC's report, he also included a silent but eloquent appendix which simply listed the honours won by former members of the pre-war squadrons during World War II, headed by Leonard Cheshire's Victoria Cross, and innumerable DSOs.

The future of the squadrons was still *sub judice* at the time when Fighter Command held its last parade in April 1968, and I was fortunate enough to have been invited by the Command. Also there was Merlyn Rees who was then Under-Secretary of State for the Royal Air Force in the Ministry of Defence. He very warmly supported the case for the squadrons for, as he told me, he himself had been a member of the Nottingham University Air Squadron. Although a few had to be amalgamated, the squadrons survived.

Long may they flourish, for both universities and the Royal Air Force are enriched by their active existence.

14

DAVID LANGDON

Per Ardua ad Adastral

AT THE OUTBREAK of the war, as part of my then employment, I was seconded, with the grandiose title of Executive Officer, to the Civil Defence R & D Depot in the borough of Finsbury, hard by the City of London.

Our job in the threatened event of bombing was to rescue people and demolish unsafe buildings. When the blitz started in earnest the Civil Defence services were stretched to the limit and for nights on end the City in the winter of 1940–1 was engulfed in the fire and general mayhem which were to afflict other parts of the country but which we then thought were aimed at us personally and in particular.

At a point when even the celebrated Cockney spirit began to flag, my thoughts turned to volunteering for the RAFVR as a safer haven. I chose the RAF because my favourite uncle had regaled me as a child with stories about his life in the Royal Flying Corps in World War I, and a book he bequeathed me, *Rovers of the Sky*, was the set-book of my early reading. I had, however, to get round the problem of being in a 'Reserved Occupation' and its implication that young and fit as I then was, I was of more use at the R & D Depot than in the armed forces.

The recruiting requirements of the RAF seemed to vary with the fortunes or otherwise of the air war. At one stage the flavour-of-the-month was for air gunners, but I did not consider it was worth applying to my authorities to lift their ban, as I reckoned my chances of survival in the rear turret of a Lancaster were roughly equal to sitting behind the sandbags in bombed-out Finsbury.

Then came a call for trainee pilots. Our depot PT instructor knew a friend who knew a friend of the orderly room sergeant at the local RAF recruiting office. Encouraged by a non-committal reply for permission from my HQ office, I presented myself to the sergeant with a note, a nod and a wink. It was when I sat waiting my turn to be interviewed that I had my first chilling glimpse of Service life.

A young LAC had marched up to the table where the interviewing officer sat, and with a shattering thump of highly polished boots, pulled off an enormously exaggerated salute, handed over a chit, stepped back a pace, repeated the salute, turned about and thumped noisily away. My heart sank.

I was to meet many stereotypes of that LAC in the months of training which followed my induction as AC2 1456437.

We all recall the traumatic days of initial training when callow youths like ourselves were transformed overnight into airmen, severing every last link with undisciplined civilian life, by dedicated NCOs who seemed all to have had identical training for the job in the same crack Guards' regiment. I recall a long line of raw recruits in the vast balloon hangar at Cardington, which had been converted into a mess hall, queueing for a midday meal. Each clutched his tin mug and 'irons' and proffered his mug in turn to an LAC standing behind a single large urn at a long trestle-table.

'Tea, coffee or cocoa?' he intoned, with that bored air of condescension all longer-serving airmen reserved for 'sprogs'. We each pondered the alternatives, trying hard to revive taste-buds so recently atrophied.

'Tea, please,' one man would timidly suggest. 'Cocoa,' another. The spigot on the urn would be aimed at each mug. The unidentifiable liquid emerging was the same for all choices.

Another memory is of the regulation haircut procedure. Here the queue was for the camp barber-shop, with a civilian barber wielding an electric clipper. Those like myself who were reluctant to forego their last vestigial tie with civilian status, made up the tail end of every intake.

'How would you like it, sir?' the barber asked, leaning conspiratorially towards my ear.

'Not too short, please,' I ventured. A pregnant pause, and I produced half-a-crown. The barber took a pair of scissors from a drawer and snipped away.

'How's that, sir?'

'Fine, thank you.'

I stepped out of the barber's shop and by some curious coincidence straight into the arms of our squad corporal.

'What do you call this then?' he thundered, poking a hard finger at the nape of my neck. 'Get back in there and tell 'im to take some 'air off!'

'Tck, tck,' said the barber, flourishing his soiled cloth over me for the second time. 'Did 'e catch you then?' The sympathy was feigned, and out came the dreaded clippers. The mutual arrangement with the corporal must have gone on ever since the camp opened years before.

Some months later, as a newly commissioned acting pilot officer, resplendent in my Gieves & Co uniform, with the thin 'scraper' ring on my sleeves and greatcoat epaulettes, I was posted back to my original training unit. This posting, contrary I believe to all Air Ministry procedure, was due either to a simple clerical error, or as I prefer to think now, a quixotically devilish ploy on the part of someone in Postings paying off some old atavistic score. I therefore appeared on a station where I had so recently been an 'erk' AC2 and soon began to attract a series of smart salutes from the same NCOs who had spared neither word nor deed in the difficult task of transforming me into an airman.

I particularly cherished the salute of my old flight sergeant, a fiery tempered, ginger haired type to whom I had once failed to endear myself when I asked him, with unusual temerity, why he had awarded 'A' Squad 100%, 'B' Squad 103% and 'C' Squad 106% at a passing-out parade. I was merely querying his grasp of elementary percentages. He dismissed this with a curt 'Because 'C' Squad was a bloody sight better than you lot, that's why.' I was never able to verify whether he recognised me in my new guise.

That heady experience, the unfulfilled dream no doubt of countless air-craftmen over the years, was short-lived, and a correct posting soon followed. This was to RAF Hunsdon, an 11 Group night-fighter station in Hert-fordshire.

This was the sharp end of Service life. Black-painted Hurricanes and Boston Havocs being serviced by fitters and armourers at dispersals, or flying off at dusk on runways disappearing into the green countryside, over beacons and ack-ack sites and white-painted station bicycles, airmen-for-the-use-of. And overall the all-pervading smell of aviation fuel.

Numbers 3 and 85 night-fighter squadrons operated from Hunsdon, and with them such famed fighter pilots as Wing Commander Peter Townsend and John 'Cat's Eyes' Cunningham, to name-drop just two. Lesser luminaries on the ground staff were Tim Molony, in civilian life Ladbroke's 'man-on-the-rails', and now Adjutant of 85 Squadron, and the Station Adjutant Richard Watts-Jones, formerly managing director of Fenwick's, the ladies' fashion store in Bond Street.

The officers' mess was in a grand country house, Bonningtons. I have a poignant memory of having the job of bar officer tacked on to my duties in Intelligence. If someone thought the connecting link between the two jobs was a knowledge of fine wines they were sadly mistaken. The previous owner of Bonningtons had graciously left the contents of the well-stocked cellar to the new incumbents, and I found myself dispensing dusty bottles, long laid-down, at a shilling a time. My conscience still pricks me, although I feel the owner of Bonningtons might well have been happy to have given away his precious bottles free of charge to those fortunate enough to have returned safely from their nightly ops, instead of my swelling the coffers of the PMC.

My final memory of Hunsdon is of No. 1451 'Turbinlite' Flight. This was then a top-secret wheeze thought up by a senior scientific boffin who had the ear and assent of the PM, Winston Churchill.

The flight was comprised of twin-engined Boston Havocs, into the nose cone of which was fitted an AI radar and a searchlight three times more powerful than the standard Army type, behind a flat disc of armoured glass three feet in diameter. The power unit was a ton of car batteries carried in the bomb bay.

The idea was for this airborne searchlight to illuminate and discommode the pilot of the enemy raider, and two accompanying Hurricanes would then go in for the kill. In practice the scheme was none too successful. Nose-heavy, the Turbinlites either crashed on take-off or proved difficult to manoeuvre in flight. Several fatalities resulted.

I recall leading one of the burial parties on its way to Hunsdon churchyard. The sergeant i/c the four aircraftmen bearing the coffin suddenly took umbrage at their slower than regulation pace.

'Come along there! Put some bleeding life into it!'

'Come along there!' he barked at them. 'Put some bleeding life into it!'

I drew a cartoon of the incident and showed it to the assembled company in the briefing room at Control. In spite of its black humour it met with unreserved approval. I sent it off to *Punch* for publication. I should have added a note to the effect that it appeared to have gone down well with all concerned at the station. It was returned with an 'Editor regrets' slip. Wisely. But to be fair he made up for this thumbs-down by publishing many of my less-controversial cartoons on Service life.

While on this subject I once received a request, by signal from Air Ministry, to illustrate a manual on 'Fighter Tactics'. Sitting on my bed and improvising a chest of drawers as a drawing board, I was busy trying to depict a type of air interception known as the 'Tizzy Angle', when I became aware of heavy

141

breathing over my shoulder. Our batman, AC2 Pedlingham (one batman per six officers) had padded silently into the room in his regulation gym shoes and was taking a close interest in my small sketch.

'Coo, sir,' he said, 'I used to be a signwriter too!'

I felt proud to be included in the same company of artists as Pedlingham, who had once been engaged on work of similar importance at Ford's of Dagenham, painting 'Ladies' and 'Gents' and such like on factory doors.

'Coo, Sir! I used to be a signwriter too ...'

One fine summer's morning I was walking down the Strand, somewhat pre-occupied. I was on embarkation leave, with yet another posting, this time to the Middle East. Striding towards me was the tall, slim erect figure of a squadron leader, military moustached, briefcase under arm. We exchanged salutes. He turned.

'Langers!' he cried.

He was René Raymond, whom I had once met at Air Ministry when we were both contributing to *The Royal Air Force Journal.* He had written a series of amusing stories of barrack-room life, which I had illustrated.

'You're just the man.'

'If it's more illustrations,' I said, 'I haven't much time. I'm on embarkation leave.'

'Hector's gone,' he countered, 'and I'm in charge of P9.'

Squadron Leader Hector Bolitho, a New Zealander and well-known as a royal biographer, had been editor of the official *Journal* since its inception. It was a lively magazine, putting across Air Ministry Orders to the troops in palatable form, and containing articles and stories by RAF personnel, including those by H. E. Bates, John Pudney, Richard Hillary and Basil Boothroyd. Unlike its larger counterpart in Whitehall, the Directorate of Public Relations, P9's remit was selling the Service to the Service.

I congratulated Raymond on his appointment and promotion.

'And I've a vacancy for a flying officer,' he said.

'Sorry, sir,' I replied, glumly. 'I'm posted abroad.'

I had long learned that in the Service if there was something you desperately needed from the powers-that-be there was scant chance of its being granted. On the other hand...

'I'll see about your posting,' Raymond said, and marched off.

René Raymond's pen name was 'James Hadley Chase'. He had become famous, and notorious, for his first novel, *No Orchids For Miss Blandish*, which had sold in its thousands and was then in process of being turned into a West End musical. A question was raised in Parliament asking the then Air Minister about the desirability of a Squadron Leader Raymond to edit the official *Royal Air Force Journal*, following the publication of the scandalous *No Orchids*.

The Air Minister stoutly defended the appointment in the glowing terms dictated by AVM Bertine Sutton, then Director of Personnel, and nominally in charge of P9 branch and Raymond.

In my view there was no finer choice of officer than Raymond. He seemed to have inherited the military bearing and attitudes of his father, who had been a colonel in the Indian Army, and I found it always a pleasure to work with him. His brief case invariably carried a batch of typewritten sheets for a new novel, but he was a strict disciplinarian, tempered by an impish sense of humour.

'You may wish you'd taken that Middle East posting,' he said to me one day, waving a signal at me. 'SEAC want to drop us over Burma by parachute with a portable press to set up a Far East edition of the *Journal*.'

My cancelled posting suddenly did appear preferable.

Soon after this scare, which failed to materialise, we were taking a lunch-time walk, from Adastral House where P9 operated, and passing Bush House in the Aldwych. A V-Bomb exploded directly above us. Raymond and I were thrown to the ground. The carnage around us was frightful. Buses were ablaze, one was hurled into an emergency water supply tank. Buildings on either side of Kingsway were shattered and there were many dead and wounded littered around.

When we recovered from delayed shock some days later, the Middle East and Burma were forgotten. Instead my thoughts went back to my comparatively halcyon days at Finsbury Rescue & Demolition Depot. I had come full circle.

15

Sir Bernard Lovell

Our Only Means of Hitting the Enemy

Thirty years after the end of the war I was dining with friends in a Cheshire village. My thoughts were far removed from the war; in fact the lady on my left was enquiring about the telescope at Jodrell Bank dimly visible through the dining room windows with its floodlit bowl silhouetted against the darkening summer sky. It was the usual kind of polite enquiry and I was in the midst of an attempt to transfer the complexities of contemporary astronomical research into plain English when the words Blenheims and Wellingtons floated across the table. I turned to my hostess: 'Forgive me for asking but who is the person next to the lady on your husband's right?' – 'Oh, he is a dear friend from Poland, Jan Turjewicz, but we call him "Skippy" because he was a pilot in the war. I think he was in Coastal Command trying to sink the U-boats.'

In a flash my thoughts left the affairs of the telescope and suddenly I was at the Coastal Command aerodrome at Chivenor in North Devon in the cold grey dawn of a day in early March 1943. I was with the CO in his office, a depressing room in a prefabricated hut with the yellowish paint peeling off the breeze-block walls and the floor covered with brown linoleum. We were anxiously waiting for the return of the Wellingtons from their night patrol over the Bay of Biscay. He was less than enthusiastic having been harassed by me and several of my colleagues for the past week fitting a new kind of ASV (Air to Surface Vessel) radar into his Wellingtons. He did not believe our 'rotating device' would do any good over the vast stretch of the Atlantic and as far as I was concerned it was an act of faith that it would do so.

This Wellington squadron had operated over the Bay in 1942 with an ASV radar working on a wavelength of 1.5 metres. They were equipped with a Leigh light, a searchlight in a retractable cupola. When the ASV detected an echo the Leigh light could be lowered to illuminate the target to make sure it was a U-boat and not a friendly vessel. If it was a U-boat, the resulting depth charge attack had a significant effect on the U-boats using the Bay as a transit area from their French west coast ports to the Atlantic shipping routes. The normal practice of the U-boats was to surface by night to re-charge their batteries and the continued harassment by the radar-equipped Leigh light Wellingtons led to a significant decrease in the merchant shipping losses. The Germans responded by equipping the U-boats with a simple receiver, known as Metox, which could detect the Wellingtons' 1.5 metre radar and enabled them to submerge before any attack developed. The fitting of this Metox in the U-boats began in August 1942 and nullified the effect of the Coastal Command patrols to such an extent that in the early spring of 1943 the shipping losses became an issue of grave concern to the War Cabinet.

There was an obvious technical answer – and that was to change the wavelength of the radar in the Wellingtons. The radar with which I had been concerned had operated on a wavelength of 10cm and had been developed with the highest priority to assist Bomber Command to locate targets deep in Germany. In the face of much opposition from Bomber Command we had taken a few of these H_2S radars and modified them for use over the Bay by Coastal Command.

The results were dramatic. The U-boats were unaware of the approach of the 10cm-equipped Wellingtons and were relentlessly depth-charged at night. Within weeks the strategic situation was transformed and by May 1943 every U-boat crossing the Bay, on average, suffered one attack. These attacks during a hitherto safe passage across the Bay coincided with the breaking of the Enigma naval codes and with the closing of the Atlantic gap with long range aircraft operating from both sides of the Atlantic. By the end of May Hitler had withdrawn the U-boats from the North Atlantic and complained in a radio broadcast that 'the temporary setback to our U-boat campaign is due to one single technical invention of our enemies'.

That was the scene so vividly re-created for me around the dinner table in the small Cheshire village thirty years later, for Turjewicz or 'Skippy' had been the pilot of one of those Wellingtons equipped with our new 10cm ASV. In Poland before the war he had learnt to fly light aircraft. When Hitler attacked he walked out of Poland and eventually reached France. When France collapsed he managed to get to England. Like all heroes he was reluctant to talk about those exploits and I never discovered the details. As those Wellingtons landed at Chivenor from their nights over the Bay in the spring of 1943 it must have been long odds that thirty years later I would be sitting around a dinner table with one of those pilots.

Although my main concern was with Bomber Command I had one other memorable encounter with the affairs of Coastal Command. We had believed that the Germans would quickly install a new receiver in the U-boats to detect the 10cm radars in the Wellingtons. The next obvious step was to prepare a similar installation working on a wavelength of 3cm. We had developed a H_2S system working on that wavelength for Bomber Command and by the early autumn of 1943 we had a prototype ASV on that wavelength installed in a Wellington. We expected that the normal procedure had been followed by the Air Ministry, that is, arrangements for a trial installation in an operational Wellington which would then be followed quickly by installations of several of this new type of ASV in a Coastal Command squadron. By October our repeated efforts to secure the appropriate Wellington for this trial installation had been met with the astonishing response that there was no operational requirement.

Air Marshal Sir John Slessor had succeeded Air Marshal Sir Philip Joubert de la Ferté as C-in-C Coastal Command earlier in 1943, and when he had the evidence in the early autumn of 1943 that the U-boats were listening to the 10cm radar and submerging before they could be attacked he came to Malvern (to where the Telecommunications Research Establishment had been evacuated in May 1942). The laboratory used by my group was in the Preston Science Laboratory of Malvern College and it was there that I first met Slessor on a Saturday afternoon, 23rd October. He demanded to know why, when this anticipated operational circumstance had occurred, he did not have the replacement 3cm version of ASV in his aircraft at Chivenor. When he discovered that we had completed our development but that some unknown persons in London had successfully sabotaged the trial installation for many months past he became very angry indeed. He removed his jacket, seized pencil and paper and in less than twenty-four hours delivered a five-page foolscap letter to the Deputy Chief of Air Staff. I still have a copy of that remarkable letter. He set out in great detail the report which he had made to the War Cabinet Committee on anti-U-boat warfare on 22nd March (1943) drawing attention to the urgent need for further changes to the 10cm ASV since he believed 'it was only a matter of time before the Germans would be able to listen to 10cm ASV'. He referred to the completion of the development at TRE and asked for disciplinary action to be taken against those responsible for the delay in providing the trial installation Wellington. He continued that this was 'either crass stupidity or pettifogging obstructionism of the worst kind I have ever encountered in this war' and ended by stating that 'no one but a congenital idiot would imagine that it was not necessary to lay on Column 7 [ie the aircraft and fittings] when Column 9 [ie the equipment] was already provided'.

This was an extraordinary letter couched in undiplomatic language from a C-in-C who was exasperated and led to instant action in the Air Ministry. Three days later I was summoned to an urgent meeting in the War Cabinet office. It was the first and only time at which I had witnessed a direct confrontation between the hierarchy of Bomber and Coastal Commands. The chairman was the Deputy Chief of Air Staff, Air Marshal Sir Norman Bottomley. On his right was the C-in-C Coastal Command (Slessor) with his staff, but Harris, the C-in-C Bomber Command, had sent his deputy (Air Marshal Sir Robert Saundby). Bomber Command had been promised 200 H_2S 3cm sets by the end of the year. The issue which DCAS placed before the meeting as a result of Slessor's letter was whether fifty of these 3cm sets should be diverted to Coastal Command for ASV use. Saundby and the Bomber Command group were enraged and argued that the most efficient use of the 3cm H_2S would be for them to use it for blind bombing the U-boat pens on the west coast of France. Slessor eventually managed to persuade

DCAS to allocate enough of the 3cm equipment for one of his squadrons. As the papers were being folded Saundby said to DCAS:

'I will report the decision to my C-in-C but I know that he will be much displeased.'

Indeed, Harris was so displeased that before I could complete my return journey to Malvern he had telephoned the Prime Minister and got the decision reversed. During those months the antagonism between Coastal and Bomber Commands erupted over the use of a few of our radar systems, but it was forty years later before I realised that this was merely one aspect of a bitter dispute about the use of the heavy bombers. In 1974 I had the task of writing the biographical memoir of Lord Blackett for the Royal Society[1] and it was Slessor who then drew my attention to the core of the dispute. In 1943, as P. M. S. Blackett, he was Director of Naval Operational Research in the Admiralty and was strongly opposed to the use which Harris was making of the heavy bombers. In March 1943 the Admiralty had launched a paper by Blackett directly to the Anti-U-Boat Committee. In this paper, prepared without any consultation with Slessor, Blackett estimated the number and type of aircraft required to have a decisive effect against the U-boats in the Bay of Biscay. He proposed a force of 260 heavy aircraft which would have required a diversion from Bomber Command to Coastal Command of 190 heavy bombers.

Slessor was greatly annoyed: 'The operational research scientist has no stronger supporter than I ... but they must stick to their lasts ... ' Slessor complained to the First Sea Lord about this 'slide-rule strategy of the worst kind'. He was convinced that he did not want 190 heavies diverted from Bomber Command but 'aircraft of the right type, with the right sort of radar equipment and with crews trained in the right way – and I wanted them quickly. *Now* was the time when we wanted to kill the U-boats, while we had the bulge over them with the 10cm ASV.'

The delay in providing Coastal Command with the 3cm version of ASV fortunately transpired to be of little consequence, such was the setback suffered by the U-boat fleet in the spring of 1943. It is one of the ironies of the war that the equipment developed with the highest priority for use by Bomber Command had such a dramatic tactical effect in the anti-U-boat campaign when a few were modified for use by Coastal Command.

My own association with Bomber Command began early in January 1942. Hitherto I had worked on the development of 10cm airborne interception radar (AI) for Fighter Command and my association with the Royal Air Force had been largely limited to the pilots who flew the night fighter version of the famous Blenheim in which we tested our experimental systems that later became so successful in the Beaufighter. That occupation changed overnight shortly after Christmas 1941 when I was ordered to form a group to develop a bombing system on the highest priority. The instructions were clear: the radar must be self-contained in the bomber so that targets deep in Germany could be located, beyond the Ruhr which was about the limit of range of the navigational and bombing systems GEE and Oboe which depended on ground stations in England.

Initially the problem did not appear difficult. The major units of the radar already being manufactured for the 10cm AI system could be modified and it seemed that the main new requirements would be a rotating scanner underneath the bomber and new display units for the aircrew operator. Bernard O'Kane and Geoffrey Hensby had made minor modifications to a 10cm AI in a Blenheim and had demonstrated in November 1941 that towns and other targets would give distinct echoes on a cathode ray tube. The belief that it would not be difficult to modify the equipment for use in heavy bombers was one of the worst misjudgements I ever made. The scanner in the Blenheim was in the nose without obstruction and the tests were made when flying at 5,000 to 10,000 ft altitude. In the four-engined bombers the scanner was truncated and housed in a cupola underneath the fuselage. This, and the fact that the operational altitudes were 15,000 to 20,000 ft created serious problems, exacerbated by the demand of the Air Staff that the powerful magnetron transmitter used in the AI equipment must not be flown over enemy territory and that the system must use a much lower powered transmitting valve, as the principles of these were already known to the Germans.

At that time we were located on the south coast and at the end of March 1942 a Halifax four-engined bomber arrived at Hurn airport for our development tests. By mid-April we were ready for our first flights and to my astonishment DCAS, and a galaxy of high-ranking officers came for a demonstration. That transpired to be symptomatic of the intense political pressure emanating from the Prime Minister that surrounded our work.

Much later in life I understood the threads that led to this pressure and made the development of the system so difficult. The source was the Prime Minister and his scientific adviser F. A. Lindemann (created Lord Cherwell in 1942). Cherwell held firmly to the view that the bomber offensive must be an essential prelude to victory. In his history of the Second World War Churchill[2] explained that Cherwell had

> begun to raise doubts in my mind about the accuracy of our bombing, and in 1941 I authorised his Statistical Department to make an investigation at Bomber Headquarters. The results confirmed our fears. We learnt that although Bomber Command believed they had found the target, two-thirds of the crews actually failed to strike within five miles of it. The air photographs showed how little damage was being done. It also appeared that the crews knew this, and were discouraged by the poor results of so much hazard. Unless we could improve on this there did not seem much use in continuing night bombing. On September 3, 1941, I had minuted:

> *Prime Minister to Chief of Air Staff*
> This is a very serious paper [by Lord Cherwell, on the results of our bombing raids on Germany in June and July], and seems to require your most urgent attention. I await your proposals for action.

The investigation referred to by Churchill, on which Cherwell based his paper, was made by D. M. Butt, who had studied the night photographs taken by Bomber Command crews during raids in June and July 1941. This analysis revealed that only one in three of the aircraft bombed within five miles of their target. The failure of Bomber Command was even more serious than this statistic implied, since as Butt pointed out in his report:

> ... these figures relate only to the aircraft recorded as *attacking* the target. The proportion of the *total sorties* which reached within five miles is less by one-third. Thus, for example, of the total sorties one in five got within 5 miles of the target, ie with[in] the 75 square miles surrounding the target.

That was the background to the Prime Minister's minute to the Chief of Air Staff on 3 September 1941, and to my own involvement with Bomber Command for the remainder of the war.

For more than half a century Mr Butt, whose report had such an effect on my life, remained an enigmatic figure. Then by sheer chance in June 1992 the veil was lifted. So many erroneous statements had been published in the press during the conflict over the statue to Sir Arthur Harris, erected outside the RAF Church St Clement Danes, that I was stimulated to write a letter to *The Times*. This was published on 30th May, 1992, and a few days later I received the following letter (dated 1st June) from D. M. Butt[3].

> In view of your letter in The Times yesterday, perhaps I should record the origins of the 'Butt Report' on bombing accuracy while I have still (just) time.
>
> At the time I was PS to Lord Cherwell. He was interested in the choice between high charge/weight ratio bombs and the traditional bombs which were nearly all steel. He had gone to Medmenham PIU (Photographic Intelligence Unit) to look at the night photographs taken when they [the bombs] were dropped, with James Tuck, his 'scientific adviser' and was horrified to find that they all showed open countryside. He and James were walking in the garden of the house at Marlow that we were then using (for the benefit of working at night!) full of gloom and despondency and intending to report to the PM next day. I told him that to base their conclusions on a sample of 10 would get them ignored. They agreed and the next day James and I were smuggled into High Wycombe BHQ and looked at 60 or 70 photos they had on record there. Same result, nearly. Prof then spoke, I think to Sinclair and Portal and they agreed on a full investigation. I was available and was sent to do it, very hugger-mugger – and very frightened, as an assistant-principal and a civilian, and not a trained statistician. However, they cooperated splendidly under the leadership of S/L Muir-Warden and dug out the most extraordinary amount of records and I got the job done in just over a week. The results shook everybody – and your researches got top priority.
>
> It ought to be called the Cherwell report, as I tried to persuade Norman Brook when he objected to a civil servant's name in the Official History.

Our work certainly got top priority and everything we wanted, be it a bomber, a mechanic or a screwdriver, was supplied with alacrity. However, top priority also meant the constant interest of the Prime Minister and the Air Staff and that was inimical to the atmosphere we needed to overcome the formidable problems of making this bombing system (coded H_2S) work in a heavy bomber. The hindrance caused by the emergency move, because of the threat of an attack on our laboratories, from the south coast and Hurn airport to Malvern and the airport at Defford, was quickly followed by a disaster. On the afternoon of 7th June the Halifax bomber left Defford for a short flight to demonstrate our experimental system to three senior representatives from EMI who had been given the contract to manufacture the system. The Halifax crashed in flames in the Wye Valley near Ross-on-Wye and killed all eleven on board[4].

Although key personnel associated with the development and all our equipment were lost the urgency was such that Churchill summoned those of us who had to make it work, manufacture it and use it, to the Cabinet Room, and declared that he must have two squadrons equipped by October. The fact that we were only two months late in meeting this demand, which seemed a fantastic one at the time of the meeting in early July, was undoubtedly the result of the pressure from Churchill – 'Our only means of hitting the enemy'. Considerable numbers of RAF personnel and civilians became involved in the tasks of development, manufacture, and flight testing, but of all with whom I was in touch during those frantic months, apart from the members of my own group, I worked mainly with and through three people.

Sir Robert Renwick (formerly chairman of the London County Electric Supply Company) who was appointed to the joint posts of Controller of Communication Equipment in the Ministry of Aircraft Production and Controller of Communications in the Air Ministry. Every week he would summon the relevant scientists, industrialists and operational RAF staff to his room in the Air Ministry in King Charles Street. Every day he would telephone: 'Any news, any problems?' The problems did not linger for long in his office, for he was in a most powerful position with direct access to Churchill.

I first met D. C. T. (Don) Bennett two days after the PM's meeting. He had just been promoted to group captain having escaped across Norway and through Sweden after his Halifax bomber had been shot down in April during an attack on the battleship *Tirpitz* in Trondheim Fjord. He was the most inexhaustible and dynamic man I ever encountered and years later when I read in Webster & Frankland's official history[5] that he was 'perhaps the greatest flying expert in Bomber Command' I remembered his impact on our flight testing programme at Defford in that summer of 1942. He had just been made CO of the newly created Pathfinder Force (8 Group) and had been sent to Defford to stimulate the H_2S programme. Hitherto we had depended on the station commander at Defford who would allow us to fly the Halifax at times which fitted in with his servicing plans. Bennett soon changed that arrangement. He maintained that the conditions were best for flying either at midnight or 6am. This schedule began on a Sunday and I have a diary note that by Tuesday night I was 'almost hysterical'. For the next three years Bennett became part of our daily life either at Defford, his HQ in Huntingdon or on the airfields of 8 Group.[6]

Group Captain Dudley Saward had been appointed the chief radar officer at Bomber Command HQ late in 1941 at a time when the initial flights in a Blenheim to test the feasibility of H_2S were being made. I first met him early in 1942 and from that moment he became of great importance to the future of the project. The close partnership that developed between us was a significant matter in the story of H_2S. It was through him that the effective integration and liaison was established between ourselves and the operational staff and service personnel of the Command. One important outcome of this friendship was our walk on the Malvern Hills on a Sunday evening in April 1943 when he told me about the new attack techniques of the German fighters on our bombers. It was then that the idea of making use of H_2S as a tail-warning device arose. He immediately sent RAF mechanics and a heavy bomber, and within a few weeks we were able to demonstrate the tail-warning device known as Fishpond. By the autumn this was operational in all H_2S-equipped bombers.

Churchill's demand for two squadrons of H_2S bombers by October 1942 was never remotely possible and three weeks after that early July meeting a more reasonable target was set for equipping twenty-four Halifaxes and twenty-four Stirlings by 31st December. In fact, by that date there were two dozen H_2S bombers in 8 Group: twelve Halifaxes of 35 Squadron at Graveley and twelve Stirlings of 7 Squadron at Oakington. The Secretary of State for Air had ruled that because H_2S used the highly secret magnetron as a transmitter, these aircraft could be flown over enemy territory only if the Russians held the line of the Volga. The defeat of the German 6th Army at Stalingrad and the surrender of General Paulus in January 1943 met this criterion and on the night of 30/31st January 1943 the H_2S-equipped bombers of 8 Group were first used to mark Hamburg.

On 9th February 1943, a memorandum was issued from Bomber Command:

H_2S ... fully meets Air Staff requirements and has exceeded expectations in that towns have proved easy to identify both by shape and relative positions. In addition to the exceptional value of H_2S for identification and bombing of the target, its great navigational value has been proved beyond all doubt.

Even so the pressure for improved definition and refinements to the system was relentless. In 1943 over 32,000 of the 53,000 sorties by Bomber Command were led by H_2S-equipped aircraft and by April 1944, twenty-three squadrons had been fitted with H_2S. When the war ended, eighteen varieties of H_2S on wavelengths of 10cm, 3cm and 1.25cm were in use by Bomber Command.

In July 1945 I was released from my wartime work and returned to the

University of Manchester. The memories of war and the Royal Air Force faded into the background of my life until firstly that night in Cheshire and again in 1990. In February of that year I was invited to take part in a symposium to commemorate the fiftieth anniversary of the discovery of the magnetron in the University of Birmingham by Randall and Boot. There I was accosted by a young man in civilian clothes: 'I believe you were once at Staxton Wold in Yorkshire' – 'Indeed, I was in the operations room of the CH radar when Chamberlain broadcast that we were at war with Germany.' The young man responded, 'I was once the CO there. Would you like to see Staxton Wold as it is now?'

So, later that summer Flight Lieutenant Peter Emmett drove me to Staxton Wold where in September 1939 I had seen the short-lived radar echoes on the cathode ray tube that six years later were to lead me to Jodrell Bank, to the construction of the large steerable telescope and the exploration of the Universe[7]. The huge aerial masts and giant transmitters of 1939 had vanished. The equipment of a new technology was performing the same task, but the men in the uniform of the Royal Air Force were a happy reminder of the permanency of a Service with which I had once been privileged to be associated.

Notes and References

1. Lovell, Bernard *P. M. S. Blackett, a biographical memoir*, Biog. Mem. Roy. Soc., 21, 1, 1975.
2. Churchill, Winston S. *The Second World War, Vol. IV: The Hinge of Fate*, Cassell 1951, p. 250.
3. I am greatly indebted to Mr David M. Butt for giving me permission to publish this letter. In his second letter of 1st August 1992 he added that the decision to initiate an Operational Research Section at Bomber Command was made the day after his report was delivered and that the subsequent analyses of the ORS for the next three months produced the same statistics as in his report.
4. Over forty years later W. H. Sleigh after retiring as chief aeronautical engineer from RSRE (the successor of TRE) made a detailed investigation of the cause of the Halifax crash. *Annex No. 4 to Aircraft for airborne radar development*, RSRE (Malvern) June 1985.

On 7th June 1992, precisely fifty years after this tragedy, a memorial window was unveiled in Goodrich Castle, a few miles from the scene of the crash. This is a memorial to those killed in the crash of the Halifax and to the many others who lost their lives when flying with the RAF Research Squadron.
5. Webster, Sir Charles and Frankland, Noble. *The Strategic Air Offensive against Germany 1939–1945*, HMSO 1961 vol.III, footnote p.299.
6. Air Vice Marshal Bennett CBE, DSO, had a brief period as a Liberal MP after the end of the war. He later played a prominent part in the Berlin airlift and, with his wife, took part in a number of Monte Carlo rallies. He died on 14th September

1986. For an account of his extraordinary career see the obituary note in *The Times* 17th September 1986.

7. For an account of these developments at Jodrell Bank, see Bernard Lovell, *Astronomer By Chance*, Macmillan 1991 and OUP 1992 (pb).

16

GAVIN LYALL

My Tiger Summer

IN THE SUMMER of 1953 we were supposed to go from learning to fly jets (Meteors) to Operational Conversion Units (Canberras or night fighters in our case: we were thought to be potential IFR aces) and thence to squadrons. But in the rapid expansion of the RAF which had, briefly, allowed peacetime National Servicemen to become aircrew, we had lost too much time waiting for airfields to be re-activated and mothballed training aircraft to be made, sort of, flyable. Our demob dates were too close for any squadron to want us.

So another long leave ended with a telegram telling me to report to Thorney Island, with full flying kit. I rang Mick: he'd had the same posting, and thought Thorney was something to do with navigators. I didn't mind the obvious deduction: that we'd be co-pilots on big aircraft with a crew, but Mick was disgusted. He wanted to join the Auxiliaries when he left, and needed to get operational on jets first.

We arrived to find Pete already there – he was married and searching for married quarters – and some even odder news: we three were to learn to fly Tiger Moths, the old trainer biplane which had been replaced by the Chipmunk on which we'd done our basic training. We would then take batches of schoolboy cadets, living in a tented camp that was being pitched just outside the perimeter fence, up for 'air experience' rides. As yet there were neither Tigers nor cadets, so we had time to look around.

RAF Thorney Island, near Portsmouth, was indeed devoted to navigation training, full of acting pilot officers, elderly one-winged instructors and a strong smell of discipline. They flew in old Avro Ansons and brand-new Vickers Varsities, the nose-wheel version of the Viking airliner, which had just replaced wartime Wellingtons. The last of these, we gathered, had been removed from the perimeter track with dust-pan and brush when it got terminally tired.

The station itself was comfortably 'permanent' (ie pre-war, with those square pillars and metal bannisters you found in both officers' messes and aircraft industry offices of that period), and actually on an island, if you counted a ten-foot-wide channel. Four of the six approaches were over the sea and we were shown, as an Awful Warning, the very patch of mud where an Anson had recently landed short. It seemed that someone had helpfully gone out in a sea mist to fire a Verey light to indicate the runway threshold, and got the Anson on the windshield, first shot.

The other nautical touch was the station yacht club, which didn't go as far as having a yacht, but did have a bar which stayed open as long as anyone was leaning on it. Add in a bus service which ran on a road from the mess across the runways (through traffic lights) to the local village and the main rail line to London, good Hampshire pubs, the summer coming in – and I reckoned I had a very nice final posting.

Waiting for the Tigers, we found we could get as many rides in Varsities as we liked. The true co-pilots, bored with four-hour navigation exercises, were more than happy to have us replace them, particularly at night, as 'safety' pilots. I imagine that 'safety' meant that, although we were unqualified on the type, we could be expected to do *something* right if the real pilot died in his sleep.

And on most trips, that seemed the likeliest time for him to go. One low-level flight on an oven-hot day took us out to Ushant, north past Land's End, then home up the Bristol Channel. Somewhere in the stoke-hold, trainee navigators were dripping sweat on to blank radar screens and making smeared marks on their charts, but on the flight deck the blinds were down over the windows and we were all asleep bar the auto-pilot.

Halfway around, the pilot woke, roused me and suggested I hand-fly the aircraft while he went aft for a leak. So I squeezed off the auto-pilot and sat there holding the wheel. Suddenly it jerked wildly in my hands: was the auto-pilot offended and trying to grab back control? I squeezed the lever desperately; whatever was happening, 500 feet was far too low for it.

The pilot came back. 'Did the controls go boomf-boomf just now?'

'Yes, sir; yes, sir,' I quavered.

'Ah.' He sat down with a satisfied smile. 'I've always wondered what would happen if I jumped on the elevator cables back there.'

I was lucky to find one pilot who needed to renew his instructor's rating and wanted a pupil to practise on. He was a Pole, one of many in the RAF at that time, and all rather sad cases. Chased out of Poland by the Nazis, now barred from it by the Communists, their only home was the RAF. But there they were still foreigners, with no hope of real advancement or command postings, living only in the present of whatever flying jobs they could cling to until time or a medical check struck them down. I was grateful to him for the circuits-and-bumps, but not for his idea that I come as co-pilot in a vic of three Varsities the station was contributing to the Coronation Review. One trip trying to fly close formation in those lumbering tubs made me remember urgent business elsewhere.

At last our Tigers arrived; eventually we got four of them. We also got a big cheerful flight lieutenant named Jim as flight commander, and an office in one of the hangars. By the normal process of not being around at the time I was appointed flight adjutant. But this demanded nothing more than making up the flying schedules to suit (a) Jim's and (b) my own convenience, and making the office look official. I did this by putting up charts showing anything anybody suggested: aircraft serviceability, hours flown, leave taken, demob dates and whether our girl friends were at home, away on holiday or at college. One rained-out week I added a three-dimensional map of the airfield, using matchboxes for hangars and soforth. Inspecting senior officers seemed to find it all very proper.

Actually, we soon realised, they'd rather not have found us at all. The Tiger Flight was a tumour on the neat pattern of flying, training, administration and engineering wings and the smooth running of the station. We learnt to keep our status as vague as possible, although later this led to me being Absent Without Leave Due To A Minor And Forgiveable Misunderstanding, *Sir*.

Meanwhile, I had a much more immediate problem: I just couldn't learn to fly a Tiger. Mick and Pete quickly got checked out and went solo, but I continued plodding round the circuit with an incredulous instructor, either flying into the ground or rounding out too high. I knew I was a slow learner, my reflexes weren't of the best ('You'd get killed in a week on a day fighter squadron,' my jet instructor had assured me) and my only other excuse is that it was an odd, backward, step from the Meteor which stalled at more than the Tiger's top speed. Anyway, the instructor clearly didn't believe what he had experienced, and sent me solo.

Unhampered by his weight, the Tiger and I frisked into the air. And about time, too, dammit: I've got my wings, nearly 300 hours, can fly jets . . . There had been a recent movie called *The Sound Barrier*, aerodynamically dubious but with some marvellous flying sequences. In one of these the son of the great aircraft designer is pushed into learning to fly, is sent solo – in a Tiger – bounces his landing, stalls, and dies in the crash.

'Just like Denholm Elliott did it,' I thought at the top of the bounce with the airspeed indicator showing 20 knots, or fifteen below the stall. I pushed the throttle and stick right forward and the Tiger, realising it had better take over, pivoted in the air, swooped to brush the grass, and climbed away. My next attempt was long, low and fast, wheeling it on like an airliner. At the edge of the grass, Mick and Pete were still doubled over with laughter.

'We were just about to order a couple of pints to your memory,' Mick said; they'd seen *The Sound Barrier*, too.

As a result, I didn't solo again for four more flights and, since the weather turned sour, these got spread over three gloomy weeks. The final humiliation was being sent up with Pete in the hope that some of his talent might rub off on me. He handled it with great tact, letting me do all the flying and barely saying a word. When the first cadet climbed into the cockpit behind me, I had less than two hours solo on Tigers.

They started us at the deep end: our first camp-load of cadets came from a Borstal school and my first passenger had lost an ear in, I imagine, a knife fight. But that was all behind him now; it was up to me to redeem him with the love of a good aeroplane. I showed him the Hampshire countryside, the ships at sea, let him handle the controls, did some gentle aerobatics – he got the full *à la carte*. And as far as I could tell, it all meant as much to him as a ride on a bus. Whatever he felt, he had learnt never to show it, and answered, 'Yes, sir' to every question, whether it was, 'Would you like more aerobatics?' or, 'Shall we go back now?' The rest of the school was the same; inevitably, they were the best behaved of all the cadets we met that summer.

My log-book shows that I flew 106 cadets from 15th July to 4th September, usually for just under half an hour each. But only two others stick in my memory. One was a Jamaican lad, built like the next heavyweight champ – except that his reflexes were even slower than mine. When he had control, the Tiger would drop a wing, get bored with him not doing anything and so pick it up herself. At that moment, he'd slam the stick over, so now we were the other wing low, and so on. I took over and we headed in. At fifty feet I felt his great hands clamp on the stick to and haul back. I pushed, he pulled. His strength was greater, but he couldn't match my experience of being terrified in the air. The Tiger and I won.

The idea of somebody 'freezing' on the stick had haunted us from the beginning, and we'd debated the idea of putting ourselves in the rear cockpits. There, the theory ran, you could unscrew your own stick, lean forward and wallop the frozen passenger unconscious, screw back in the stick and land safely. But such complications apart, it was easier to change over cadets in the rear seat, and flying in the front, we weren't in the line of any sudden airsickness.

That was something else we'd feared, but in the event I think I got only two instances: say two per cent – granted that we didn't fly in rough weather nor forced aerobatics on unwilling cadets. Talking it over, we concluded that it was mostly a matter of nerves and we could tell which ones were vulnerable. Indeed, they usually told us: 'I hope I'm not going to be sick,' or 'If I get sick, can we come straight down?' You bet we can, sonny, and you can clean out the mess yourself – though in fact I let their schoolmaster-officers do it.

The third cadet I remember was one with a cast-iron stomach who nearly pushed *me* over the edge with cries of 'More, more!' after each aerobatic. It was too early in the day and I could feel my breakfast rolling back and forth like the Chinese passengers in Conrad's *Lord Jim*, about to find the ladders and rush up . . . 'I will now demonstrate straight and level flying,' I said firmly. 'It takes great skill to do; sit quiet and learn something.'

We flew with one other sobering thought in mind: that we could never, no matter what happened including engine failure over the sea, ask a cadet to bail out. They had parachutes and dinghy packs, but these were just wrapped around them by their schoolmasters, so a harness adjusted for a six-footer might be draped on a four-foot customer. Even if they found the ripcord, the opening shock might break their backs or just spill them out of the harness. So we knew we had to stick with the aircraft, which in a water landing with a fixed undercarriage would probably mean a half-somersault and us trapped beneath. So if I worked up the courage to do a Lindbergh to the Isle of Wight, it was at a height that made the *Queen Mary* below seem a matchstick and I could probably have reached Heathrow without stretching the glide.

That I remember so few cadets isn't only fading memory: most were just goggled faces in the rear-view mirror and a voice on the intercom, dumped into and hauled out of the rear cockpit by their schoolmasters while I kept the engine running. We couldn't brief them beforehand, and in half an hour could only show them how the controls worked: it was just 'air experience'. Yet I believe we tried to make it a memorable experience, and it must have been, for most of them in those days, their first flight. I doubt I so inspired one rear-viewed face enough that he's now an air chief marshal, but I can hope that somebody is telling his air-package-holidayed children (or grand-children by now): 'Ah, but you've never flown in a *real* aeroplane . . . '

Shamingly, I can't improve on that cliché: the Tiger *was* a 'real' aeroplane – except when it was being an unreal aeroplane, which was just as much fun, only less predictable. For my self-esteem, I'd prefer to have operational status on night-fighters or Canberras in my log-book, but privately I wouldn't swap that Tiger summer for a chauffeur-driven Concorde. Flying the Borstal-trained Chipmunk would have bored us out of our skulls, for all the gadgets it had and the Tiger lacked – which is odd, because the more knobs, dials, switches and gizmos an aircraft had, the happier I usually was.

The Tiger had no brakes, flaps, radio, blind-flying panel or self-starter, and had a skid instead of a tail-wheel. The skid wore out on concrete, so we flew off a triangle of grass between the runways and 'taxied' across those with a burst of throttle and the tail up. No radio meant the control tower couldn't tell us to behave except by firing off a barrage of red rockets and a senior officer in a staff car; this happened only when one of them cut too close across the bows of a Varsity or landed straight off a spin – the easiest way to lose height in a Tiger.

I could have used some brakes only once. I was landing the way I had taken off half an hour before and right in line with the wind-sock (I'd checked). Obeying the old rule of 'round out when you can count the individual blades of grass', I found them going too fast to count. I realised I had landed down-wind before anybody told me, but they told me anyway; I'd forgotten that the sea-breeze could change to a land-breeze (or perhaps the other way round) swinging the wind 180 degrees in a few minutes. Thereafter I checked the wind-sock's direction as well as line.

All this and swinging the prop with calls of: 'Switches *off*. . . switches *on* . . . ' made it seem we had slipped through a time-warp from the Jet Age to the Dawn Patrol. And that summer was an odd plateau in my life anyway; for once, if briefly, I was no longer crawling up what we now call 'the learn-ing curve', nobody's pupil, no tests or exams to worry about. I just *was*, a pilot and an officer, for the first time in my life being paid to do a job, and one that was pure fun. It gave me a remarkable feeling of status and freedom.

I added the trimmings: grew a moustache (it would have been over-confident to do that as a pupil) and bought a peaked cap (crown bent down to show I'd worn it under headphones on my thirty missions over Berlin).

And if I was Biggles on duty, I did my best to be Bertie Wooster – on a PO's pay – in my own time. I popped up to town to catch a show at weekends, and ordered a tailor-made pair of slacks. Alas, I must have forgotten to take off my American-pilot-style sunglasses when choosing the cloth. The expected quiet lovat green turned out to be swimming-pool blue, and I only dared wear them for lonely walks on Hayling Island beach.

Until just now, I had become convinced that the summer of '53 could only have been so bright in the sunshine of memory. But going back to my log-book shows I flew on eighteen out of twenty-three possible days (no weekends – or so I thought) and it would have been two more except for that little matter of being AWOL.

My reading of the flight's status on the station had been that we did the duties (such as orderly officer) for no wing but took the holidays of all. So I returned from August Bank Holiday by Tuesday lunchtime; Jim was glad to see me: 'Where the bloody hell have you been? – you're flying,' and five minutes later, I was. I discovered that they had flown both the Saturday morning (unheard-of; perhaps even un-British) and all Monday. Luckily Jim couldn't take it any further without losing a baby-sitter: I was happy to swap the rumpus of the mess for his married quarters where I could read and write in peace.

The flight's independent status came unstuck on only one other occasion. An officious RAF Regiment pilot officer announced that he was going to hold a ground combat course and would Flying Wing send him, as per regulations, four aircrew officers next Monday? So rather than disrupt their own flying schedules, Flying Wing promptly decided we belonged to them and would provide the four.

By this time we were reinforced, for a week or so at a time, by Reserve officers. They were splendidly undisciplined wartime types in splendidly undisciplined wartime uniforms and attitudes towards Authority ('If the officers of the Tiger Moth Flight wish to continue to take morning coffee in the Instruction Block, will they please get their hair cut?' – signed ——, S/Ldr. *That* sort of Authority). Two Reserves, Pete and myself, were detailed by Jim to become ground combatants.

It started with a lecture on precautions against mustard gas and showed every sign of getting worse. But at the coffee break, the RAF Regiment PO approached us, and the conversation went much like this:

Him: 'You're the chaps who fly those little biplanes, aren't you? Any chance of, er, a ride?'

Us: 'It might be arranged. But, as we're chatting informally, may we comment on the rest of this course? Strange though it may seem, we aren't very keen on lectures about gas and how to give aiming orders. We don't mind shooting guns; indeed, we might go as far as enjoy it, if it isn't spoiled with a lot of mystique about Range Safety. And we'll even agree to play cowboys-and-Indians with blanks and thunderflashes, provided it's a nice day and we don't have to walk very far. Are you receiving us?'

He got his ride, and earned it the day one of our Reserves, a bit hazy about the First Immediate Action when a Bren jammed, waggled the trigger and clouted the gas regulator simultaneously. The mystique then was how that burst of fire missed the officers' mess.

Suddenly, the cadets and Reservists were gone, and so were Mick and Pete: Mick to convert to Vampires, which his local Auxiliary squadron flew, Pete having decided to make the RAF his career (he died five years later as an instructor on Jet Provosts). The station adjutant told me I could demobilise myself as soon as I'd got a medical check and about fifty signatures on various forms – mostly attesting that I'd handed back equipment I wasn't entitled to and hadn't actually got.

I spent nearly a week collecting signatures in the mornings, then deciding which of my private air force of four Tigers I would take for a flip in the afternoon. I had friends at another Tiger Flight at another Navigation school some 60 miles away, and decided to visit them for lunch, taking a navigator friend to find the way. That was a mistake: without his radar, drift sight, radio and crystal ball, he was lost before we took off. But he had the only map and couldn't pass it forward against the slipstream.

Admittedly, I'd compounded things by getting only a local weather forecast (a 50-mile radius) when there was a warm front waiting at 51 miles. The cloud pressed us down and down over what looked like the surface of the Moon, and I knew the wind must be shifting. I asked where we were.

He studied the craters below. 'I *think* we're over the anti-aircraft range on Salisbury Plain.'

But then we spotted and identified a white horse cut in a hillside and, blessing whoever thought of marking them on RAF maps, navigated horse by horse into Hullavington. Where I landed on the soccer pitch instead of the light aircraft area; luckily the season didn't start so early in those days and the goalposts weren't yet up.

On my last day in the service it looked as if Navigation Authority's worst nightmare had lasted into breakfast: a bunch of characters in mixed flying clothing, leather jackets and check shirts sat smoking at one of the tables. They turned out to be American F-86 Sabre fighter pilots, brought from Germany to unfamiliar countryside to spend the last week pretending to have been shot down over enemy territory and evading the hunt by our army and police. They'd had a rough time, particularly from the American military police (willingly pretending to be the KGB) when caught.

We pilots pounced on them. Jim and I offered rides in the Tigers (my passenger was a tough, stocky little Lieutenant Wilhite) while others trundled off in Varsities.

'Multi-engine time? Who needs multi-engine time?' sneered Wilhite, the true fighter pilot. He flew like one, too, constantly twitching the Tiger so as to peer suspiciously into every corner of the sky, and chortling: 'Me and Eddie Rickenbacker, boy; me and Eddie Rickenbacker!' He tried a slow roll and I untangled us from an inverted stall with the gravity-fed engine spluttering,

but let him do the landing. Thinking the prop went round the opposite –
American – way, he kicked on the wrong rudder when he cut the throttle.
One wild swerve, the skid clipped the runway edge, and my last flight in the
RAF was over.

That evening, I went out with Wilhite and two of his mates to a local
restaurant, and they were still hungry from their week in the wilds. 'But don't
order steak,' I pleaded. 'Go for the fish, like me.' I had read about American
steaks, and this was Britain 1953. But they didn't believe me until they saw
the little charred scrap on their plates.

I told them that, tomorrow, I would be out of uniform, and they stared.
Why hadn't I ordered champagne? Why wasn't I getting blind drunk?

I couldn't explain; I don't think I even tried. I had joined up because I had
to, thinking two years were being taken from me. Now I felt instead that they
had been given to me – and the future outside looked cold. In a few weeks I
would be a nobody at the bottom of another ladder at Cambridge. Perhaps I
should have tried to sign on, as Pete had: kept what I had achieved and taken
on new challenges. But would I have been taking them on only because they
were challenges, not because they'd lead to what I wanted to do with my life?
How does a man feel when he's climbed Everest just to prove to himself that
he can, but then wishes he'd spent the time writing an opera?

I didn't know what I wanted to do with my life, only that *my* challenges
and answers lay outside the Service. So thank you very much for having me,
and Yes, I've handed in my aircrew wristwatch and all the rest and got
signatures to prove it. But you can't take back my Tiger summer.

17

JACKIE MANN

'Not Again!'

I JOINED RAFVR (741491) on 6th April 1938 at Woodley, Reading, whilst an apprentice with Phillips and Powys Aircraft, and learned to fly at 8 E&RFTS on Miles Hawk and Magister aircraft, graduating to Hawker Hart, Hind and Audax biplanes. On the outbreak of war I was mobilised, and early in December 1939 was posted to 3 ITW Hastings, where I remained until March 1940. Then I moved on to 9 FTS at Hullavington, where I continued to fly Hart variants.

On completion of the course I was sent to 5 OTU at Aston Down for conversion to Spitfires. After an hour dual in a North American Harvard I went solo in a Miles Master for half an hour, then solo in a Spitfire.

In mid-July 1940 I was posted to 64 Squadron at Kenley. Towards the end of the month my Spitfire was hit by enemy cannon shell; the solid nose cone of one shell became lodged in the bottom of the control column, practically blocking its movement so that elevators and ailerons were almost unusable, although I was able to fly it back to Kenley. On the final approach to the airfield, however, I was forcibly reminded of the aerodynamics of the Spitfire. With power cut right back and speed reduced, the starboard wing started to drop. This was normally easily corrected by use of ailerons, but now these were virtually inoperable. Finally I touched down on the starboard wheel and wingtip. Very fortunately the wing did not cause a cartwheel, but instead bounced me back on both wheels, and so I was able to walk away.

On 25th July, I claimed a Messerschmitt Bf109 destroyed, and on 5th, 8th and 12th August, Bf109s. The 109 on the 5th was a frightening experience. I opened fire from dead astern at a range of about 200 yards and saw pieces of the enemy aircraft breaking off until the cockpit canopy came off. I ceased firing expecting the pilot to bail out but after a few seconds when he had not done so, I opened fire again with a short burst, upon which the 109 literally exploded in front of me. The camera gun recorded the whole episode.

On 16th August, after a mid-Channel skirmish with 109s, the squadron had become dispersed and I found myself crossing the south coast at 18,000 feet with no other aeroplane in sight (not an unusual experience) when – *whoomff.* Assuming enemy attack I broke into a sharp right-hand evasive turn, but still could see no other aircraft. But what I could see was a ball of black smoke from the top of which trailed a streamer in white which followed the flight-path of my Spitfire. Obviously the engine cooling system had been damaged and I was leaking glycol. I immediately throttled back and put the aircraft into a glide and headed for the nearest airfield, Hawkinge. This was our forward base so I knew it well.

While I was gliding down, I had time to think. The only conclusion I could reach was that I had been hit by our own anti-aircraft fire despite that, on checking, I established that my IFF (Identification Friend or Foe) transmitter was still operating so I should have been identified by British ack-ack batteries. I also found that I had been injured, particularly in the right calf, by shrapnel which had penetrated my flying boot.

I landed safely at Hawkinge, having lowered the undercarriage and flaps by the emergency system but without brakes. I then had the minor misfortune of hitting, with the starboard wingtip whilst still rolling at about 15–20 mph, an eight-foot diameter cable drum, which had been left on the airfield during mine-laying operations. I was given first aid by the station medical officer while 64 Squadron were sending a communications aircraft to transport me back to Kenley.

On arrival there I was put into an ambulance and transported to the Royal Navy Hospital at Greenwich for the removal of the shrapnel. A few days later I learned that a Royal Marines battery based on Dungeness had claimed a high-firing record on having shot down an aircraft at 18,000 feet on the date I was hit. I suppose I was sent to Greenwich on the basis that the Navy put the shrapnel in so the Navy takes it out!

On 18th August the Luftwaffe made a heavy raid on Kenley. 64 were airborne at the time but I was grounded. I had gone to the loo in my quarters and had just settled down when the air raid sirens wailed. To save myself from flying glass, I reached forward and put the black-out blind over the window, but within seconds one of a stick of bombs hit the building, which collapsed around me (including the loo). Having dug myself out, I crawled to the nearby sick quarters where I was treated for superficial cuts and bruises.

On 20th August 64 were withdrawn north to Leconfield where I rejoined them after the stitches in my leg were removed some five days later. On 12th September I was posted to 92 Squadron at Biggin Hill whither they had just moved from Pembrey.

In the late afternoon of 14th September 92 were scrambled to meet an incoming heavy Luftwaffe force. I was flying No. 3 to the flight lieutenant leading the squadron. The 109s passed high overhead, then came down behind us. One by one the other three sections called the leader on R/T and informed him they were breaking off.

The leader did not acknowledge the calls but maintained a steady climb and eastbound course. Finally, with 109s closing behind us, his No. 2 called and also broke off. I could see, dead astern, at least two 109s in my reflector and expected to be fired on, so I too called to the leader and broke into a steep left-hand turn which I held for about 270° until I found myself behind two 109s in close formation. Immediately I opened fire and saw strikes on the enemy but had to break off when my aircraft was hit. It felt to me that I'd been kicked up the backside!

On the way back to Biggin, I managed to get a hand into the seat of my trousers, and on withdrawal found the fingers covered in blood. Having landed safely and taxied into my dispersal I was greeted by my ground crew, whose first question was, 'Did you get anything, sergeant?' To which I responded, 'Yes, a bullet in the... ' Meanwhile, another mechanic had a quick look around my Spitfire and came back and dramatically exclaimed, 'It's British ammunition.' So, for the second time, I had been shot down by friendly fire!

This time more seriously wounded, I gave money to a corporal and asked him to send a telegram to my parents to say I was off to hospital. No ambulance was available so I was moved into the back of an open truck but after a few yards couldn't endure the vibration and was transferred to the cabin; and so to Farnborough (Kent) hospital. On Monday morning 16th September at my home near Northampton, my mother answered the front doorbell and was faced by a uniformed policeman who asked to see my father.

With a mother's instinct she said, 'It's Jack, isn't it?' to which she was given the dismal reply, 'Yes, I'm sorry to tell you that he is dead.' Father, with the help of friends, organised a motor hearse, with coffin, and drove, with Mother and elder sister Madge, to Farnborough to collect the 'body'. Arriving at the mortuary they were told by the attendant that he had five RAF corpses there whose condition was such that they couldn't be identified and any one of them could be taken!

Father understandably demanded more information and was then directed to the nearby police station. Fortunately the officer in charge there had been on duty when I was admitted to the hospital two days earlier and was able to tell them that he was sure I was still there but as a patient.

In the meantime most of the projectile had been removed from my 'lower back' (about an inch or so from my spine) so, despite being bedridden and facedown, we were reunited.

The family, hearse and coffin returned the hundred or so miles to Northampton where friends and neighbours had arranged a lying-in room and wreaths and flowers had already arrived. (Incidentally they had driven back through London during a heavy bombing raid.) The telegram which I had caused to be sent arrived on Tuesday morning. Scotland Yard, who accepted responsibility for all RAF casualties, eventually apologised for the mistaken identity.

After Farnborough was hit by a bomb (without casualties) I was moved to Orpington hospital where I met Squadron Leader Tom Gleave who had been badly burned on 31st August leading 253 Squadron. In November I was discharged and sent on leave but the wound opened again whereupon I was sent to the RAF hospital at Halton. After inspecting the wound with a fearsomely long probe the wing commander MO decided it would be best to leave the remaining metal fragments and, after two or three weeks' treatment, I was sent again on leave. At the very end of 1940 I was instructed to report back to 92 Squadron at Manston. Arriving there early January 1941 I was informed by Squadron Leader Johnnie Kent that 92 were fully staffed. After a phone call he advised me to report to 91 Squadron at Hawkinge, which had just been formed from 421 Flight. Their role was to maintain a standing 'Jim Crow' patrol of two Spitfires along the French coast and Channel and south-east corner of Kent, to report on incoming raids or intruders.

About mid-March I was on patrol as No. 2 to my flight commander Flight Lieutenant Bob Holland DFC. We were at 22,000 feet over the Dungeness area when we were jumped out of the sun by enemy aircraft. Immediately I half rolled and, flicking my radio transmitter on, warned Holland of the attack. Then found my Spitfire was in a spin from which I couldn't recover. With the R/T still on, I was talking to myself saying, 'I'm going down, I can't see,' which I repeated a couple of times before I could pull myself together.

It was minutes before I could establish that, although I could move the control column normally, I had no aileron control. I was down to 4,000 feet before I managed to get the aircraft to fly straight and level but the lowest speed I could maintain that attitude was 140 mph. Remembering the Kenley incident, I had no option but to attempt a crash landing at that speed – but in an open field!

I could see plenty of open space below me but as I neared ground level could also see that the area was criss-crossed with anti-glider-landing wires. In the final seconds, after checking my safety harness was tight, I lifted the aircraft over one set of wires and forced it, with wheels up, onto the ground under the next lot. Soldiers from a nearby Royal Artillery ack-ack battery were standing by when I climbed from the cockpit. My right elbow was slightly injured by shrapnel, otherwise I was unhurt. A quick check on the aircraft showed the aileron balance cable had been cut by the enemy fire.

On 31st March the Royal Navy asked for a report on Boulogne harbour. Sergeant A. W. P. (Dagger) Spears and I were standing by for the next patrol so we took off. We had decided to climb over Kent to about 24,000 feet before starting across the Channel, but on the climb Spears found his oxygen supply was not working and had to turn back. Ground Control asked what I wanted to do. I replied that I'd carry on alone. Still climbing GC again called to say there were about a dozen 'bandits' near me. I checked carefully around but could see nothing and, as I was close to my planned altitude, I said I would continue. Over Boulogne in a diving attitude and at full speed at 10,000 feet I made a couple of circuits of the harbour.

This was empty of large shipping which I believe was what the Navy wanted to know. They were keeping a wary eye open for the whereabouts of German capital ships.

About halfway back across the Channel I suddenly found there were six 109s behind me. I'd been flying with the cockpit canopy slid back and my goggles on my forehead for better visibility. Immediately I half rolled, and tried to close the canopy. This would come only halfway where it jammed before jettisoning itself entirely. Before I could get my goggles down, a cloud of dust and grit came up from the cockpit and hit me in the face and eyes.

Then my goggles were caught in the slipstream and snatched off. During this period I was attempting to outmanoeuvre the 109s. At around 5,000 feet one of the 109s went past me in an inverted dive. Later, when on the ground at Hawkinge, the Navy confirmed seeing this crash into the sea. Also the 'Y' section reported hearing German pilots calling one of their comrades without getting a reply. So I was credited with scoring a 109 – without even firing at it!

On 4th April Spears and I were again rostered together when we were scrambled to intercept two enemy aircraft approaching Deal from the east. We were vectored to various points on the coast (Ramsgate, back to Deal etc) but could find no enemy. After about twenty minutes of shuttling we were informed by Control that our objectives had gone home and we could do likewise. I was leading and could see Hawkinge some 15 miles away and started to descend followed by Spears, my number two, whose role was to keep my tail clear of enemy attack.

Unfortunately and unbeknown to me Spears was attacked and had to bail out with a cannon shell through his right arm, leaving me a sitting duck. He was shot down by Adolf Galland, the German's 58th victory. The first intimation I had was when my Spitfire was hit by six or eight shells in the starboard wing root. Following evasive action I could see torn sections of the wing upper surface standing upright! There were no personal injuries but I too should have bailed out particularly when I found a few minutes later that the fuel tank between the engine and me had been damaged and was leaking a lot of petrol into the cockpit. By then I was too low to use a parachute but decided to put the aircraft down in a farmer's field with undercarriage up.

I was still a hundred feet up when, with everything set for a forced landing, I slid back the cockpit canopy. In retrospect this was foolhardy for within a second or two the cockpit petrol burst into flame and I was sitting in an inferno. All I could then do was to close my eyes tightly, hold the aircraft's attitude, close the throttle and hope for the best. With the remains at a grinding halt, and after hitting my head on the gunsight which dazed me, I rapidly evacuated it.

Instinctively I went through the foreign territory escape drill and, realising my parachute was still in the cockpit, went back to retrieve it and then buried it in a ditch so the Germans couldn't find it! At this time my clothing was still on fire but luckily I was wearing both silk inner gloves and gauntlets and could beat out the flames. In doing so I discovered my folding Kodak camera in my tunic pocket; I extricated it and took two snapshots of the burning wreckage, one from the starboard quarter and one from astern. These were subsequently developed by the Hawkinge Intelligence Office and are very interesting: the cockpit is ablaze, the starboard wing is missing, the starboard elevator is shot off, the port elevator is half missing and the rudder is two-thirds missing. But one can still see the 91 Squadron identification letters DLB!

Gathering my flying equipment (flying boots which I had kicked off in order to extinguish my burning trousers, flying helmet which had protected my head, ears and cheeks, oxygen mask, and microphone which had covered my lower face, mouth and nostrils and goggles, which as normal for landing had been on my forehead), I walked in my socks across a couple of fields, including negotiating a barbed wire fence, until I encountered a road across which was a cottage.

In answering my knocking on the front door, a middle-aged lady thought I'd had a motorcycle accident. After installing me as comfortably as she could in her entrance hall, she produced her bicycle and rode off toward the RAF sick quarters which were only a couple of miles away. Halfway there an oncoming RAF ambulance passed her – my aircraft had been seen coming down by staff and was still emitting clouds of smoke together with exploding ammunition. The lady turned around and came back to where the ambulance had stopped by her cottage, by which time the crew had rushed over to where they assumed I was. In turn the lady hurried to tell them that I was in her cottage. Moments later the Hawkinge Medical Officer, Flight Lieutenant Jacobs, came in and said, 'Who is it?' I responded, 'Mann.' I'll never forget his distressed exclamation, 'Oh, not again!' It was the third time he'd had to treat me!

So, loaded into the ambulance and dosed with morphine, I was taken to the Royal Victoria Hospital, Folkestone. There my legs, particularly the right, were coated with tannic acid, my eyelids with (I think) mercuricrome and my scorched fingertips with whatever was necessary. The doctors at the Royal Vic were clearly worried about my eyes and when I recovered from the anaesthetic I found they were heavily bandaged. Every day they were bathed, re-dressed and bandaged again. Apparently the eyelids were badly burned and could not be treated until the scar tissue had fully formed.

While this occurred the eyelids contracted but vision was still blocked by discharging mucus until, after about ten days of sightlessness, during the daily bathing I suddenly said, 'Nurse, you've got a shiny nose.' She was so excited that she dropped the dressings she was holding and rushed down the ward calling, 'He can see! He can see!'

A few days later I was transferred to the Queen Victoria Hospital at East Grinstead where I was placed into what became the famous Ward III of the RAF Burns Centre. There I was initiated into the new saline treatment for burns which did not involve the use of tannic acid. In fact the reverse was true. After a few exposures to the daily saline bath the existing tannic covering started to curl up at the edges from where it was carefully cut off by scalpel when it was revealed that the underlying flesh had begun to rot! After a few days, I passed out in the bath. The attendants quickly removed me back to bed which was then surrounded by the 'seriously ill' screen and the doctor summoned. He diagnosed me as suffering from delayed shock and prescribed suitable injections and blood transfusions. The following day the screen was removed and I was well on the way to recovery from shock.

I missed only two days of the saline baths when on 25th April the *London Gazette* published the announcement, to my very great pleasure, that I had been awarded the Distinguished Flying Medal. A month or so later I began a whole series of skin grafts starting with top eyelids using skin taken from the inner upper right arm and performed by the maestro Archie (later Sir Archibald) McIndoe. After another month the lower eyelids were grafted (left arm) by Squadron Leader George Morley. By this time all the tannic cover had been removed from my legs. The left leg had healed but the more seriously burned right was showing considerable reluctance and grafts were necessary. For these 'pinch grafts' were taken (seventy-two of them) from the unburned area of the upper left thigh (where I still have the draught-board pattern) and spread over the area from mid-calf to upper thigh. Sixty-five of them grew successfully and new skin grew from them.

An old friend who visited me made a trip to the wine shop in the town where he bought their entire stock of Harvey's Bristol Cream sherry (five bottles) and arranged that one should be sent each Saturday to me at the QVH. The second bottle arrived on Saturday, 19th July. On the following day a grogging party was called for in the surgeons' mess in an adjacent hut and a Czech fighter pilot, Frankie Truhlar, collected my bottle of sherry as a contribution. And so was formed the Guinea Pig Club of which I'd become a founder member.

I was discharged from QVH in late November and in mid-December received notification of posting, effective 1st January 1942, to No. 1 ADF (Aircraft Delivery Flight) at RAF Hendon. The unit was moved to Croydon March/April and I stayed with it for two and a half years which were probably the most happy, interesting and educational in my flying career.

In my time with it I flew twenty-four different types of aircraft plus variants (including seven marks of Spitfire) and graduated to twins (including Rapide, Oxford, Anson, Blenheim and Mosquito). ADF pilots were immensely assisted by the issue to them of cockpit drill manuals as provided to the ATA (Air Transport Auxiliary).

In the spring of '44 I was sent on a flying instructor's course on Oxfords followed by a week instructing; in turn two weeks' night flying, at which I was relatively inexperienced; then to a Transport Command training station on Wellingtons. During this I was promoted to flight lieutenant. It was normal practice for BOAC to select a small number of crews from these courses for secondment. My crew was one of three selected. I was despatched to Montreal to join the BOAC Return Ferry Service which flew American four-engined B24 Liberators. During 1945 I completed twenty-six two-way crossings of the Atlantic, Montreal-Prestwick-Montreal, as First Officer. In January '46 I was sent by BOAC on a conversion course onto DC-3s (Dakota) at Bristol. At the end of this a request came in for three pilots to fly Rapides for Channel Islands Airways. Based on Jersey, they operated to Southampton and Croydon.

In No. 1 ADF I had flown 30–40 hours on Rapides and on the Transport Command course had qualified for a Civil Pilot's licence so I was an automatic choice for CIA. With them I spent three to four months living in Jersey during which British European Airways was being founded, including a takeover of CIA. A BOAC official suggested it would be advantageous for me to switch from BOAC to BEA. My next move was to BEA's base at Northolt where, for a year, I became a first officer on Dakotas again until I got a captaincy. I stayed with BEA until 1948 when I resigned and joined Middle East Airlines in Beirut, Lebanon, flying Dakotas as captain. After a year I was appointed Chief Pilot. In 1950 MEA became an associate company of Pan-American and rapidly began to expand its fleet firstly from seven Dakotas adding, in 1956, three 4-engined Hermes which I flew for five months before they were replaced by turbo-prop Vickers Viscounts. The Dakotas were gradually eliminated and in March '61 MEA bought Comet 4Cs which replaced the Viscounts. Thus I became a jet pilot. To me the Comet became a four-engined Spitfire – though no aeroplane could ever replace the 'Spit' in my affections.

My flying life ended with over sixteen thousand flying hours.

18

LORD MERLYN-REES

Operations Officer in Italy

LOOKING BACK at my years in the RAF from 1941 to 1946, it is tempting to see them as a straight line with a beginning and an end; a progression all connected together.

Well, 1941 was a long way from 1946 and it seemed even longer in 1946 when vaguely one remembered 1941. Mine was a disjointed career and never glorious. But, risking the straight line approach, I spent five years plus in the RAF, from AC2 1576563 in 1941 to Squadron Leader 119433 in 1946. My first phase was in the No. 1 (full-time) course in the newly-formed Nottingham University Air Squadron.

Eventually, in June 1941, after attesting at Birmingham and collecting our uniforms at RAF Hucknall we returned to the university and our headquarters at Beeston, just outside the gates. The adjutant was a New Zealander, John Davison, who had shown great bravery after the crash of a Blenheim and had been awarded the George Medal. Our gunnery instructor, Sergeant Eborall, bore the scars, both physical and mental, of operational tours in Hampdens.

We were in the RAF and by osmosis we picked up the spirit of the force. No line-shooting was required to tell us that we had entered the war unprepared to deal with all eventualities. The Battle of Britain was over, the casualties had been great; casualties in the, then, small Bomber Command continued to be high and went on that way. Modern aircraft were not yet available.

Osmosis is the right word for our changing attitude to our maturing life and work in which we flashed messages in morse code and waved flags in semaphore or marched to the command of NCOs from the Sherwood Foresters. We stripped guns, we recognised enemy aircraft and we learned to navigate under the direction of the Nottingham University Professor of Mathematics, Professor Piaggio. My strong early recollection is of an RAF which was meritocratic and technically based. I was very content. I felt at home. Then we were all split up and consequently lost touch with each other.

For me it was even worse. I was not allowed to continue with the aircrew course because of one very bad eye. In no narrow patriotic fervour, but because I was now part of it all and had as a youngster argued about Spain and the need to stop Hitler, I tried everything. I had another medical, but to no avail, and soon I was commissioned as an administrative and special duties officer, then, with older men (at least thirty years of age!), passed through the officers' school at Uxbridge. I proceeded to become an inexperienced operations officer in 11 Group Fighter Command, at RAF Debden.

Oh, the misery of being first at HQ Fighter Command and then HQ 11 Group. The work there was interesting enough as a supernumerary ('spare') acting pilot officer, but mealtimes in the mess with no one below the rank of group captain or perhaps wing commander were not easy.

RAF Debden was better as I worked within a closed community of men and women, many of whom had volunteered as AC2s in the years before the war and were now senior NCOs and officers, very good at their task. I saw this particularly in August 1942 at the time of the Dieppe raid, when in our Debden operations room together with others in 11 Group, under the ultimate command of our own commanding officer out in HMS *Berkeley*, control ship in the English Channel.

Squadron Leader J. H. Sprott, DFC, from World War I, who received an OBE for Dieppe, was a brilliant man, both in himself and at his job, and I could not deny the value of the work we were doing. But I was too young to be watching the war from an operations room and a table covered with radar and Observer Corps plots.

I talked to the CO and tried to change to aircrew again as a radar observer, but once again it was no good.

Then a chance came (via perhaps Sprottie) and off I went to a new world: I was posted to No. 1 Mobile Operations Room Unit. We were based at RAF West Malling, with caravans and radio trucks in a nearby field. At the start we slept in the traditional mess but eventually off we went on Exercise Spartan to practise for the Second Front.

There were airfields and aircraft that existed only on paper, and where they were being constructed had no aircraft; there were moves under canvas from Surrey, Hampshire and Berkshire to Oxfordshire. We were denied the use of the usual RAF facilities and collected army rations for 'preparation' in the field. We even practised using pigeons to send messages in case the signals facilities were poor or put out of action. I can recall on one occasion going by truck down to Southampton from west of Oxford to obtain food. This in itself was a new dimension of RAF life.

Eventually the three weeks' or so exercise was over and off we went to the ex-Balloon Unit at RAF Chigwell. We were there with other similar units, servicing commandos, and were trained to use a rifle, a revolver and to drive all sizes of vehicles and motor cycles.

I can recall double declutching my way down Oxford Street and around Marble Arch in a 30-cwt truck. The corporal said it was better to learn on a difficult vehicle! We were introduced to the mysteries of petrol engines on the one hand and unarmed combat on the other. There was talk (but only talk in the event) of us wearing combined operations badges.

The living conditions were bloody, as hundreds of us slept in bunk beds spread all over the huge hangars. Heaven only knows who had dreamed it all up and evidently some bright spark wrote to his MP for there were questions in the Commons and articles in the London evening papers. As a result we had lots of 'important visitors' but nothing changed. A few of us, with 'behaviour unbecoming' I suppose, used our newly-acquired rope-climbing and rope-swinging techniques to escape in the evenings for a quiet drink.

Shortly we were off in troop trains, waved off by the station commander and his staff whom we had never seen before! From Glasgow we sailed over to near Newfoundland, then down off the Azores and through into the Med. We were put ashore for a route march in Algiers to regain our land legs, then back aboard to our tightly-packed sardine quarters. I have no memory of how we were fed but I did my orderly officer duties with our own chaps. If there were grumbles we were all in the same boat!

We waited off Malta and for the first and last time I saw the Grand Fleet at anchor. Surely it was going to be Sicily – or was it Sardinia, or Italy itself?

Then off we went and a day or two after the main landing we went ashore at Augusta, Sicily. To the accompaniment of hostile Italian Macchi aircraft (that aircraft recognition course helped) and after a long wait in the hold we clambered down rope nets into landing craft. The temperature was in the 90's and 100's.

On shore we were met by disdainful beachmasters (one of whom was Major Denis Healey I discovered later) who viewed our Arctic-type battle clothing with amazement. One asked if we had prepared for Narvik – we were not amused.

Up into the hills we marched, through white-taped beach exits to a vineyard where at night we lay under the 'bushes'. Our equipment had not arrived; had it been sunk as was that of our sister unit, Mobile Air Reporting Unit (MARU)? Certainly at night the bay was festooned with tracers to the sound of naval and army artillery guns firing at German night raiders. Ships were sunk, an ammunition ship went off with a sound like that of doomsday.

Up where we lay the debris of the guns rained in on us but our casualties were only slight cuts and abrasions. A Ju88 came hurtling towards us, and after it hit the ground two of its aircrew were found dead.

At last our equipment did get through and we set up shop on a hilltop at Mellili. At first we controlled the night fighters and very successfully. Living in the field, however, was a different art and one which we had to learn the hard way. Latrine digging daily was a necessity. In those early days we had no rations for they had been loaded with our vehicles on the ship which had gone astray. Let us say we looked around locally, but I was sent off on a Harley Davison motor bike to find the DID – an army food distribution depot down at Syracuse.

The heavy traffic had worn trenches on the narrow volcanic road so I rode on the narrow track in between. I found the depot and told the CO that I would be back later with a truck to collect food and supplies later, then tightroped my way back to our camp.

I noted the POWs from the Hermann Goering Division mending the roads. They were particularly interested in my blue RAF hat, as were their Military Police guards. I gave them each an appropriate salute!

From our hilltop I watched the Desert Air Force P-40 Kittyhawks going over to pound the escape routes west of Mount Etna. We knew little of the wider pattern of the war but obviously Sicily would soon fall even if the Catania airfields were not yet available.

Then, much to my surprise, I was told I was posted as operations officer to 324 Wing, still down on the flat area south of Syracuse whence its Spitfire squadrons, 111, 43, 72 and 93 Squadrons, were still operating.

Why the sudden posting nobody then knew at MARU, and when I arrived at 324 in a 15-cwt truck it seemed my predecessor had moved on. Perhaps, years later I can now surmise, to go to 244 Wing where their airfield and operations tent had been badly bombed.

Anyway I was operations officer of 324 Wing and another longer episode of my RAF life had begun.

I was to go with 324 over to Salerno, then on to Naples, Lago, and Anzio via Rome; to Tarquinia, Grossetto and Piombino in Italy; then Calvi in Corsica and Ramatuelle, Sisteron, Lyon and La Jasse in France. We would then come back to Italy, to Florence, then across to Rimini, Ravenna and Treviso; followed by Klagenfurt and Zeltweg in Austria. In the end I became one of the wing's oldest inhabitants in service time if not in age.

It was in this closed and isolated world of army/air support with the civilians usually miles in front or miles behind that I lived for nearly three years until after VE Day. Apart from one or two places, we were cut off from the rest of the world with everybody working from dawn until dusk, and with no chance for home leave for three (married men) or four years. For long periods we were without mail and the outside world was only brought to us by the British 8th Army News or the American Stars and Stripes.

We moved up frequently with the army and all of us became experts at the required mobility. The main reason for our expertise was experience. No one told us to avoid crowding near the graded or wire-surfaced or pierced steel planking strips (PSP) made for us by the army engineers. We conserved water, used it sparingly and somehow kept our bodies and clothes clean.

Our experience, like Topsy, just grew. I suppose we looked scruffy but the job was well done and I was very content with my role. Indeed, when I was asked to go back to Bari in 1944 to undertake an intelligence, operational role with the unit which dropped soldiers/agents into Yugoslavia I gently turned it down. I had asked how often I would get over the Adriatic myself and the answer came back sufficiently vaguely to mean not at all. I stayed with 324.

But back to the Sicilian campaign and 324 Wing, where eventually there arrived a wing intelligence officer and an air liaison officer who, with me, briefed the aircrew down at the side of the runway.

When this campaign came to an end I drove in a jeep up the east coast, past Etna and the villages destroyed by the artillery and the fighter bombers, over the mountains following the route of the 78th Division to a new dirt strip at Falcone. It was close to Milazzo from which in LCTs our forward units set out for Salerno.

The early part of the campaign on the mainland was more than difficult. We knew all was not well, not only on the beachhead but at the front a few miles inland. Regimental names now became meaningful and I shall never forget, for instance, the Hampshires as they moved up to Bottipaglia.

Salerno was a long way from RAF Debden and 11 Group. I still have some of the log books of the operations we engaged in on 324 Wing. The simply penned and often pencilled notes illustrate the basic system we used. A phone call from the American wing that controlled us and then a quick briefing. Nothing complicated.

So we maintained readiness for 'scrambles' on the ground. Our aircraft sometimes 'swept' behind the bombline but more often patrolled with fewer aircraft. We gave cover to the medium bomber Bostons or the Mitchells, sent off to deal with bridges behind the front. I note that we also gave cover to minesweepers about their work. On occasions we were asked to strafe gun positions on the way home.

After Naples we rarely saw enemy aircraft over the landing grounds. They were too busy defending the Reich but nevertheless over the years a large number were destroyed by 324 and the other DAF wings in the air beyond the bombline and on the ground.

We did very well from the pre-information from the 'Y' system provided by our two cipher officers, Croall and Van der Veen. We had our casualties too and they are noted from time to time in the log book. They were fine young men who would have been good for our country after the war.

So it was up through Italy into Corsica and then into the South of France. We came back over to Italy, to Florence, and then in a fighter/bomber role through to VE Day. A number of incidents in these years I remember in particular. While at Lago we had a forward unit at the Anzio beachhead where aircraft taking off and landing had to avoid shell-holes; smoke from a cigarette, it seemed, was enough to bring the odd blast from the hills. It was 'sitting duck' country and particularly for the Army fighting in almost First World War conditions.

I had returned to Lago after the problem arose of Spit IXs with new Merlin engines at Anzio which were unable to take off because, it was said, of 'sand in the petrol'.

In the 111 Squadron mess tent at Lago one night, 'Spanner' Farrish, the engineer officer, took more than his fair share of ribbing about this from the lads. The day after I was in the Ops truck by the PSP runway when a Spit IX taxied up to take off.

What was all this? No one had asked me. As it raced up the runway, LAC Cliff Shasby (who was my invaluable assistant over the years) and I thought the pilot was a midget. In fact it was Spanner without a parachute under him. I knew it; off to Anzio! He wanted to get the U/S Spits there serviceable. He was not a pilot but managed the trip with the aid of 'Pilot's Notes'!

I wound the telephone to inform the Ground Controller – 'Spanner Farrish is airborne,' I told him nonchalantly. I left out my guess as to his destination. On went Spanner to Anzio (Nettuno) vectoring 270° and the 090° straight in to make a perfect three-pointer during shell-fire as the squadron commander of 601 Squadron crashed in a shellhole. Group Captain Duncan Smith DSO, DFC, OC 324 wing, had chased up to Anzio after Farrish and observed all this.

Spanner's court martial was a success – for him. Duncan Smith was suitably hard with words but like the rest of us he admired him.

As for the South of France, after the initial landing and the misapplied attention of the American naval guns at us when we flew in from Corsica to Ramatuelle, Tim Lucas, our Army liaison officer, made himself at home with the American Rangers and the French Maquis. The 'German' units, it seemed, were often 'Russians' in German uniform.

The squadrons harassed the Germans retreating up the Rhône valley, strafing trucks, horsedrawn vehicles, armoured cars, etc. We still had our casualties but it did not stop some pilots speaking to me and thus to the group captain about the plight of the horses. The enemy soldiers could get away but not the animals. He took it seriously and not pompously; the roads were blocked and there were plenty of other targets to harass.

We were ordered up to Sisteron to act as a 'task force' over a wide area, so we set out with the RAF Regiment. We 'liberated' the mountain areas without opposition. It was then over to the Rhône valley and up to Lyon. I led a small convoy and one night we slept under our trucks in the town of Montelimar.

At early light an old English lady came asking for the officer in charge. I emerged; unshaven and unwashed, to hear her disbelieving exclamation, 'You do not look like the English officers I knew!' She was right! Cliff Shasby observed to her that there were many other changes at home.

At Lyon (Bron) on the bomb-splattered airfield we had to stop to await news of our future. While we waited, shades of things to come: General de Gaulle landed in his Hudson and Duncan Smith and I were in attendance, only to be utterly ignored.

At night in Lyon the various wings of the French resistance fought each other. Peace had broken out in a part of France where collaboration was not unknown.

In the streets near the airfield also I came across a hastily earth-covered bombhole with the limbs of children poking through the earth – shot by the Germans for cheering our low-flying bombers! Nearby there were the bodies of workmen, shot for the same reason.

Then it was back to Italy, in fact to Florence. Once again we were on our travels; our equipment had gone ahead by sea and an advance party was to fly east in a DC3. The Spitfires were to refuel in Corsica. On that 2nd October 1944 it all went wrong. We were flying against the light.

To put it briefly, Florence Peretola 'airfield' with its gutted buildings and bomb pock-marked surrounds was smack alongside a mountain. There was nothing there but a recently constructed wooden flying control 'tower'.

The refuelling all took too long and while 111 (one of whose flight commanders was Frank Cooper, later Sir Frank Cooper and permanent secretary to the Northern Ireland Office and Ministry of Defence), 93 and 72 landed with no problem, 43 Squadron arrived in the circuit in darkness.

On the ground I stumbled in search of flares and we erected a makeshift flare path from the lights of some trucks and jeeps. The first ten landed safely, but the eleventh hit the cab of a truck and somersaulted on to its back. No. 12 came in, hit the wreckage and blew up, killing both pilots and the pilot of 111 Squadron, who had gone out to help extricate the first pilot. No. 13, thinking the flames were to assist the landing, hit the same truck, crashed and suffered head injuries against the gun-sight.

Then the Americans diverted the rest of 43 to Pisa where there were night-flying facilities. They might have acted earlier, but only knew of the problems through R/T chatter.

It was a gloomy time at Florence in a nasty winter. It was good to get back to the 8th Army and DAF in October/November 1944.

In the period up to VE day, 324 operated in its new role working even more closely through 'cab rank' with the Army. Our fighters were patrolling behind the front line ready to be called in to attack a ground target, tanks, guns, infantry – just like calling up a cab. To this day I look at NE Italy through the eyes of very large-scale maps. It was all valuable to the army but we were not without our casualties.

Eventually the Germans collapsed in the face of overwhelming Allied forces and we went up with the forward elements of the 8th Army to the north-eastern tip of Italy. We went so fast that we were dependent on the large US bomber force to bring us POL and food.

I have a box brownie photograph somewhere of me standing on the bonnet of my jeep looking back down into Italy. I reflected on the campaign carried out by those whom Lady Astor deemed the 'D-Day Dodgers'. How foolish politicians can be! Little did she know of the work of the men of 8th Army, and of the Desert Air Force working in appalling conditions to keep the aircraft flying.

But then, after a last look back into Italy; on by the lakes to Klagenfurt where once again over the gates into an airfield.

There was harassment from the Yugoslav forces who foolishly claimed the areas as theirs. It was all sorted out eventually but never will I forget the hatred of the Slovenes, Croats and Serbs in a world where normal human relationships had broken down. I did not like what I saw of 'middle Europe' and we could not cope with the chaos left over from the war and the thousands of retreating former friends of the Germans all, it seemed, wearing the Iron Cross.

At first in Austria our commanders kept alive the idea that we would militarily control Austria with our planes and a small army presence. It would be prewar Iraq all over again. It never proved necessary, for the Austrians, themselves former fervent supporters of Hitler, began the process of convincing the world that Hitler was a German and Beethoven an Austrian.

At some stage in those early days Group Captain Barnabas de la Poer Beresford, DSO, DFC, took me aside and told me to be ready for a small airborne landing at a Hungarian airfield. In the event it was not necessary and adjustments to the 'line' were made with a none too co-operative Russian officer to enable us to move into Zeltweg which had housed units of the Hungarian Air Force. The place was littered with hundreds of old Luftwaffe aircraft with their backs broken by the Russian soldiers.

It was from Zeltweg that the wing flew operationally again – as did 244 from the Udine area of Italy. The Yugoslavian air force (which in the war I had not come across) had shot down a US transport plane flying from Vienna down to Italy. It was the route their heavy bombers had used many times as was shown by the number of crashed and burned-out planes I had seen in the mountains. We were ordered to keep the skies clear for legitimate passage but once the announcement was made nothing further happened.

Shortly after all this I became CO of the headquarters unit of the wing as we returned to a peacetime air force. Zeltweg became a contented place under the benign control of Barney and then of Group Captain Brian Kingcombe, DSO, DFC, late OC of 244 Wing; both made the transition to peacetime command look easy. There were no fears of mutinies as in 1918. Our educational and sports (including skiing) facilities were good and we even had home leave.

By the summer of 1946 all the stalwarts who had carried the wing had returned to civvy life – Squadron Leader 'Tiny' Le Petit, senior admin officer, Jim Evans, engineering officer, Francis, equipment officer, Perry, armament officer, and now it was my turn. I reflected on the offer of an emergency (and then a permanent) commission. But it was not for me: it was time for a return to university.

The inexperienced youth had disappeared into the mists. The RAF had done well by me; by the end I had repaid some of my debt.

19

CLIFF MICHELMORE

The Victoria Cross Squadron

IT WAS SOME years before I learned that they were classified, unofficially of course, as 'expendables' by senior officers at Bomber Command Head-quarters. From the moment it went into production in 1937 the Fairey Battle had not been a welcome addition to the ever-gathering strength of the Royal Air Force. Nevertheless by the end of 1940 they had produced over 3,000 of them by which time the German Luftwaffe and their ground defences had long since proved the senior officers at High Wycombe right. In modern warfare with closing speeds of 150 mph these single-engined lumbering four-tonners were underpowered, underarmed and overstretched. They were, in short, out of their class, and written off even before the war began as expend-able. The same sad fate befell many of those who flew in them. They too were expendable.

When the Second World War broke out it was this aircraft, in company with the twin-engined Blenheim, that formed the striking part of the Advanced Air Striking Force's 256 light bombers. That attacking power had, for protection, some Hurricanes.

I had joined 12 Squadron at Andover in 1938 just as they were re-equipping and bidding a fond farewell to the long-serving, old fabric-covered biplane, the Hawker Hind. They let them go without reluctance because the all-metal aircraft were rapidly taking over. The Battle was a low-wing monoplane and, except for the fabric-covered control surfaces, was all metal. Its hydraulically operated retractable undercarriage, flaps and bomb-racks, the variable pitch airscrew and sliding cockpit hood made one feel, at least, that this was a truly modern aircraft and one designed well enough to take on the job of the RAF's short-range bomber. It was when it was put to the test that it was sadly found wanting. The Rolls-Royce Merlin II engine which was installed in August '38 gave it barely 1,030 hp which was never man enough for getting the aircraft, with its crew of three and a bomb load of four 250-pounders, airborne, let alone getting up to the top speed of 254 mph in level flight. Everyone declared it pleasant to fly if you were to ignore the odd outbreak of 'Merlinitis'; this was an alarming situation in which the engine would suddenly cut out. The cause was a design fault which allowed a lick of flame to escape from an inlet valve and set fire to the mixture in the induction trunk; a fault cured after extensive and frantic modifications were introduced almost on the eve of the declaration of war.

Its armament also proved inadequate. A front-firing .303 Browning was fixed in the starboard wing and the pilot could line up the target through the same ring and bead sight that was used for dive bombing. In the rear the wireless operator/air gunner had a Vickers 'K' gas-operated gun on an awkward swivel mounting and later the observer, on his stomach in the belly of the aircraft, was given a rear-firing swivel mounted Browning which had to be lined up in a mirror sight. A practice camp at West Freugh and a Redland/Blueland exercise was to expose the Battle's shortcomings. We also had another exercise at Catterick where we tested out our gas-spraying capabilities using a stinking aniseed mixture in place of gas. Unfortunately one driver/airframe pushed the jettison button instead of the firing button and an enormous canister plummeted earthwards into the garden of the officers' mess.

Austria and Czechoslovakia were over-run by Germany, Italy bagged Albania and Abyssinia and then came Poland. At the signing of the armistice in 1918 Marshal Foch predicted that the German border would only remain intact for twenty years and now he was proved right. France had run out a protective barrier to invasion in the form of the Maginot Line designed by a sergeant from the First World War, André Maginot. It consisted of deep underground bunkers and barracks with gun emplacements covering all the lines of approach. But the Line stopped at Longuyon and from there to the North Sea, a matter of 200 miles, was left undefended. No attack was expected across the Flanders plain or through the Ardennes. '*Ils ne passeront pas*' boasted the propaganda posters and lapel badges backed up by the slogan '*Nous vaincrons parce que nous sommes les plus fortes*' – We shall conquer because we are the stronger. In truth the French, we were told, had 1,000 bombers. The RAF had produced some Hurricanes and Spitfires to replace the old fighter biplanes. The German strength on the ground and in the air is now well-known. We were heavily outnumbered.

We went to France as soon as war was declared. The aircraft flew in to Berry-au-Bac and everyone else went by road or by a Handley Page 42 four-engined biplane airliner and Armstrong Whitworth Ensign requisitioned from Imperial Airways and both of which had been hurriedly dressed in camouflage. Buckets of brown and green paint were splashed on them with brooms. It was a week-end! The landborne airmen were relieved that they were not expected to get aboard the trucks marked '*Hommes 40 ou Chevaux 8*'.

Berry-au-Bac was up the road from Rheims towards Laon on a canal. They were certainly not expecting us. There was a small fuel store, a handful of sullen French reservists, who looked as though they had been left over from the last war, and an old bus. We were, after all, a 'mobile' squadron complete with its own HQ, stores trailer, cookhouse, workshop and operations room but we were not ready for war and that was certain. No accommodation had been arranged, no food, no refuelling and no chance to change currency. The officers were mostly billeted in private houses, the NCOs in the Town Hall and the 'erks' were given a palliasse, pointed towards a stack of straw and told to get on with it. They ended up in a half-built hall with a cement-dust floor. Later the officers settled in a château and the NCOs in private houses.

The airfield was littered with the debris left over from the war twenty years earlier, and the local military cemetery with its dead. Helmets – German, French and British – unexploded shells, fragments of barbed wire still strung between screw pickets, metal torn from machines of war and on one occasion a bone or two were found when we were building ramps on which to push the aircraft back into the woods so that they would be hidden from view. Each aircraft crew built itself a dug-out along the margin of the woods as somewhere to sit out of the rain, but soon the river rose and many were flooded. Then the workshops were set up as were the cookhouse and ops room. We were, it appeared, as ready for action as we would ever be. The first action was the leaflet raids over the Rhine. One observer was heard to say that they had to be certain to undo the bundle just in case it hit a German on the head and they had to be careful to make sure that the leaflets landed in the river; one air gunner took with him a half a dozen empty bottles which he dropped through the hole in the bottom of the fuselage designed for the camera. 'That will give them a bit of a scare when they hear those whistling down.' He was later reprimanded by the CO. But even the leaflet raids came to an end when on a recce op 150 Squadron suffered losses at the guns of some Messerschmitt 109s over the Rhine at the end of September.

As the rains came and the mud bogged down the aircraft there was a feeling of gloom and frustration. At home there was a sense that the war would never come to anything and that it would just quietly fade away. We had some affiliation flights with the French Morane 406 fighters and the newly arriving Hurricanes; we moved from the muddy morass of Berry-au-Bac to the relatively dry ground of Amifontaine but we were still within 'liberty bus' distance from Rheims, Laon and Soissons and those of us who were footballers got to travel to Paris to play. Servicing the aircraft was extremely unpleasant out in the winter weather. The Merlins hated the cold as much as we did and despite being cooped up in warm tents with a heater they took it out on us by refusing to start. Batteries went flat, oil became thicker and wireless operators complained that their sets needed calibrating regularly as frequencies became capricious.

Winter suddenly swept across the fields and the aircraft could only be distinguished by the top tip of the propeller blade above the heavy drifts – so they tell me. I was in the advance party for some bombing and gunnery practice down at the Mediterranean port of Perpignan near to the Spanish border. We were sternly warned not to invade the Spanish air space nor try to cross the border.

Gradually the weather improved in the spring of 1940. There were more recce flights from German aircraft and one was shot down by the local anti-aircraft detachment much to their surprise I suspect. Defence gunners had now arrived and were scattered around the perimeter; they were often called on to 'standby' as an attack was expected but none came. Back home Neville Chamberlain declared on 4th April that 'Hitler had missed the bus'. Five days later he caught the bus, train, plane and everything else by way of transport as he invaded Denmark and Norway. By 10th May it was our turn. Out of a clear blue early morning sky they came; six Dorniers flying low level over the village, over the airfield at Mal Maison which they pounded to hell. Our old dispersals at Berry-au-Bac were pummelled at the same time. 'Lucky Twelve' cried our colleagues as we escaped unhurt and with our aircraft intact.

The Germans had attacked exactly where the Maginot Line wasn't. The flimsy defences thrown up by the British could not stem the advance. Through the Low Countries they came. Then the German attack was switched through the Ardennes with 44 divisions, seven of them armoured and four motorised. Rommel's panzers crossed the Meuse near Sedan and the roads were jammed with the pathetic sight of lines of refugees fleeing, once more, the invaders. From above came the paratroops and the gliderborne troops.

Four of our aircraft went to attack the advancing columns. Only one returned. Flight Lieutenant Bill Simpson, Flight Commander of B Flight, was dragged from the burning wreckage of his Battle by Sergeant Edward O'Dell and his AG, Robert Tomlinson. Both were awarded the DFM and Bill Simpson the DFC. Bill eventually returned and was one of those treated by Dr Archie McIndoe at East Grinstead. His aircraft was 'V' for Victor, and as one of McIndoe's 'Guinea Pigs' so too was Bill a victor over his severe burns and injuries.

By 12th May the AASF was down to 72 aircraft and the tide of the German advance had not even been hesitated, leave alone halted. The gliderborne troops had captured two out of the three bridges across the Albert Canal at Maastricht. The Belgian Air Force had been re-equipped from their old Fiat biplanes with old Fairey Fireflies and seven out of nine of them had been shot down in attacking the bridges. The French asked for an attack on the bridgehead at Sedan, by now heavily defended.

Signal 12 Squadron   Time 0915 Z   date 12.5.40
Attack two bridges over Albert Canal. One mile west of Wilre, one mile west of Vailwammes. Additional information regarding targets obtained from Michelin Guide for Belgium. STOP.

A former 12 Squadron colleague of mine assures me that he saw that signal.

No. 12 Squadron was selected for the mission to attack the bridges at Vroenhoven and Veldwezelt which remained intact; the retreating troops had failed to blow them up and air strikes had proved ineffective. The six 'readiness' crews were briefed and Flying Officer Norman Thomas led three aircraft from A Flight and Flying Officer Donald Garland B Flight's formation. Thomas was to attack Vroenhoven by dive-bombing and Garland Veldwezelt at low level, with both sections going independently. Hurricanes of 1 Squadron from Berry-au-Bac were the escort and cover. In the event one A Flight aircraft was left behind because the airscrew refused to go into coarse pitch and by the time the reserve was ready the flight was off and away.

Accounts of the action vary which is not surprising given the circumstances. Of the five aircraft only one returned to Amifontaine and that brought back horrendous battle scars. There was a gaping hole in the wing so that you could see into the petrol tank, the rudder was held on by a single bolt, shrapnel and bullet holes had ripped through mainplanes and fuselage. From the rear gunner's hatch could be seen long scratch marks down to the tailplane where LAC Gordon Patterson, the W/AG, had baled out; he had been wounded but managed, together with the observer Sergeant Mansell, to get out. Mansell made it back to base but Patterson, later awarded the DFM, was taken prisoner.

Mansell, in a broadcast, later described part of the action:

When we were about twenty miles from our target thirty Messerschmitts tried to intercept us but we continued on our course while the three fighters [Hurricanes] waded into the attack. The odds were ten to one against us, but even so several of those Messerschmitts were brought down . . . the barrage was terrific over the target, the worst I have ever struck. The big bridge looked badly knocked about and was sagging in the middle. It had been hit by the bombs of the three bombers ahead of us.

In another account of the action:

Flying Officer Garland led his section at low level, line astern and met extremely heavy anti-aircraft fire from about 400 guns which contrary to intelligence advice had been installed in the bridgehead. Garland's bombs hit the target but his aircraft crashed on or just beyond the bridge.

The other two B Flight Battles were brought down.

Of the fifteen aircrew who left from Amifontaine that spring morning six were killed in action, two returned to base and the rest all ended up as prisoners, five of them injured and burned.

The following day we were read the following message:

OC 12 Squadron   13.5.40   ACM Sir Cyril Newall CAS
Personal. I send my warmest congratulations on the brilliant attack carried out by pilots and crews of your squadron yesterday stop.
As the Squadron's first CO I am proud to see the gallant and courageous spirit which exists and which I know will continue to bring further honour and credit to the squadron stop.

Flying Officer Donald Garland and Sergeant Thomas Gray had the Victoria

Cross conferred on them in the *London Gazette* on the 11th June. The citation ends:

> 'Much of the success of this vital operation must be attributed to the formation leader Flying Officer Garland, and to the coolness and resource of Sergeant Gray, who navigated Flying Officer Garland's aircraft under the most difficult conditions in such a manner that the whole formation was able successfully to attack the target in spite of heavy losses.

What of Wireless Operator/Air Gunner LAC Roy Reynolds who was in the back and who went unrecognised and unrewarded? On the fiftieth anniversary of the raid his family were presented with a commemorative silver salver signed by as many of the squadron who were in France as could be found. It was a belated but much overdue recognition.

As the Germans advanced so we retreated. Night operations replaced day attacks. By June we ended up west of Vendome and casualties mounted. By the time we were attacked at Sougé and suffered severe casualties to personnel and aircraft we had lost twenty-three Battles. We had also lost in the first few days of the real war many of our original aircrew who were awarded two VCs, two DFCs and three DFMs.

On 16th June the ground party left Brest for Plymouth and the following day a handful of Fairey Battles with the squadron marking (PH) left for Finningley. We were returning with nothing more than we stood up in and our pride.

As the ground party made its weary way up from the dockyard at Plymouth to an assembly park a bystander asked the squadron warrant officer who we were.

'We, madam, are the Victoria Cross Squadron. That is who WE are.'

C. NORTHCOTE PARKINSON

'A Significant Role'

THERE WAS A period during World War II when our ill-behaved opponents began to drop bombs upon our country. We discouraged this practice. We also wondered whether the falling bombs would be replaced some day by armed parachutists. Should we have soldiers at hand to deal with them? We shouldn't (or so it seemed at the time). Nor had we men enough to guard our airfields against ground attack. We needed men who would serve to guard our airfields just as we had Royal Marines to guard our naval bases and our ships of war.

When war began (3rd September 1939) I was a master at the Royal Naval College Dartmouth, teaching naval history. The war came nearer to us in June 1940, after the evacuation of Dunkirk and the fall of France. When the Dartmouth summer term ended I went to London to ask for a commission.

I made no progress in my search until September when I applied to the Air Ministry for a commission in the Air-Sea Rescue branch of the RAF. I was told to apply in person on a given day. The effect of this on the War Office was instantaneous and dramatic. I was commissioned as 2nd lieutenant on 24th September, being posted as an instructor in 166 Officer Cadet Training Unit at Meeanee Barracks, Colchester. Reporting there, I was given a platoon of officer cadets with defensive duties at a road-block on the Ipswich Road. I was made lieutenant on arrival and promoted captain on 25th December with seniority from 25th September. Colchester was under spasmodic air attack and it was decided to move the OCTU to the Isle of Man. From there we turned out batches of subalterns at four-monthly intervals, each batch a shade less convincing than the previous batch. Late in 1941 the supply of raw material gave out, and the OCTU was transferred to the RAF for the training of ground defence officers. The officer training of what was to be the RAF Regiment was set up initially at Butlin's Holiday camp at Filey in Yorkshire. This answer to Goering's Luftwaffe regiment was headed by an air commodore, a colonel, and two lieutenant colonels, the instruction being entrusted to majors, captains and subalterns. The whole organisation was presently moved to another camp at Grantham, where it was presently dissolved. I was myself transferred to 22 Group at Buntingsdale Hall, Ternhill, Shropshire. Here there were an air vice marshal, a group captain as Air I, supported by me as Air II. The Group extended to Grantham, Filey and

Eastchurch. For the defence of Eastchurch (in Sheppey) I was specially responsible. To reach Sheppey I used to fly in a Vega Gull aircraft, in which I had the role of navigator. As Number Four in the Group I felt entitled to make an occasional suggestion. In doing so I urged that the RAF Regiment should stage a raid on the French coast. Whether it was ever to do so, I have no idea, but the immediate result of my speaking out of turn was that I was posted as GSO II to the War Office. This was in December 1944 and I was still on the General Staff when war ended in 1945. The object of my ill-timed suggestion was to give the Regiment a first and humble battle honour. If the raiding party could take a prisoner or two, preferably from the Luftwaffe, with (say) a light machine gun or mortar, the existence of the new unit would begin to be known. In the light of this suggestion promptly rejected, I may claim to have almost achieved something in World War II. I had done nothing (aged five) in World War One although I stood close, at one time, to King George V in St Paul's Cathedral.

Looking back on my military career, which I began as a second lieutenant in 1931, I feel that I was possibly right about blooding the RAF Regiment at an early date in its history. I was also eager to devise for it a uniform as distinctive as that worn by the Royal Marines. About this I said nothing at the time – having already spoken out of turn – but I was also probably right in what I silently thought. Should we have another World War, I propose – at the age of eighty-two – to keep out of it. I played, after all, a significant role in World War II. I must be content with that.

21

LORD RAYNER

Training for Life

LIKE MANY other young men in wartime I volunteered for the RAF at the earliest age regulations permitted. Almost inevitably I applied to join for training as aircrew whose wartime exploits made them very much the heroes of youth. The end of the war in Europe seemed to be in sight and on news of my acceptance after a rigorous selection process I cherished the illusion that I had been one of a few selected from the many volunteers. However, this illusion was soon shattered when in due course I was asked to attend a further selection committee to see if I was worth keeping on reserve for ultimate training as a pilot.

This time with perhaps a little more reason for pride I was successful in being retained on reserve but sent home to await the call for duty. However, a year later with the war now finished I was informed that I could no longer be held pending training for air crew but would now be called for National Service with the RAF.

Whilst on initial training I was asked if I wished to apply for a commission in the Accounts Branch or in the RAF Regiment. Understandably in youth I was not thrilled by being in the Accounts Branch dealing with pay and rations, important though this service may be. However, lack of detailed knowledge of the activities of the RAF Regiment led me to have a glamorous view of its role and I sought to be selected for the RAF Regiment Officer Training Course at Grantham.

My recollection of my life there is one of enjoyment and the pleasure of meeting a wide range of people, as many of my fellow cadets had already experienced wartime service and had a mature view of life, as the OCTU consisted not only of recently called up National Service men but also experienced air crew NCOs who had sought a transfer to the RAF Regiment. These older officer cadets with their first hand experience of the challenges of wartime service and their knowledge of countries abroad provided a stimulating environment for a young man brought up in the restrictions of wartime Britain.

The OCTU staff of officers and training NCOs were also of a very high calibre. They had been seconded from the Foot Guards to ensure that our standards of training matched the best. They undertook this task with great dedication and I have no doubt that the RAF Regiment in the early days of its development and training achieved its high standards with the help of the Army who ensured that the RAF set off on the right path and at the outset a fine tradition was established which has continued to grow and flourish.

The experienced fellow officer cadets were not used to carrying out instructions the hard way. I remember one exercise where we had to march across the countryside collecting messages that had been left in the nature of a tough treasure hunt. My group proceeded to a nearby pub where some were well known. We sat in the back bar whilst locals were persuaded to cycle round the course and bring the clues back to us. I turned this experience later to good account when as an officer I was on a battle course; a group of us were left on the top of the Yorkshire moors and challenged to return to base. Between us and the camp servicemen were at large to spot and take us back again to the starting point. I unhesitatingly suggested that it would be foolish to march in the direction of the camp; rather, we should walk in the opposite direction and use the resources to be found in a local pub to ensure a more convenient way of returning to base. Although without money, we persuaded a local to drive us in his horse box back to a place near the camp. We must have looked trustworthy and indeed we were and we rewarded him for his time and the use of expensive transport.

On commissioning I was sent to Headquarters Middle East to be a training officer available for duty throughout that substantial command which stretched from Malta to Nairobi; to Iraq and of course Palestine and Egypt. My first assignment was in Palestine which in the autumn of 1946 was preparing to become the State of Israel on the withdrawal of British Forces. I was stationed near a pleasant small town, Hadera, which was very continental in background. Its cafes made the local RAF personnel at home and its council allowed us to use the town's swimming pool.

During my three months in Palestine Christmas arrived and being a serious prospective candidate for ordination in the Church of England I was anxious to take a group of men to Bethlehem on Christmas Eve. To my amazement my trip was heavily oversubscribed and we set off to visit Jerusalem and then to go on to Bethlehem in time for the midnight service.

As always, I laid careful plans for rendezvous times knowing that we could not go round as a large group. When the time came for departure back to base there were only the handful of servicemen who had remained with me throughout the evening. The rest were missing. I was relieved to learn that there was no mystery where they might be found. No Christmas service for them at Bethlehem – they had been entertained by ladies who were in plentiful supply on these occasions. Fortunately some of the men knew where to find the missing airmen and we were able to return to camp before dawn in time to hand out morning tea to those who had spent the night at the base.

My next posting was to Malta for a similar training assignment. The RAF headquarters mess and accommodation were in a magnificent building in Valetta overlooking the Grand Harbour. As most of the group of headquarters personnel were accompanied by their wives very few lived in the mess and as a result we enjoyed a very spacious lifestyle. Malta, recovering from its wartime experiences, still had scarcities of some fresh foodstuffs, and with an early demonstration of my entrepreneurial skills I persuaded a regular training flight to Benghazi to let me come with them as I had learnt that eggs were plentiful and cheap there. This mission enabled me to supply the mess with all the eggs it needed, and to sell them profitably to the married families and supplement our standard of living in downtown Valetta.

All too soon my few months' assignment ended and I was asked to return to base in the Canal Zone. The journey on this particular trip was indeed luxurious as we joined a civilian liner, and for three or four days lived in high style as the shipping companies worked hard to restore the pre-war standards of first class life at sea.

On arrival back at headquarters I was informed that as the adjutant was due for demobilization I was the declared candidate to take over his job. Ever a businessman I pointed out that the rank for the post was flight lieutenant and because of the rules of length of service qualification I would remain a pilot officer for another year on the appropriate pay. My protest was to no avail – I became an underpaid adjutant sorting out the office that was in desperate need of administrative skills.

Except in passing I have not mentioned the fact that throughout this period of my life I was a very serious candidate for priesthood in the Church of England, due to read theology at Cambridge and very much committed to the life style I believed was demanded by my vocation. Needless to say, my no drinking, no swearing and no smoking profile led to a number of good-humoured practical jokes at my expense. The most embarrassing was a Sunday evening after service when I was engaged in a serious conversation with the padre and was offered my usual drink of lime and lemon. Such was my absorption with the conversation that I failed to notice that it had been heavily laced with gin. Perhaps a more experienced drinker would have proceeded with caution but I, unaware of the possible hazard, consumed the first and accepted a second with some devastating results.

Amongst the tasks I undertook was a Sunday evening service at the base as the padre had to conduct a service elsewhere. In pursuit of this responsibility I rang the bell, played the organ, read the lesson and asked my long-suffering friends to endure a weekly sermon. What they made of all this I do not know but I suspect it was a cause for some amusement as I was ever encouraged to continue in this particular form of good works.

When the time came for me to leave the RAF Regiment I did so with great affection for the institution of which I had the privilege to be part and for the friendships that I have made and indeed retained until today. I regard my $2\frac{1}{2}$ years' service with the Royal Air Force as an important part of my training for life. I would have been less knowledgeable about my fellow men and had a much narrower view of life in my early twenties without the travel, companionship and challenges of my brief career with the RAF Regiment.

22

LORD RIX

Laughter in the Ranks

I JOINED THE Royal Air Force on Saturday 22nd July 1944, with a suitable theatrical flourish. My sister Sheila, by now a WAAF officer, had a Free French major in tow. It was just before he went back to France to continue the fight on his own soil – but he was very keen on Sheila and very keen to impress all the family that his feelings were genuine. Once he got back to France that keenness rapidly evaporated but on Saturday, 22nd July 1944, he was still on the boil and volunteered to drive me to Scarborough some thirty-odd miles from Hornsea. So there was I in a dirty great staff car – chauffeured by a Free French major, with a WAAF section officer riding shotgun. I sat at the back in regal, if somewhat car-sick, splendour. We duly arrived outside the Prince of Wales Hotel, Scarborough where 34 Flight, E Squadron, No. 36 R & C Wing was stationed. A squad of men was drilling smartly on the promenade outside. Their instructor saw our staff car slowing to a halt, two officers in front, and began to wonder nervously who on earth was in the back. The rear offside door opened. Corporal Collinson (for such was the corporal's name) decided discretion was the better part of valour, called his men to a heel-stamping attention and brought up the most tremendous salute. Out of the car stepped 1593333 AC2 Rix B.N.R. and politely enquired from the corporal where the guard room was. Much suppressed laughter in the ranks and the corporal told the new recruit, in no uncertain terms, where he could find the bloody place. Actually, he was a splendid chap and we became good friends even though he was the drill instructor for our flight!

The motley collection of new arrivals settled themselves, uncertainly, on the appointed benches and waited for all the horrible things that were going to happen to us. They did – but not before I saw someone else with long hair sitting beside me. Long hair, in those days, denoted you were 'arty' so I enquired if he was an actor. He turned out to be a pianist called Tommy Watt – newly departed from the superb Carl Barriteau band. We have remained friends ever since but then we were more pre-occupied with the horrors of our first RAF haircut. It was *just* as ghastly as we had expected and even in July the wind whistled round our shaven necks. All the other delights came, too, in rapid succession. Kit issue and those lovely boots that not only blistered your feet but also blistered your ankles and shins as well. Buttons that had to be polished and polished – I wish I'd had shares in Duraglit – and vests and underpants I used to great comic effect when I finally returned to civvy street. One compensation. Because we were potential aircrew, we wore little white flashes at the front of our fore and aft caps. This gave us a great feeling of superiority over lesser mortals – although not one of our bunch ever qualified as a pilot. The war ended before we were needed, so everyone was made redundant. Even in those days, that ghastly word was in common usage.

For the moment, though, we wore our flashes proudly and clattered off to Sick Quarters for our FFI and jabs. For the ignorant among you FFI means 'Free From Infection'. You are all lined up, having first stripped off, and told to raise your arms above your head. This rigmarole is to make sure you haven't pox, clap, crabs, or some other sweet-sounding infection.

After the FFI – inoculations and vaccinations – your left arm was scrubbed clean with soap for that delicious scratching vaccination needle and your right arm was wiped clean with spirit for that delicious blunt TAB and ATT jab. You were then informed you were on forty-eight hours' light duty. As far as I could ascertain, light duty meant being doubled out into the road, doubled back to the billet and told to swing those arms as high as possible to keep the jabs going round. Several strong men fainted, several weaker men developed temperatures but it was only *then* that we were informed all inoculations and vaccinations were voluntary. This information was dropped in amongst all the other mass of knowledge we were supposed to assimilate at our first lectures.

However, during my lengthy Medical Examination (as opposed to the FFI and jabs) it came out, not unnaturally, that recently I had suffered an operation for chronic sinusitis. My ears, nose and throat were sprayed, illuminated, X-rayed and examined from every possible angle and finally the doctors said I would have to be taken off training for a few weeks to see how things developed. If my sinuses did not clear . . . well, bad luck, but flying in unpress-urised aircraft was completely out of the question and I would have to be re-employed.

I was re-employed. This meant being sent to the re-employment centre at RAF Eastchurch on the Isle of Sheppey and the nearest equivalent to a concentration camp we had in the RAF. It's now an 'open' prison. In those days it was a closed one. You see we were the unwanted ones. Some redundant, some medically unfit or some, in the ghastly jargon of the day, LMF – Lacking Moral Fibre. My fibre had never been put to the test, thank God, but here were hundreds of aircrew, many decorated, stripped of all rank, brevets and dignity because they had, say, asked not to go on a particular mission. It was awful to see them with the faded sections of their uniforms showing clearly the badges that had recently been sewn there. Like the marks when you take a picture off the wall on moving day.

For me, moving day didn't take long. Being medically unfit I was offered alternative jobs which did not exactly ring any bells: cook, medical orderly and down the mines as a Bevin Boy. I chose the latter.

So there I was. Called up July 1944. Demobbed February 1945.

A few days later, dressed in my lovely grey chalk-striped suit and green porkpie hat which clearly showed I had been in the forces, I was making my way for training at Askern Main Colliery near Doncaster. There we were given practical tuition underground or lectures on the surface. My first visit to the pit bottom was not, exactly, a success. We were all herded into the cage (the mining equivalent of a lift – but it has open sides with bars) and I was wearing all the regulation gear. Steel-capped boots, belt for my lamp, water bottle and snap-tin, all topped by a helmet, and, to complete the ensemble, pigskin gloves. Not that I thought I was going to the office – but as an actor I felt I should protect my hands from all that coal-dust. The cage jerked upwards and then plummeted into the depths. Down, down we rushed and suddenly we were going up again. Later I discovered that was an illusion and was caused when the wheelhouse applied the brake. Then, a splash and there we were at the bottom of one of the deepest pits in England – 960 yards – or so we were told. We stepped out into a version of the underground at Piccadilly Circus. Whitewashed walls, electric light, neat little arches leading to various parts of the mine. This happy similarity didn't last long as we soon discovered trudging along the roadways. For the moment, however, we were highly delighted. The instructor gathered us together and then looked at me:

'What the bloody 'ell's them things on your hands?' he enquired.

'Gloves,' I said. 'I'm an actor, you see, and I must protect them.'

'The only protection you need is to be a bloody sight fastern'n me, lad,' said he. And he held up one hand with the three middle fingers missing. 'That's wheer t' bloody roof came down fast. Me hand wheer on top of a tub and me mates had to hack them fingers off.' By now I felt distinctly sick. 'You'll get them bloody pansy gloves stuck in machinery. Chuck 'em away, you silly sod.'

But we learnt a little at a time. No 'new boy' was allowed near the coal-face. We were used for shovelling rubble – caused by ripping (the enlarging of the roadways to the face) – into moving tubs after the shot-firer had done his work. We learnt, too, about the construction and the 'safety' in pits and the future envisaged for them. Nationalisation was just around the corner.

Then, out of the blue, my medical papers arrived from the RAF and I was told to report to the medical wallahs looking after the Bevin Boys. Again my nose was picked over, at considerable length, and this time it was decided that if altitude would hurt my ears – so would depth. I was hoofed out of a job I was not enjoying but, shall we say, appreciating. To make matters worse it was decided I was fit for ground duties. So, even though the war in Europe was over, back to the RAF for me and, strangely enough, I had a ball.

I had long longed to be a doctor but my stupidity at Latin, Chemistry and Physics overcame my desires. Now I was forced to become that *very* poor relation – the Nursing Orderly. We were even poor relations to the SRNs for our training was perfunctory and much shorter. I say 'forced' because my

192

particular alternatives were cook – I can still only boil an egg – or paratrooper. Heights make me dizzy.

I suffered my three months' course as Med/Ord U/T N/Ord at RAF Halton with consummate bravery. With only Tring and Halton to choose from as points of activity and only 2,000 WAAFs to choose from for proclivity, life was a struggle. Somehow one managed and whilst I was there I joined the station dramatic society and gave my well-rehearsed guest performances in *Nothing But The Truth* and *Night Must Fall.* This drew the authorities' notice to the fact that I'd been an actor in civvy street and someone decided I'd make a good instructor. So, one day, there was our squadron leader, a doctor, of course, bursting into our classroom and demanding that I give a lecture. Even then, my detractors would say, I went for the easy laugh and gave an hysterical turn concerning the use of bottles and bedpans. I say 'hysterical' because my audience laughed a lot. Luckily the squadron leader was no critic, dismissing the laughter as merely sycophantic, and decided I'd make a good lecturer. All I had to do was three months 'field' work in hospital or sick quarters and I could return as a full-blown corporal instructor. Would I accept? Would I accept?!! I'd have paid a premium.

Field work at RAF Hospital Cosford. This consisted of cleaning out the sluice rooms, emptying bottles and bedpans (where were my easy laughs now?) bumping floors and generally acting as anybody's dogsbody. But it could have been worse and whilst I was at Cosford the war against Japan ended. We all repaired to the nearest town and there was much dancing in the streets of Wolverhampton *that* night. Those who weren't dancing were occupied in other pleasurable ways. At Cosford, however, things got a little out of hand. Many of the patients had been prisoners-of-war and when they heard the news they almost went berserk. Much of the furniture from the officers' mess was piled into a great pyre and the flames lit our unsteady way home as dawn was breaking. Accompanying this eerie scene was a recording of Glenn Miller's 'When Johnnie Comes Marching Home' played again and again and again. I never hear it now without being transported back to those unreal days.

For they were unreal. The war was over – but the rigours of peace were about to descend on us. With no war to unite us I noticed an almost immediate change in our relationships, one with another. Politics became important again and friends who had been happily discussing women or gin or other normal subjects suddenly became desperately involved about who was responsible, say, for the shortage of butter – the Conservatives before the war or the new Labour lot after the war. Bloody silly really . . .

My three months at Cosford ended by my being posted to a far corner of Scotland – Milltown, near Lossiemouth. The journey took three days. First a slow train to Carlisle. Then a twenty-four hours' wait, because there were no further trains to Elgin, followed by the slowest of all trains to the north. I really do believe that train driver grew vegetables along the track and tended them every few yards. Ten hours later I arrived at my destination, to be greeted by a jovial Geordie MO, a cheerful Cockney corporal and an old sweat leading aircraftman – 'Pop' – who eventually became a Chelsea Pensioner, but even in those days he must have been eligible, so great was his age. The four of us were the sick quarters' staff of Milltown, but really there was nothing to do except go to the flicks in Elgin or to admire the beautiful russet tints which coloured the trees that autumn.

Christmas was now approaching and the sick parades virtually ceased to exist – so much so that the MO told me I could take an extra four days' unofficial leave and go home for Christmas. I arrived at Elgin station to be greeted by a panting 'Pop' who had cycled down to catch me.

'You're posted,' he gloated, 'that's cocked up your Christmas' – evincing the true Festive Spirit. Indeed, I thought it had, for my posting was to MTE & D RAF Halton as a trainee instructor. I arrived – two days later, smarting at my loss of leave – to be interviewed by the same squadron leader who'd been moved by my bedpan lecture.

'You do want to be an instructor, don't you?' he enquired.

'Yes please,' I replied, 'if I can go home for Christmas.' I was lucky. He still remembered my lecture . . . I became a trainee instructor *and* was granted ten days' official leave for Christmas. It was the start of a very fruitful twenty-two months.

After lecturing for the first year, I was promoted from instructor to corporal in charge of medical staff postings. This meant I worked one day a week – docketing all the movements in and out of the station. I also sat on Medical Trade Test Boards, asking simple questions about splints and first aid *and* bottles *and* bedpans, and awarding marks to the hopeful candidates. The warrant officer and the squadron leader asked the more difficult questions. I was hardly overworked but fortunately our CO was an Australian, mad on cricket and the Officer Commanding Central Medical Trade Test Board was a Scot, mad on the theatre. I came up from under my bottles and bedpans smelling of roses. I was captain of cricket and ran the station dramatic society. As I noted all the postings, it was easy. If a good cricketer or a good actor appeared on the books I reported this to the SWO. He in turn reported it to our Australian wing commander or our Scottish group captain and the lucky airman was on the permanent staff. We had the best cricket team and the best amateur dramatic society in the RAF. All from a total of eight hundred! I'll never forget visiting RAF Cardington to play cricket. With ten times our number of men to choose from they expected to annihilate us. We shot them out for sixty-three and made the necessary runs for the loss of one wicket, a dubious lbw. They didn't realise till then that all of us played or had played County Cricket, Minor County Cricket or League Cricket. Next to God, there's nothing like having the CO on your side.

I had a *marvellous* summer. The weather was glorious, cricket abounded (Compton and Edrich went berserk) and frankly I *enjoyed* getting up early – the sun was always shining and to crown it all, my demob number was getting nearer and nearer. But all the time the jobs were going to actors pouring out of the forces. I became very depressed at my prospects of finding work easily, or even at all, but running the station dramatic society, plus memories of Wolfit, had given me the idea that I might like to become an actor-manager.

I had one hundred pounds saved. I went to my father. 'If I put up a hundred quid – would you and Uncle Bert put up, say, another nine hundred. I can get a rep going for that.' Much to my surprise, he agreed. I was in business.

The last rites of my RAF service took place in October. By November I had headed paper and an attic over a chemist's shop in Hornsea, which served as an office, but no theatre. But I was full of confidence. I wrote to everyone offering my non-existent company. My SWO's last words to me were prophetic:

'You'll bullshit your way through h'anything,' he said, and, you know, he was right! By Easter Monday 1948, I had my company and I had my theatre – if the King's Hall, Ilkley could claim such distinction. Marriage, *Reluctant Heroes* and the Whitehall Theatre were just around the corner. Who could guess that Whitehall would be in my title when I was made a life peer some 42 years later. Not me, I'll be bound – nor my station warrant officer. A pity he's not around to reflect on the accuracy of his prophecy . . .

23

IAN SMITH

From the Western Desert to the Western Front, via Italy

W HEN WAR WAS declared in September 1939 I was an undergraduate at Rhodes University in Grahamstown, the Cape Province of South Africa. As a school boy one of my dreams was that I would become a pilot in the RAF. This had now become a realistic probability. There was an air of tremendous expectation and excitement. Most of us were sufficiently mature to comprehend the importance and gravity of such a momentous decision, but at the same time we were reconciled to accepting that someone, some nation, would have to give a lead in making a stand against this upstart tyrant in Germany if we were determined to protect freedom in our world. That was part of our history – our fathers had been in the forefront in the last Great War 1914–18, now it was our turn. Once the die was cast, we were more than ready to respond to the call from our mother-country.

Our end of year examinations were about to commence, and once completed I would be returning home for the long Christmas vacation, and this would enable me to make my plan. However, on arrival I was confronted with the news that our Government had announced that all Varsity students must complete their degree courses before they would be considered for enlistment. Moreover, Rhodesia had been chosen as one of the sites for the Empire Air Training Scheme, and preparations were commencing. There were many obvious advantages – a very high proportion of clear, sunny days, an equitable climate, and a well developed infrastructure. So my best bet was to return to university for another year, by which time, according to available assessment, the pilot training would have commenced.

There was an interesting local episode, typically Rhodesian, the day war was declared. One of the biggest gold mines in our country, the Wanderer, operated in our district. That night about a dozen of the learner miners and apprentices boarded the train for Salisbury and presented themselves for service. However, the mine management had been alarmed of the event and immediately contacted the authorities. Accordingly the over-enthusiastic volunteers were put in the cooler for the day, and thence on to the return night train back to the mine. Vital services had to be maintained, and gold production was high on the list in order to produce the finance to pay for the war. We were dealing with tremendously spirited young men, amongst the best rugby players in our team which had won the provincial championship that year, but they, along with everyone else, got the message that we were confronted with a most serious situation, and there had to be order and planning. The Government immediately introduced a system of conscription to ensure that key industries were maintained – conscription not to enlist people into the services, but to keep them out. Three of those who boarded the train that night were personal friends of mine. Eventually they were released for pilot training and were subsequently posted to Britain. In turn they were reported missing from operations over Germany, and never returned to their homes.

Let me record a few interesting facts:

24.08.39 – Special sitting of parliament at which a bill conferring on Government the power to govern by regulation was passed through all its stages. The sitting ended with a unanimous affirmation 'to stand by the Motherland in this hour of grave national emergency'.

27.08.39 – No. 1 Squadron Southern Rhodesian Air Force departed from Salisbury for Nairobi. This was to become 237 Squadron RAF (*Primum Agmen in Caelo*) ie first in the field.

03.09.39 – War declared.

04.09.39 – Southern Rhodesia declares war, the first to follow in Britain's foot steps. 'Britain's wars are our wars'.

The record shows that Southern Rhodesia along with New Zealand holds pride of place in the percentage of population which fought in the war.

It was not surprising that on a number of occasions during the war years I heard the comment: You Rhodesians are more British than the British.

So it was a case of back to university for another year. However, when I returned home for the Christmas vacation, foremost in my mind was the need to make a plan to circumvent our Government's decision that students should first complete their courses. I travelled to Salisbury, consulted with friends, took the normal pilot's test, filled in all the necessary application forms avoiding any mention of university and with a great sigh of relief was notified of my acceptance and subsequently received my call-up papers.

Initial Flying Training School was on Tiger Moths at Guinea Fowl, and Service FTS on Harvards at Thornhill, respectively 12 and 24 miles from my home – most convenient.

My next move was to the Middle East, and after a short transit stop at Cairo, on to an OTU course at Baalbek which was situated in a pleasant valley between Damascus and Beirut. Apart from an interesting visit to the famous Cedars of the Lebanon, and the friendliness of the inhabitants of Beirut, I never ceased to be fascinated at flying over one thousand feet below sea level with the associated strange readings on the instrument panel – the Dead Sea.

The dreadful history and suffering of the people of the Lebanon in recent times is all the more stark and grotesque to those who visited and took away with them pleasant memories of the beautiful country and the pleasant people.

There is something missing in our modern civilisation with all of its tremendous advances in science, industry, the humanitarian fields, and power-ful world organisations tasked with preserving justice, and freedom and the protection of human rights, but is nevertheless impotent when it comes to handling such problems.

My next posting was to 237 (Rhodesia) Squadron. They had been pulled out of the Western Desert for a break and posted to Teheran, capital of a country which was then known as Persia. From there we moved westwards to Kirkuk, one of the big oil fields of Iraq. Apart from getting some more hours in on Hurricanes, that great, versatile aircraft with which the squadron was equipped, we enjoyed ourselves playing rugby against the London Scottish and London Irish Regiments, at Habbaniya, the large permanent RAF base to our south near Baghdad, and a few others in the vicinity who were able to muster a team and give us a game.

Our next move was back to Egypt to catch up with Montgomery's 8th Army. We were re-equipped with the Hurricane Mk IIc which carried the very formidable fire power of four 20mm cannon, and our first base was El Alamein. Most of our work was on convoy patrols, with the odd chase after a Ju88 on a photographic reconnaissance mission over Alexandria. However, once it got its nose down on its return flight to Crete, there was no hope of catching it in a Hurricane. We took two of the cannons out of a few of our aircraft hoping that the reduced weight might enable us to get up on to the target quicker, but there was no luck. Unfortunately radar was not yet available in those parts, and so by the time we got the orders to scramble it was too late to be effective.

There was a bit of excitement when we carried out a low level daylight raid on Crete, with long range fuel tanks which were jettisoned prior to crossing the hostile coast, but expectations of catching a Ju88 somewhere in the line of fire did not materialise.

We then moved along the coast to Benghazi for a period before returning to the Delta for what was referred to as the Defence of Alexandria. But what was more important was that we were converted on to Spitfires, and this was an indication of more exciting things to come. The culmination was the squadron's posting to Corsica, where we were equipped with the Spitfire IX. Without detracting from the wonderful service rendered by so many other types of aircraft, including our beloved Hurricanes which we had left behind, the Spitfire was the most beautiful aircraft ever made – a dream thing for those of us who had the privilege to fly it.

My stay on Corsica was all too short, for on a train-busting raid in the Po Valley I was hit by flak, necessitating a bale-out in the Ligurian Alps to the north of Genoa. Before long I contacted and joined up with the Italian *Partisani*, thereby spending five of the most interesting months of my life.

Towards the end of September 1944 there were some snow falls on top of the mountains, so concluding that I didn't wish to be hemmed in for the duration of the winter, my plan was to go westwards, as the American invasion into the South of France had been successfully carried out. There was strong opposition from my *patrioti* friends who enjoyed having an *Englasie majore pilote* to parade around with them, but once they had reconciled themselves to the fact that my decision was final, they assisted with advice and letters of introduction to other groups of *Partisani*.

There was a young British corporal in the vicinity who had indicated a desire to accompany me if I chose such a course, so I took him along, and en route we picked up three others – a Frenchman, an Austrian and a Pole. After walking for twenty-three days, four of us crossed the Alps into France, spending the final night sitting, shivering on blocks of ice. We met up with an American recognizance party as we descended. The Pole, a youngster of about seventeen years, didn't make it. The previous day when we passed through a particularly dangerous point under the scrutiny of German sentries his nerve cracked and he turned back.

We were taken to the nearest American base and treated to a most welcome meal in the warm atmosphere of their canteen. However, thereafter we parted company, as aircrew were to be returned to their bases by air, others by road and sea. We had grown to understand one another and trust had been built up, so there was a sense of emotion over the farewell. I appreciated their genuine gratitude expressed that without my assistance they would still be behind the enemy line. As they were now in safe hands, I could leave them with a clear conscience.

Unfortunately my wish for a posting to Britain and the Western Front did not materialise. In spite of a number of interviews at as many levels as possible I was confronted by the fact that 'Regulations' (and I certainly had cause to curse them that day) stated that I was to be returned to the command from which I was operating at the time I was shot down.

The following day I was on the old Dak (DC-3) – I think it fair comment to say that no other single type of aircraft could claim to have made a greater contribution to the war effort – from Marseilles to Naples.

At the reception centre I was informed that I could be moved immediately to Cairo and thence to Rhodesia. Fortunately this time my luck was in, firstly with a very reasonable flight lieutenant, who took me through to a most understanding squadron leader who listened with great patience, and ultimately with a kind smile on his face said that he thought it would be possible to find me a place on the next ship to Britain. But this didn't sail the next day, and when one is in a hurry to get moving each day seems to take as long as a month – the way things were going the war could be over before I arrived!

Eventually we were in London. The Air Ministry believed that a refresher course at an Air firing School in Shropshire was desirable, and although I wasn't convinced, it was clear that there wasn't much chance of changing the decision. Fortunately, after about ten days the CFI called me in and said that from the reports he had received it didn't appear as if there was much more I needed to learn about the game, and my next stop was a transit station south of London, and thence a posting to 125 Wing at Celle in Germany.

Johnnie Johnson DSO, DFC was the group captain, George Keefer DFC

(Canadian) the wing commander, and I found myself in 130 (Punjab) Squadron with Frank Wooley DFC as squadron leader. They were stirring times, but unfortunately at that stage of the war German aircraft in the skies were few and far between. Occasionally one might see a Me262 (Twin jet) zooming down from above, and it was quite a formidable sight. We were flying the Spitfire XIV with its Griffon engine and tremendous power, which was necessary to get on top of the enemy, but detracted from the smoothness and quality flying of its predecessors.

All of a sudden the war ended, almost prematurely for my state of mind. I had lost out on one and a half years of flying, firstly with a period of about nine months in the 15th Scottish Hospital in Cairo after a crash in the Western Desert, followed by a similar period after baling out in Italy, and to me these were times of lost opportunities, for which I was hoping to catch up. However, those were momentary thoughts. It was wonderful to know that the madness of killing people, especially innocent people, had come to an end in Europe, and husbands and fathers would be returning to their homes and families.

The wing broke up with the various squadrons going in different directions, and there were interesting and happy times for us. We were the first Allied squadron to land in Copenhagen, where we spent a fabulous time over a week-end, then stop-overs in Amsterdam and Brussels on our way back to the south of England, where we all had leave to go where we wished. On our return we were re-equipped with the beautiful Spit IX – the Mark XIV was required for the Far East.

Our next stop was Aberdeen, the Granite City, where we spent a few weeks before flying across the North Sea, the first squadron into Norway. Our base was at Kristiansand in the south, where we were to spend four glorious months. It was the middle of summer with twenty hours of sunlight each day, living on a peninsula jutting out into a fiord, eating crayfish and prawns and many other appetising dishes, surrounded by great kindness and hospitality from the local community who immediately adopted the squadron.

A memorable occasion was a visit six of us made to Stockholm one week-end. One of our pilots was a Swede, Chris Christensen, and during a visit to his home he succeeded in making a plan. And what a memorable event. It was the first time RAF pilots in the splendour of their uniforms had been seen in Sweden, and wherever we went the red carpet was rolled out. Unfortunately it created such a stir that it came to prominence.

We were busy arranging the next trip for another batch of our pilots, when a message came through from Oslo telling us to stop – there had been a protest from the Russians!

I had derived much pleasure from being in a squadron, and previously a whole wing, composed of different peoples from different countries, hearing their ideas and learning about their philosophies – what kind of a world were we hoping to achieve? We had a few Australians, a few New Zealanders, a few Canadians, and others from all over Britain. There was no divergence in our thinking. We were part of the British Empire, believed in the principles on which it was founded, and the world would be a better place for everyone if this concept could be promoted. Rhodesians were certainly in the forefront when it came to making a stand along those lines.

Suddenly there was a distinct change in the weather, winter was clearly approaching, so we flew to Oslo and spent a week there before returning to England.

The time had come to make plans for my return home and reunion with my family, for it had been a long break and a few anxious moments, on their side. Moreover, arrangements had to be made for my final year at university. I made the trip to London and visited our people at Rhodesia House in the Strand, and before the year was out was on a ship through the Mediterranean via Port Said to Durban, and straight on to a DC-3 for Bulawayo. The rains had come, the grass was so green – what a wonderful breath of fresh air.

24

DUDLEY SUTTON

'Morning, Shakespeare...'

I JOINED THE RAF in 1951, following a difficult period of teenage depression, living in digs and doing a boring job measuring bolts of cloth in the rag trade. I spent a large part of my free time watching really depressing films in small art cinemas in and around the West End, as they were often the only warm places in the long cold winters of bed-sitting-room London. I had seen a poster of a young pilot with two fighter aircraft forming a 'Vee-sign' vapour trail in the background and that did it.

My father, who had been in the RAF Regiment during the war, was furious that I was not trying for a commission. He had spent his time in the ranks, somehow educating three sons through the public school system, an advantage that he had not been able to enjoy, and could not see how anyone with my 'privileges' – privileges which had cost him so dear – would not take a commission, but preferred to serve in the ranks. The truth was that I was far too lazy to try to pass the exams (I had no qualifications as I'd had to leave public school early because of a temporary cash flow problem through his business at the time) and couldn't even do long division, let alone the maths required of the modern fighter pilot.

They must have been desperate for engine mechanics, because that was the course I was sent on after square-bashing at West Kirby. I was actually quite fascinated by the whole process; by living with twenty-odd blokes from totally different backgrounds, who spoke totally different English and frequently appeared to be far better educated than I – though I did understand what the officers were on about, because I was familiar with the tone. I was able to explain that when an officer comes into the work-place or the billet, and stands there flicking his fingers, looking sheepish and, if he was as young as were most of our officers, as like as not blushing as he speaks the immortal words 'Carry on chaps', he didn't know (a) what to say, (b) what he was supposed to say, (c) what to do and (d) what he was supposed to do.

It was thus that I became a sort of interpreter between the men and the officers. I doubt if the men would have put up with me as well as they did had I not been able to fulfil this important function and I am sure that this was why I was able to get away with so much, such as playing opera in the billet and quoting from plays that I did not understand but liked the sound of. I was already unconsciously in love with acting and I believed that it was the fact that this love was unconscious that was at the root of much of my depression.

Most of my life I had been involved in drama, either acting or designing sets and, upon being posted to No. 2 Air Navigation School at Thorney Island in Hampshire in 1952 to service the last of the few Wellington bombers still staggering through service, I was delighted to discover that the station boasted an Amateur Drama Society.

Wellington bombers were stunning. Supposedly one of the earliest uses of the geodesic system made so popular by the American architect Buckminster Fuller: astonishingly strong body frames but very light, with an almost egg-shaped cross section. I would sit in the cockpits for hours, day-dreaming secret night flights over enemy territory, to drop secret agents far behind enemy lines... One of my jobs was to stand within a few feet of the engines when they were being run up to maximum revs for warming up before take-off: one of us would have to stand there, often in the relentless drizzle, with a mobile fire extinguisher in our charge. As the engine reached very high revs, the tremendous sound would create a strange kind of vortex, like the middle of the maelstrom, when one enters a weird world of 'white' noise or anti-noise – the silence in the centre of the hurricane – and it was into this 'silence' that I began to spout speeches from Shakespeare which I was studying during the long periods of hanging about that is the engine mechanic's lot, especially in peace-time. The pilots must have thought I was crazy, the sergeants were pretty certain I was crazy, the blokes knew it. But, my God, it stood me in good stead later in life at the Royal Academy of Dramatic Art (no less!)

It was in the RAF that I learned to read – not that I was taught, I already knew how, but that I was given the space. Also, there was a very good young Education Officer at Thorney, bright and kind, who took me under his wing. Even our sergeant put up with my 'bookishness' with pretty good humour. 'If SAC Sutton would be kind enough to put the book down, we might endeavour to get these aircraft into the sky and save Britain from the Russians...' He was quite wicked really and could reduce the crew room to tears of laughter with a mere look.

One of his great delights, once he'd lined us all up on parade, was to walk up and down the line (there were only a few of us), peer deep into our eyes, make some wickedly cutting remark and yell at us if we so much as smiled. Whenever he came to me, knowing my habits, he'd say, 'Morning, Shakespeare, what have you got for us today?' Then he'd pull at my battledress blouse in the knowledge that there would be a book hidden there, a book that would slip to the ground, its pages fluttering in the wind. With a deep sigh and a 'Dear, oh dear, oh dear', he'd bend wearily down and scoop up the book, look at the title and sing out with great mock scorn: 'Oh Gor Blimey – *Ballet for Beginners!* Dear, oh dear, oh dear, better not let the Russians find out about this, my life, won't they be scared? For God's sake, put it away!' Then he'd do a couple of mock ballet steps away down the line.

There was never any malice in it, or in the billet, just amused tolerance at this nutcase with a squashed nose who used to go on stage at the Station Cinema, as often as not playing the love scenes in a comedy, holding in his arms the doe-eyed daughter of a squadron leader or a wing commander or a warrant officer: they were all doe-eyed and I was in love with them all, for all the good it did me – for a depressed and confused young mechanic, clearly in the wrong job, was not an exciting prospect for a Night Out.

The education officer sent me to drama classes in nearby Chichester, where I lived in terror that the blokes would come past, look into the street-level windows and see me prancing around a studio with a bunch of pre-pubescent girls, in a dance and mime class. Luckily that never happened – it would have taken more than a little explaining.

When the depressions became too great, following diagnosis of Manic Depression by the MO, I was allowed to buy myself out: or, at least, my father, whose fortunes had more than recovered, was allowed to buy me out and, hopefully, my squashed nose was about to be pointed in the right direction.

One of the people I had to see on my way out of the RAF was the education officer who had to help me to fill out a form and, when the question required me to answer as to what job I was going to do after leaving the RAF (this would still be a few months away), I told him that I hadn't the faintest idea. 'But you are going to be an actor,' he laughed. 'Everybody knows that.' And it all began to fall into place. I panicked: 'But how?' I asked. 'By applying to the Royal Academy of Dramatic Art,' he replied, as if it was the most obvious thing in the world. Fear leapt in my soul, 'But I can't go anywhere *Royal*,' I said, terrified at the grandiosity of the name Royal Academy etc. 'Well, you're in the *Royal* Air Force, aren't you, you twerp,' he laughed. 'Let's write them a letter, then you can take it to the *Royal* Mail and send it off.'

When I told them in the billet what I was going to do, they all laughed. 'What, with a face like that?' was the general feeling, but nobody said don't do it.

Three or four years later, I was so grateful for my time in the RAF and, thanks be to God, that I never did take a commission, because I came into the theatre at the great Renaissance called The Kitchen Sink, when writers from the working class sprang onto the scene for the first time, when actors appeared who had not been to Public School, when directors, designers, writers and actors who had not had commissions changed the face of the theatre and created the wonderful television and films that became the pride of post-war Britain in the fifties, sixties and seventies, and I, with my RAF experience of four years in the ranks, four years' amateur drama, four years of reading and dreaming and reciting Shakespeare in the company of Wellington bombers at maximum revs, was ready for them all, and one thing I was never to do when joining a cast of actors, writers, designers and directors from all walks of British life, was to stand in the middle of the floor, flicking my fingers, blushing and saying, 'Carry on chaps!'

25

LORD TEBBIT

'If you want Peace, Prepare for War'

IT WAS IN June of 1949 that I was called up as a National Serviceman into the Royal Air Force. I was just eighteen – and the RAF only thirteen years older. The Second World War had finished only four years earlier; the Cold War had just begun and the Korean War was soon to come.

Now, forty years later, many of the events of those days are still sharp and clear in my memory, but perhaps of even greater significance are many of the incidents and circumstances which completed the moulding of the character of the boy Tebbit into a man.

Because I left school at sixteen, the RAF became both my finishing school and university. In many ways it gave me much that university could not have done. I learned discipline, both how to take and to give orders and the two-way street of loyalty to both those of superior rank, from whom I took orders, and to those entrusted to my command. Events were kind to me and being selected to be one of the tiny élite of National Service pilots I learned the skills which gave me a living for almost twenty years. But the training of a combat pilot is not just a matter of acquisition of skills, it is a moulding of character. The process is not unlike the tempering of steel and I still harbour mixed feelings that I was not called upon to experience its final stage of service in action.

Looking back at those years, I am always struck by the sense that they were years of such enormous change, the completion of the transition from the pre-war to the post-war era. The weaponry, tactics, navigation, indeed the very aircraft, were (with the exception of the jet engine) no more than extensions of pre-war developments. Indeed, the whole business of flying was more like the art of pre-1939 aviation than the technology of today.

Of course that was hardly in my mind when, alongside a representative sample of my fellow eighteen-year olds from all classes and all parts of the country, I presented myself at RAF Padgate to become 2435575 Aircraftman Second Class Tebbit. We were, of course, all white, all culturally as well as technically British, all English-speaking even if at times the Scots and Geordies had difficulty in comprehending the rich accents of those from the far West Country.

The transition from a nonetheless motley civilian mixed ability crew of every class, character and ability, first into a homogeneous mix of disciplined

205

servicemen, then to be separated into the trades and skills, began at once. It must have been hardest for those from the most privileged backgrounds (although those from public schools had already undergone a not so different experience) but the cultural shock was quite sharp for all of us.

Within a week we had grasped the rudiments of Service life and the first great sifting process began. Together with those others who, like me, had volunteered for pilot training, I headed south again to RAF Hornchurch in Essex, the aircrew assessment centre. For several days we were interviewed, questioned, examined and required to display all kinds of mental and physical fitness and agility. At the end of it I was told that whilst I had not been found suitable for pilot training I would be accepted for any other aircrew category – subject of course to my willingness to enlist not for my two years of National Service but eight years as a regular officer. At eighteen, eight years is a lifetime, and with my heart set on journalism and politics, I thanked the RAF for its offer but said, no thank you.

So it was back to Padgate to continue basic training as a raw recruit, pounding the barrack square, learning the habit of discipline, the instant obedience to command, and the skills of weapon handling. The spit, the polish, the drill so bitterly resented by the ignorant are essential in welding a collection of ill-assorted individual civilians into a fighting force whose members can rely upon each other to react coolly and rationally under great stress and danger. The fighting formations may have changed from the eighteenth- and nineteenth-century redcoats' square to those of today, but discipline and training which prevent fear from becoming panic have not.

In retrospect I think that it is discipline, which gives steadiness under fire – literal or metaphorical – through the understanding and control of fear and the habit of two-way loyalty, which are the attributes that I am most grateful to have gained during my service career.

All that I came to realise much later. In the summer of 1949 things looked somewhat different from under the hat of an AC2 at Padgate, disappointed at being rejected for pilot training and practising that detachment of mind from body which makes military drill training bearable. Then it all changed. For reasons unexplained to this day, some half dozen of us were called from the barrack square to the adjutant's office to be told that we had been re-assessed. We were no longer rejects – we were acceptable for pilot training if we still wished to volunteer.

We would have volunteered for almost anything, even a jump into the fire, to escape the frying pan of Padgate – let alone volunteer for pilot training. Within days we had caught up with our colleagues to form No. 36 Pilot Course, RAF Wittering, ready to begin five months of ground training.

Our course concentrated on the basic knowledge required to fly and fight, aerodynamics, aero-engines, weapons, meteorology, navigation and, on military training, drill, weapon and combat training. Throughout the weeks and at the final examinations students fell out to be remustered into the flightless branches of the Service – a process of attrition that steadily trimmed our numbers right up to the time of joining our squadrons.

As officer cadets (the policy at the time was that all pilots should be commissioned) we lived in the officers' mess. Times were changing but officers were still expected to be gentlemen (even if they were not and never had been always so) and junior officers needed permission to marry or indeed 'live out', which was discouraged. Dining-in nights and guest nights were a mixture of the formal and the wildly disorderly requiring nice judgements on the part of cadets in particular in identifying the boundary between high spirits (to be encouraged) and hooliganism (to be deplored).

It was some three miles to the nearest town and even had we been able to afford cars (which, with two exceptions, we were not), as cadets we were not permitted to keep them on camp so most time off was spent on the station. Nor were we allowed to wear civilian clothes for our first three months and our distinctive white webbing belts and white cap bands often led to being misidentified as Service Police – which did not always lead to enhanced popularity amongst the many ex-servicemen in the town. However, with hard play and hard work the time passed rapidly and after a short break cooling my heels impatiently at home I was posted with the rest of 36P to RAF South Cerney in Gloucestershire – No. 2 Flying Training School.

Again I found myself in an air force in transition. South Cerney was the last all grass airfield to be used as an FTS. The redoubtable Tiger Moth had been retired and our basic trainer was the Percival Prentice, a great big rather ungainly 46-foot wingspan, low wing, fixed undercarriage tail dragger, with side by side seating for instructor and pupil as well as an observer's seat behind. It was certainly not overpowered by its 250 hp Gypsy Queen engine and its handling was stodgy rather than vibrant. It was difficult to fly it either really badly or really well, with aerobatics, particularly in the rolling plane, quite a challenge to perform well. Its outstanding characteristic was its spin. The Prentice stalled as one might well expect, with plenty of warning, shaking and rattling, then mushing away unless held tight. Then the nose drop; when it came, it was quite sharp. A decent touch of rudder or judiciously crossed controls would easily initiate a conventional spin in a steep nose down attitude. Recovery was swift, stick well forward and a boot of opposite rudder left one in a good steep dive with rapidly building airspeed. However, if left in the spin for more than five turns, the Prentice would suddenly lurch nose up and commence a slow flat spin, from which recovery was always slow, sometimes difficult and from time to time according to even experienced instructors who had baled out, quite impossible. At the very least it required full rudder and stick, sometimes rocking of the stick in time with opening and closing the throttle or even lowering of flap. Even at best recovery from the flat spin took several turns of anxious waiting.

My instructor, Bob Ross, did not bother one with such worrying thoughts as on a bright December day we prepared for my first flight – 'air experience'. In those days civilian flying was for a tiny minority, the days of mass travel were still years ahead and like almost all of my colleagues I had never been airborne. Would I be sick? Air-sickness on the big Boeings cruising smoothly at 35,000 feet may be a rarity today but the hardy passengers in unpressurised rattling piston-engined aircraft bouncing along in low level turbulence seemed almost to expect to be sick as part of the adventure of flying. Fortunately I kept control of my stomach – indeed to this very day the nearest I have been to air-sickness was but a couple of years ago whilst in a helicopter being buffeted by turbulence from strong winds in and out of a low cloud base, when I think had our arrival at Battersea been delayed another ten minutes I might have succumbed.

We managed a second flight that December day and by then I knew that more than anything else I wanted to win that most coveted of all badges, the RAF pilot's brevet.

Bob Ross was a good instructor – and a delightful man to know – and he soon brought me to understand my strengths and weaknesses as a pilot. I was not a natural, instinctive pilot, but a careful plodder. I had to understand why a plane reacted as it did, what forces acted on it, before I could work out how to make it obey my will. But within a dozen hours of instruction I had gone solo and from there progressed through basic training and on to the Harvard.

I owed a good deal to Bob Ross who went on to the Empire Test Pilots' School at Farnborough (where he won the McKenna Trophy) before being killed whilst test flying a Gloster Javelin all-weather fighter. Exploring the extremities of the flight envelope Bob Ross was unable to regain control and leaving it desperately late to bale out followed his aircraft into the River Severn estuary and was lost.

The Harvard and Prentice were really as chalk and cheese. With twice the power, shorter wingspan and crisp controls the Harvard could be flown beautifully – or with disastrous consequences. I think I achieved the latter condition rather more often than the former. Never having flown a single piston-engined fighter it is one of my regrets that neither Spitfire, Hurricane, Mustang nor Fury appear in my log books, but at least the Harvard felt like a proper fighter. The tail wheel undercarriage (conventional as opposed to tricycle we called it in those days) and the large diameter radial engine restricted the forward view on the ground necessitating regular swings of the nose from side to side whilst taxiing. The cockpit smelled of hot metal and engine oil, and on start-up – a marvellous ritual requiring three hands or a prehensile foot if the engine was cold – it coughed and spat as a real aero engine should. In fact I met no other engine like it until I flew the DC-7C many years later.

In short the Harvard was a 'real' aeroplane. If given its head it would bite. If mastered with positive but smooth handling it would obey the pilot's every whim. I explored every facet of its character – many such as the flick entry into the inverted spin or the common ground loop inadvertently.

During the Harvard phase of my training I sensed I was not far above the pass-fail line and was given a change of instructor. Barry Byrne, my new instructor, was a brilliant pilot, his forte being aerobatics in cloud. Since the airdriven gyro horizon and directional gyro toppled at such times, leaving one with airspeed, altimeter, P10 compass, turn and slip and rate of climb/descent, this was quite a challenge for Byrne's pupils. However, as he constantly reminded me, loss of control ended in either a spin or spiral dive. Provided, therefore, one learned how to deal with each of those there was nothing to worry about.

He was, of course, right and in due course I achieved my instrument rating and then in November 1950 my 'wings' and was commissioned as a pilot officer. All sorts of distinctions have come my way since but few – perhaps none – have compared with having been commissioned as a pilot in the Royal Air Force.

The passing out parade of 36 Pilot Course was a parting of the ways as we were allocated to fighters or 'heavies'. Some of us went to Middleton St George near Darlington for the Gloster Meteor conversion course, others to fly Oxfords in preparation for Transport or Bomber Command. Early in the new year I was posted to Middleton St George for conversion on to the Meteor. The only jet to see service on the Allied side during the war, the Meteor had taken the world's airspeed record at 616 mph in 1946. It was a combination of old and new technology. The Derwent engines were the harbingers of the jet age but the weapons and radios, aerodynamics and controls showed no advance over the Spitfires and Hurricanes of 1940. As to navigation systems – well, mental dead reckoning – map reading and radio bearings from ground DF stations were all we had.

At speeds of Mach .8 and with a low level endurance of little more than 30 minutes (although with belly and wing drop tanks one could make Malta with only one stop) Meteor flying in poor weather was always potentially exciting. The concept of reserve fuel was based on that of a missed approach and a tight circuit rather than a diversion, which encouraged concentrated thought and swift decision making.

There was a huge gap between the Harvard single piston-engined trainer and the Meteor twin jet fighter and it is a tribute to the instructors of the era (many of whom had little more jet experience than their pupils) that we did not suffer more casualties. Curiously I found myself at home with the Meteor quite quickly and it consolidated my love of flying. There was little controlled airspace in those days, and none at higher altitudes where we were free to roam at will with only other military traffic to share our freedom of the skies. I indulged in vast sprawling aerobatics, loops 10,000 feet and more in diameter over London, high speed runs from east coast to west pushing at the limits of the high speed envelope until at Mach .83 or .84 aileron snatching and pitching culminated in the Meteor rolling on to its back and plunging earthwards until warmer and thicker air reduced the Mach Number and restored control.

Even at altitude, high speeds sharply shortened endurance and in poor weather the high level QGH procedure was used for a quick return to base.

After being homed overhead at 30,000 feet by VHF DF we commenced the outbound leg of a teardrop turn to home back in, hopefully aligned with the runway in use.

At the commencement of the inbound turn we began a fearsomely hairy descent. With throttles closed and speed brakes out, initially at Mach .78 and then 350kts, the descent to 2,000 feet for the inbound run took less than three minutes during which the three pointers on the old-fashioned altimeters wound around at such speed that fatal misreading errors were all too common. Even on breaking cloud one's troubles were not always over as the cold soaked airframe often became covered in thick hoar frost which the windscreen de-icing system shifted all too slowly. If fuel permitted a blind low level run would burn off the ice; if not then a curved approach with an open hood gave a 1930s' flying club touch to the landing. Despite such hazards and the potentially fatal combination of powerful engines set well out on the wings giving the Meteor the asymetric characteristics of the de Havilland Mosquito only more so, it was an almost viceless aircraft, unbreakable (short of collision) in the air despite any amount of abuse and simple in the extreme.

Once I had learned (more or less) how to avoid letting my own aircraft kill me it was time to move on to the Operational Conversion Unit at Stradishall in Suffolk to be taught how to use the Meteor to kill one's enemy. There in a lovely English spring and early summer we learned to fight. We sweated pints flying in battle formation – the big wing tactics developed ten years earlier – in which the basic two-plane units deployed over a quite wide front would nonetheless be manoeuvered through sharp turns. Close formation take-offs and landings, gunnery, tail chasing and aerobatics were our daily diet until by June of 1951 we were ready to be posted to operational squadrons or back to civvy street.

I looked back at my two years with the fondest memories of comradeship and deepest gratitude to those who had taught me to fly – and in doing so made a man out of the boy who had been called up only two years earlier. Most of them were wartime pilots, some, like the Poles and Czechs, patriots still burning with hatred of Nazis and Communists alike who had plundered and enslaved their countries. Many were eccentrics still coming to terms with the end of the war. There was much hard drinking, bawdy sing-songing and frenetic wild parties, madcap driving and dangerous games, as they struggled to readjust from the hot to the cold war.

As I handed in my kit I thought that part of my life was over – but it was not to be. Flying 150 hp Chipmunk trainers in the RAFVR was thin gruel after such a rich diet and within six months I was in the cockpit of a Vampire of No. 604 (County of Middlesex) Squadron, Royal Auxiliary Air Force at RAF North Weald.

Happy as were my days in the RAF, my days as a 'weekender', flying first Vampires and then Meteor 8s were amongst the best of my life. The friends I made in those days remain friends forty years later. In my four years as an Auxiliary I survived a total write-off accident on take-off and a mid-air collision, not to mention all manner of Friday and Saturday evening parties – generally more hazardous than flying.

At the seventy-fifth anniversary of the RAF I hope that many other young men (and today even young women) will find in the RAF the comradeship, the challenges, the rewards and the sense of fulfilment from dedication to a profession and a cause – the defence of the United Kingdom – which I found in my time.

Per Ardua Ad Astra. Yes, but the motto I have carried through life remains equally valid: that of 604 Squadron, *Si Vis Pacem Para Bellum* (If you want peace, prepare for war). I trust my more recent erstwhile colleagues in Government keep the latter in mind.

26

DAVID TOMLINSON

Friday, 12th April 1957 – Undimmed from David Tomlinson's Subconscious

I LEARNED TO fly before the war on an Avro Tutor, a plane very similar to a Tiger Moth. My instructor was David Llewellyn who had made a record flight to South Africa. He was not only an excellent teacher but also a very kind and, most of all, patient man. Although to this day I remain nervous of heights, I had absolutely no fear of flying at all. I must though admit to a slight frisson when David first put the plane into a spin, a manoeuvre necessary when learning to control a plane in an emergency. At a safe height, about 5,000 feet, the aircraft is stalled by closing the throttle, pulling the nose up and then putting on full rudder. The result is that the plane goes spiralling down – round and round towards the ground. To come out of the spin you apply the opposite rudder and move the stick forward. The first time, as a pupil with David, I thought I would never be able to do it.

'It's the easiest manoeuvre you'll ever do,' David Llewellyn said.

I was relieved to find that what I had been taught did indeed work. The plane came out of its spin. Some aircraft are very difficult to control but not the lovely old biplanes. They behave beautifully.

I soloed and got my licence before I was twenty.

At the end of 1940 I enlisted in the RAF, just a hair's breadth ahead of conscription. My experience in the Guards had made me very reluctant to get involved with the military again, but war was a different matter. This time I wanted to fly, but at first I was posted to Newchurch on Romney Marsh, not all that far from Folkestone. I was on radio location duty (the forerunner of radar), tracking aircraft that came into English airspace. I longed to be a pilot – after all, I already had a flying licence – and was at last selected for flying training in Canada.

There, I was first stationed at Assiniboia, Saskatchewan. The nearest cities had very evocative names – Moose Jaw and Maple Creek. Assiniboia itself seemed the prototypical one-horse town.

I did my elementary flying training in a Fairchild Cornell, a Canadian-built version of the USAAF PT-19 and PT-26 primary trainers, and not unlike the Miles Magister to look at except that it had enclosed cockpits. I passed the course and was sent on to Weyburn for further training. There we flew Harvards. At the end of the course I got my 'wings' and was commissioned as a pilot officer and put in charge of twenty-seven sergeant pilots.

It would have been reward enough for my six months of diligence to get my 'wings' but there was more: We were chosen to do a goodwill tour of Canada.

Back in England, I spent the rest of the war at Booker, near High Wycombe, as a flying instructor under our charming commanding officer Wing Commander O'Donnell. Life there was delightful.

Twice I was seconded to a film unit.

The first film was *Journey Together*, a Ministry of Information film, written by Terence Rattigan and directed by John Boulting. Only three civilians appeared in it – Ronald Squire, Bessie Love and Edward G. Robinson, who arrived by bomber from the States and took no salary for his role.

The other film I made while still in uniform was *The Way to the Stars*. Once again I was directed by Anthony Asquith. It was the story of an RAF bomber station and about the co-operation between British and American forces in Britain. Even before the filming started we all realised thankfully that the war would be over before it was shown. Terence Rattigan wrote the screenplay.

In 1946 I was demobilised, and I returned to acting.

It was Friday, 12th April 1957. A distant relation who lived near by was eager to fly so I took him to Luton Aero Club and I hired a Tiger Moth. To keep your pilot's licence active you have to fly so many hours a year. I was therefore quite keen on the flight. Since the war I had done about seventy hours of flying and I still loved it. I have never forgotten when David Llewellyn took me above the clouds. It was a magical experience.

We took off with me in the front cockpit as in my instructor days. My passenger was in the seat behind me. We flew over Mursley and then southeast of the village climbed to about five thousand feet and did a loop. We then did a slow roll. After that I went into a shallow dive and levelled out at about three thousand feet. All I remember is feeling peculiar. The next thing I remember was waking up and I was lying in the hall of Brook Cottage.

The plane had crashed into a spinney at the bottom of my garden. It had landed upside-down. The engine was completely torn away and embedded in the ground. The wings were shattered.

I had blacked out. I knew it could happen when you are doing aerobatics. The blood rushes to the head and this was obviously the cause of my passing out. But it had never happened to me before in an aeroplane. My passenger, helpless in the back seat, was terrified. He thought the plane was skimming the trees rather too close for comfort.

'Aren't we cutting it a bit fine?' he asked nervously over the intercom. I heard nothing.

He looked forward and it seemed to him, according to evidence that he subsequently gave, that I was in a perfectly normal position but when he leaned forward, he could see that my head was slumped forward and I was out cold. We then hit the trees.

Neighbours pulled me out of the demolished Tiger Moth and my passenger emerged, still conscious and unscathed. I had concussion and was taken immediately to hospital, with my wife Audrey trailing anxiously behind the ambulance. But it was really a precaution. I was bruised and had a slight haematoma and that was it. Of course, if the trees had not cushioned the crash, the plane would have gone straight into the ground and it would have been a very different story. We were very lucky.

'David Tomlinson pulled out of this – ALIVE', screamed one newspaper headline framing a photograph of a very dilapidated Tiger Moth, the following day. I hoped that its readers would not share the apparent disappointment! But it was no laughing matter. Officialdom stepped in and I was presented with summonses alleging:

1. I operated an aircraft in a negligent manner so as to endanger life or property.
2. I flew over a congested settlement below fifteen hundred feet.
3. I flew closer than five hundred feet to structures at Mursley.
4. I carried out an aerobatic flight over a populated area.

All of these charges were totally false – but I could understand how they had come about. If I had had a pupil who crashed near his home my reaction would have been simple: I would have had a suspicion that he had been showing off to his family. However, I was not an inexperienced pilot. I was a middle-aged, ex-training instructor who knew better than to take chances. I was not a fool and I was certainly not suicidal. I had flown over the vicinity of the house at a safe height. I had enough experience to know that in a Tiger Moth you can't loop and spin unless you are at a safe height because it always loses height performing aerobatics. A Tiger Moth is not like a Pitts Special. That's a high-powered aircraft and if you are clever you can do aerobatics in one of these aircraft quite near the ground. In a Tiger Moth you don't attempt any at less than four to five thousand feet. Still, I could understand the accusations. Even my brother Peter, an experienced Spitfire pilot during the war, should have known me better. He wrote to me and said, 'What the hell were you up to?'

The only person who stood by me absolutely staunchly was my ex-commanding officer, Wing Commander O'Donnell, who believed everything I told him. He knew how proud I was of my abilities as a pilot and he also knew that with my experience flying Tiger Moths I wasn't likely to kill myself in one.

The wheels of justice then as now ground slowly. My hearing was not to be until the autumn. Audrey and I went down to Folkestone to stay in a small hotel where I could recuperate from the concussion and watch my bruises heal out of sight.

My father, a solicitor, represented me at the committal proceedings when the local magistrates took depositions from various witnesses. He had no real pretence to advocacy and knew that the inherent weaknesses in the police case were best left uncovered until my trial at Aylesbury Quarter Sessions. Undoubtedly he was right but I found it frustrating to listen to apparently uncontradicted assertions by the Prosecutor and some of the witnesses with which I profoundly disagreed. I was depicted as having done a classic 'beat-up'.

On Tuesday, 1st October 1957, I faced the four charges of dangerous flying at Aylesbury, pleading not guilty on all counts. It was a worrying time.

Mr Peter Lewis prosecuting retreated a little from the 'beat-up' aspect preferred by his predecessor before the Justices. He said to the jury: 'What Mr Tomlinson was doing over Mursley was *possibly* for the benefit of Mrs Tomlinson and the family...' Then he added that my general method of flying 'was so negligent and careless that there was a likelihood of danger to life and property'.

I knew that was untrue but would I be believed?

The hearing lasted two days. Audrey was in court. My father had briefed F. H. Lawton, QC, later to be Lord Justice Lawton. A blue and red toy plane was produced so that witnesses could demonstrate what they had seen. The sight of grown-ups swirling the toy through the air demonstrating as they stood in the witness box what they said I had done would have been comical had it not been so serious. One witness said that she had seen the Tiger Moth over the fields beyond the house. She gyrated the toy plane in an impossible and unlikely demonstration of how she had seen it go higher.

'The engine just seemed to stop and it just twirled down,' she said. Down plummeted the toy. More helpfully, it was said that at no time was the plane seen to perform stunts over the village.

Luton Flying Club's chief instructor testified that he was completely satisfied with my competence to fly.

The film of *Three Men in a Boat* had recently opened and in it I had given one of my dim-witted upper-class twit performances as 'J'. Jimmy Edwards and Laurence Harvey were the other two men in this adaptation of Jerome K. Jerome's classic which turned the polite humour of the original into a successful comedy.

Fred Lawton told the jury, 'When you earn your living playing the fool, you like a rest when you get home. That is just the position with Mr Tomlinson. You must not think for one moment that because he earns his living playing the fool for our entertainment that he plays the fool when he is at home. You may think that a man of Mr Tomlinson's age – he is now about forty – married with young children – that the last thing he is going to do is to risk his life and the life of a passenger in the way the prosecution has described. You will hear that if Mr Tomlinson was, in fact, doing what the prosecution witnesses said he was doing he was clearly risking his life – virtually committing suicide. No experienced pilot with Mr Tomlinson's knowledge of flying, especially in Tiger Moths, in which for many years during the war he taught many pupils to fly, would have behaved in the way suggested in this court.'

I was cross-examined and told the court exactly what had happened.

'My first manoeuvre was a loop. Then I did a slow roll. I was then over four thousand five hundred feet. I was not over the village at any time. Later I went into a dive and levelled out over two thousand five hundred feet. Then I didn't feel completely well and decided to fly level to recover myself. I was never closer than one thousand yards to the village. I decided to return to Luton and told my passenger. I remember nothing after that.'

The Chairman, summing up for the jury, said: 'Mr Tomlinson is an experienced flyer and is not likely to have done stunts over his own house to show off.'

The jury was out for forty-two minutes and brought back a verdict of not guilty on all counts. My father gave me the thumbs up. The tension of the last six months was gone and I was believed. The jurors, to a man and woman, requested autographs. I felt very peculiar signing autographs in court.

Audrey took the toy plane home from the court for the children and I was at the Westminster Theatre as usual that night, in time for the curtain-up.

Looking back now, I find it hard to understand why the decision was made to charge me, notwithstanding the close proximity between the spot where the plane came down and my home. Long before I was *compos mentis*, my passenger had said that I was clearly unconscious and this was reported the day after the crash. He continued to talk to the press and one remark was reported in a most unfortunate way in the *Daily Telegraph and Morning Post* the day after the verdicts: 'I think he will not fly so low again.'

I had just been acquitted of deliberately doing that!

The *Daily Mail* got it right. He had said: 'I don't think he will ever fly solo again, just in case it should happen a second time.'

But he was wrong. One day, later on, I was making a film on location at an aerodrome near Elstree. There was a pilot there with a Tiger Moth.

'Can I do a circuit and landing?' I asked him.

He had never seen me before in his life.

'Certainly,' he said.

So off I went. I did a perfect three-point landing and it was just like old times.

27

SIR GEORGE WALLER

Five Years in Coastal Command

WHEN I WAS at Cambridge I had friends who joined the University Air Squadron and I thought of applying to join. However my spare time was already taken up with rugby football or rowing or other such matters and I discovered that I could join the Reserve of Air Force Officers (the RAFO) and be taught to fly during the University Long Vacation. My application was successful and in 1931 I joined for five years; I learnt to fly at Hatfield, being paid as an acting pilot officer while doing so, and completed 50 hours flying on Tiger Moths. Then six months later I had to learn to fly an operational type and did 12 hours on a DH-9J, a relic of the First World War but then still in service in India. For the next four years I had to report and do twenty hours' flying each year.

I did not renew my commission in 1936, though the international crisis in 1938 made me join the RAFVR. When the war came, however, I had not flown for three years. I was called up in September 1939 and was posted to Cranwell in January 1940 to learn about single wing aircraft, with two engines, flaps, superchargers and retractable undercarriages, which had not come my way in 1936. I completed 100 hours flying on Oxfords including 2 hours night flying and landings.

When I finished at Cranwell I was keen to get on to flying boats and I opted for a General Reconnaissance course as a first step to Coastal Command. I was posted to the School of General Reconnaissance in Guernsey to do a GR course. The course had only been going for a week or so when France fell and the school had to leave the island. A week or so later it reopened at Blackpool. I duly completed the course, having done, in addition to lectures and desk work, 50 hours' flying as a navigator-passenger. I finished in the top two or three thereby hoping to get on to flying boats, but instead was posted to 502 Squadron, an Anson squadron just about to be reequipped with Whitleys which were then to do similar work to flying boats although they were landplanes. Our aircraft were equipped with a new development in radar known as ASV Mk2. When flying at about 500 feet this was designed to detect a surfaced U-boat or a ship at a range of 15–20 miles. In the winter of 1940–1 this gave rise to great expectations. These expectations can be judged by the fact that on one occasion there was a telephone call from the prime minister, Mr Churchill, asking why we only had ten (out of fifteen) aircraft serviceable. In fact this was normal with the way our flying and maintenance was planned.

At first we carried anti-submarine bombs which had to be dropped from a minimum height of 500 feet, but later we were equipped with 250lb depth charges which made it possible to fly much lower, usually around 50 feet, and attack with greater accuracy. Sadly the squadron did not attack many U-boats, but we were consoled by being told that this was because U-boats saw us before we saw them and had to dive. This being before the days of the Schnorkel meant that the submerged speed would be about 3 knots instead of 16–18 on the surface and accordingly the U-boat would be delayed and would not be able to meet the convoy it was hoping to attack. It would also reduce its fuel and therefore its time at sea.

We were not able to fly quite as far as the flying boats but we could fly to about 20° west. We were stationed in Northern Ireland at Aldergrove, and later Limavady and did not suffer attacks from enemy aircraft because our flying was west of Ireland out over the Atlantic. We flew north from Lough Foyle and then west. The last sight of land was of Tory Island off the north-west of Ireland. Our sorties were eight to ten hours in length and accordingly we would not see land again for at least five or six hours. Each aircraft did carry an inflatable dinghy which would be available if an engine failed. Whitleys didn't go far on one engine!

Morale among the aircrews was an important factor. The squadron had been flying Ansons in the Irish Sea in daylight and the change to the Atlantic in all weathers and partly in darkness in a more powerful aircraft but one that could not maintain height if one engine failed, was a substantial change. Furthermore there were few visible achievements to counterbalance the long hours of flying in all weathers. Between late 1941 and mid-1942, our squadron sank just two U-boats and damaged three others.

The squadron had a new squadron commander and although he flew a substantial number of hours on operations he was faced with a problem. I captained one of three crews detached for some weeks to Wick in the north of Scotland and when we returned to Limavady we found morale in the squadron very low and the CO was not popular. A few weeks later one crew took off during the night for a scheduled flight of seven or eight hours. Three-quarters of an hour after taking off the aircraft returned and the squadron commander who lived nearby heard it and went down to the airfield to see the pilot and find out what had happened. The pilot said that he had returned because one engine was misfiring. The CO said that was rubbish, an excuse that was being given too often. The pilot, a pilot officer, and a young stockbroker in peacetime, was very upset. The following morning the pilot was in the mess when a message arrived that the CO wished to see him. He reported to the CO who apologised to him and said, 'Please forgive me. This is something that happens too often and investigation shows that there is nothing wrong. But you were absolutely right to come back. There was trouble in that engine.'

The pilot went back to the mess where he said, 'If the wing commander is prepared to apologise to me, a pilot officer, then he is good enough for me.'

This marked a turning point in the popularity and respect of the CO and of the morale of the squadron. So much so that some months later when there was a rumour that he was going to be posted, there was nearly a mutiny!

We flew with a crew of six, captain, second pilot, navigator, radio operator, front gunner and rear gunner. The radio operator and the navigator were the principal operators of the ASV. It was part of everybody's duty in daylight to look out for enemy U-boats and for shipping. Our aircraft had an automatic pilot and once the course was set the pilots too would have plenty of time to keep such a lookout. If our duty was to meet a convoy then of course our duty was to find the convoy and its escort and having found it we had to pay particular attention to the area ahead of the convoy. Our radar was a great help as it would detect a convoy or its escort 50 miles away. There was, of course, radio silence so navigation depended on dead reckoning in the first place. We had to make regular checks by measuring the wind speed and direction. To achieve this it was necessary to divert sixty degrees from course in one direction and then check the drift. Having done that to change back by a hundred and twenty degrees and check the drift. Then go back to the original course and check the drift. The three drifts would enable the navigator to work out the direction of the wind. The navigator would plot our position and revise our course and direction; he could check our position at night by astro navigation. We could also check our latitude at midday by sun sights.

Aircraft returning from the Atlantic were the sole source of information about weather approaching the British Isles from the west. We were always asked to report on the weather which we had experienced and we were asked to obtain the barometric pressure at the limit of our sortie. This was done by flying very low and resetting the altimeter; not very accurate but better than nothing at all. On our return having regard to the radio silence we were always concerned about the identity of the landfall because that would enable us to set course for base. We had to avoid flying over the Irish Free State because it was neutral. At night, however, if necessary we flew over Ireland and no exception was taken. The lights of towns and villages told us exactly where we were. The risks were not very great though the strain of long flights 300 miles from land at about 1,500 feet or less in an aircraft that would not maintain height if one engine failed did increase as time went by.

Our tour of duty was 500 hours on operations. The experience was entirely different from other commands in the RAF where contact with the enemy was much more frequent and the risks were far greater. Nevertheless the strain of the work we did was such that the satisfactory completion of the tour was a great relief giving one a break from operational work. I completed my tour in just over thirteen months. Most of my flying was without incident but there were some experiences which it is worth recording.

During our detachment to Wick I had one narrow escape. We were at Wick to do a regular patrol across to Iceland and back, searching for U-boats sailing into the Atlantic from Kiel or Bergen. On one occasion we were returning to Wick in low cloud, flying at less than 1,000 feet, able to see the sea below but with no visibility ahead at all. We should have been aiming for a landfall at the eastern part of the north coast of Scotland, passing about 50 miles north of Cape Wrath. My navigator, who was at that time not very experienced, had given me the course to fly. I had queried it, but was assured it was correct. I continued on course but unhappy about the course because of the hills in the north of Scotland. A little while later feeling more unhappy, I said, 'Are you sure the course is right?' He replied, 'Good God, I've forgotten the variation', ie, an error of 14 degrees. Having regard to all the hills in the north of Scotland I immediately turned and flew due north until he had worked out the course correctly. When he had done this, we later made a landfall near Wick and landed at Wick. In being debriefed I was told, 'You must be the aircraft that turned north just off Cape Wrath.' It is difficult to say what 'just off' involves, but it probably means in less than two minutes we would have flown into the side of Cape Wrath – a very lucky escape.

I remember being sent to provide an anti-submarine escort for the battleship *King George V* with the C-in-C Home Fleet in command returning after the sinking of the *Scharnhorst*. When we were approaching the neighbourhood of the KGV we encountered a German bomber aircraft, a He111, which immediately disappeared into cloud. When we were in sight of the KGV we attempted to signal a warning by Aldis lamp without success. The signal from Flying Officer Waller to C-in-C Home Fleet was never received!

There was another occasion when we were sent to escort the ill-fated HMS *Hood*, which we did. Nothing happened but it was a change from the normal anti-submarine patrol.

One day I was detailed to join a submarine, *H-31*, in Londonderry to take part in some trials of the Leigh light, a searchlight installed on the wing of a Wellington to enable a low level attack to be made on a U-boat at night. I joined the submarine and met the CO. He asked me if I had ever dived before. I said I had not but would be interested to do so if necessary. After dark the submarine went to sea in Lough Foyle and the aircraft was going to make six runs over the submarine going in various directions and putting on the searchlight as it approached so as to light up the submarine as it approached and flew over. The aircraft made four approaches lighting up the submarine each time. On the fifth run the plan was that the submarine would dive as the aircraft came in. However when the aircraft completed the fourth run it signalled that that was the end. 'Good,' said the submarine skipper, 'we don't need to dive. Oh, I'm sorry, you wanted to dive.' I replied, 'No thank you. I was ready if I had to, but not otherwise.'

We returned to base and on the way I told him that if he would like to fly at any time it could easily be arranged if he rang me at Limavady. He replied, 'Me fly? No thank you. Not without a direct order from their Lordships at the Admiralty.' Each man to his taste!

In due course I completed my tour. The same crew had flown with me for the whole of the thirteen months and each member would be finishing his tour at the same time. Often the flight was uneventful and, if the weather was good, making a landfall which we were expecting. But sometimes in bad weather the landfall was not where it should have been and we had to identify the error produced by strong winds. The completion of 500 operational hours was, in my case at any rate, a relief and I was grateful to stop for the time being.

On completion I was posted to a staff job at HQ 19 Group Coastal Command at Plymouth. This was the location of a joint Naval/Air Force headquarters. 19 Group was responsible, under HQ Coastal Command, for anti-submarine activities to the south into the Bay of Biscay and into the Atlantic to the west of Cornwall and South Wales. The work was largely routine and my personal duties were concerned with the state of training of the squadrons in the group. The squadrons were located in airfields in Devon and Cornwall and South Wales. There was a Communication flight at the airfield at Roborough, outside Plymouth, and flying the Miles Mentor or a Tiger Moth, both single-engined light aircraft, was a rather nice change from a Whitley.

I had to visit the various squadrons in the group, sometimes on my own, sometimes in the Mentor with the AOC as my passenger. I had one rather unfortunate experience. The AOC rang me to say he wanted to go to Carew Cheriton, in South Wales. I checked and found that his aircraft was not available. I told the AOC, and he told me to find another one. I could only find a Tiger Moth which had not been flown for a few days. I told the AOC and he said, 'We'll go in that one.' In due course we took off and at 300 feet the engine cut. There were quite a few scattered trees round Roborough airfield which presented a problem, but I remembered the lesson never to turn back. So we carried on into wind and finally crashed on a tree. Neither of us was hurt and the AOC said that I must go home for the rest of the day and he would go back to do some work. Whether the engine stopped because of water in the petrol (because the aircraft had not been flown recently) or because I pressed the wrong lever has never been established!

The most satisfactory thing about the work in 19 Group Headquarters was that while I was there aircraft with the Leigh light became operational in 19 Group and one was able to learn about the initial success of attacks on U-boats leaving port on the French coast and attempting to cross the Bay of Biscay on the surface by night. The tactical result was that such U-boats had to try and dive before such an attack took place. Usually, the first the U-boat crew knew of the aircraft was the sudden blinding light. Diving reduced the number of successful attacks but also seriously delayed the U-boat's approach to the Atlantic.

When I had been at 19 Group HQ for some nine months I was ready to go back to a squadron and was wondering where it would be. I felt flattered when I was posted to Headquarters Coastal Command. I rather expected that this would be a twelve month stint and then back to flying, but this was not to be. My immediate boss, the Command Training Officer, said I was not going before him and I was at Headquarters until the end of the war.

At HQCC I had been promoted to wing commander and was number 2 in the Training branch headed by the Command Training Officer. We were responsible for the Coastal Command OTUs and we shared responsibility with the Personnel Department for the posting of trained crews to the appropriate squadrons and for the posting of individuals when particular flying experience was required. Every now and again there was a query about some crew, whether it was to go overseas or not. If for some reason one crew was not to go, then another had to be sent in its place. One day I had a telephone call from a member of staff at the Air Ministry. The Secretary of State's son was finishing at OTU and he wished to know where his son was going. I made some comment about having to alter his posting. The answer on the telephone was, 'Certainly not. On no account is any alteration to be made. His son will not tell him where he is going as he regards it as secret. The S of S just wants to know.'

Another telephone call was from my old squadron commander who had been promoted and was in charge of a unit concerned with the towing of gliders, with Whitley pilots. He said who he was and then said, 'What the hell do you mean by sending Flying Officer X to this unit?' I said, 'Well, you asked for a Whitley pilot, I knew he had had considerable experience as a Whitley pilot, and there was no adverse report.' He said, 'But you knew he is no good. He was one of those who flew round Tory Island for five hours instead of going out on his Atlantic patrol.' I did not know this, but it explained a great deal about the morale in the squadron and how he, as squadron commander, had identified the undesirables and eliminated them.

The HQCC Communication Flight was stationed at RAF Northolt and the Coastal Command OTUs and other units which we had to visit were located at various places all over the British Isles. I had made a private resolution that I would if possible make all visits by air flying myself. And I was very reluctant to cancel a visit once arranged. One such visit stands out in my mind. I was going to visit Stornoway and I was going to fly round the north of Scotland thereby avoiding most of the mountains. I flew from Northolt to Dyce where I landed to refuel. I had got my weather report before I left. It was not very good for the early part of my flight, but a good forecast for Stornoway and the Hebrides. While I was being refuelled at Dyce I thought I would just check the weather. It was similar to my original forecast but a bit worse. I decided to go on and said so to the Met man. He said, 'You go directly against my advice.'

I took off with those words ringing in my ears. I flew north from Dyce and was soon in cloud and flying over the hills before reaching the north coast. I flew further north than my estimate of the coast and then came down through the cloud until I could see the sea below. Once I was below the cloud base I could see a long way in all directions but no sign of land. I flew west and then south, still no sign. I was responsible for all accident reports in the Command

and the longer I continued not knowing where I was, the more I imagined a court of inquiry with the Met officer giving evidence and saying, 'I told him he was flying definitely against my advice.' I flew on and on. The clouds disappeared and the sun was shining and there in the distance were the Hebrides and I landed at Stornoway in perfect 'staff officer's weather', not a cloud in the sky.

The day to day work which I had to do was not concerned directly with operations and therefore did not provide many interesting recollections. There was one, however, which has always remained in my memory. The Command was about to have a Liberator squadron doing anti-submarine work, and the question arose as to what should be the operational tour. The Whitley tour of 500 hours in 502 Squadron was mentioned and I was told my chances of surviving the whole tour had been 50%. I said that is ridiculous, it was much safer than that. I was told I was wrong and that I should bear in mind that the chances of surviving a tour in Bomber Command were 4%. I have never forgotten that figure.

In September 1945 I was demobilised, made a fresh start at the Bar and have never again piloted an aircraft I am sorry to say.

28

KENNETH WOLSTENHOLME

Pathfinder

WHY DID I join the Royal Air Force? That is a question most airmen have asked themselves during their time in the Service. As for me, I went voluntarily, unpushed and uninvited.

It was at the time of the Munich crisis. Just about everyone was convinced the Second World War was inevitable, despite the promise of 'peace for our time'. Only the *Daily Express* believed that 'there will be no war this year, next year or in the foreseeable future.'

Now any ex-serviceman will advise you against volunteering for anything, but I reasoned that at my tender age of eighteen I would be among the first to be called up so I decided it would be for the best if I chose the Service I was to join. The Royal Navy was out immediately. The only sailing I had ever done was in a rowing boat on Heaton Park lake near Manchester and I reckoned that war was going to be bad enough without the risk of seasickness. The Army didn't last much longer. If I had to go to war I couldn't see why I should walk there.

So the RAF it was. I joined the Royal Air Force Volunteer Reserve and began learning to fly Tiger Moths (one of the greatest flying machines ever built) at Barton Airport just outside Eccles, the town near Manchester which gave us the famous cakes. Every Saturday and Sunday, we fliers of the future met in a flying club atmosphere. We studied the theory of flight and for one 30-minute spell – two if you were really lucky – we would be in the air actually flying.

It was a wonderful way to spend a weekend, and to make it more wonderful we were paid the princely sum of 10s 6d a day, which is $52\frac{1}{2}$p in modern money. On top of that, even though we had no uniforms, we were immediately given the rank of sergeant pilot, a distinct advantage when war actually broke out.

Break out it did. On Friday, 1st September 1939, Poland was invaded by the Germans and Britain mobilised its forces. On the wireless, which is what we called the radio in those days, all members of the RAF Volunteer Reserve were ordered to report to their town centres immediately, so I packed my bag (although I hadn't the faintest idea what I should take), said farewell to the family, which included a very tearful mother, and caught the bus to Manchester.

What happened next was pure farce, right out of a Robb Wilton sketch. We keen, but rather fearful, young lads turned up to be met by a warrant officer and an airman who were completely nonplussed because no one had told them what to do with this influx of youngsters of doubtful talent. But give the warrant officer his due. He pulled himself together and showed us why a warrant officer was more feared in the RAF than the Chief of the Air Staff. He got us 'fell in', proceeded to bring us to 'attention', then to 'stand at ease' and finally to 'stand easy'. (There is a subtle difference between the latter two although we didn't know it at the time!) He then repeated the whole procedure... and finally asked, 'Could you all come back tomorrow morning?'

All it needed was Captain Mainwaring and the cast of *Dad's Army* and we would have been in business.

Anyway, I had left home at half-past six in the evening and I was back home by ten o'clock. My mother looked at me as if I had settled the crisis on my own... and then she burst into tears again.

Saturday, and it was back to Manchester for a few more rounds of 'Attention... stand at ease... stand easy' before we were sent home once more and asked to report again at nine o'clock on the Sunday morning. By this time even my mother was beginning to see the funny side of it all, but Sunday, 3rd September 1939 was for real.

This time, standing to attention, we sergeant pilots, dressed in our various assortments of 'Sunday Best', heard Neville Chamberlain, the then Prime Minister, utter those fateful words, 'And that consequently this country is at war with Germany'.

Then we went home to have Sunday dinner with our families.

In fact it was a few weeks before any of us left home, and when we did it wasn't to climb into some aeroplane but to go to what was called an Initial Training Wing. I was posted to Trinity Hall, Cambridge – yes, the University – where I met a dreadful man called Warrant Officer Tynan, whose sadism put Hitler to shame.

For hours on end he had us marching up and down, about-turning, wheeling and should an aircraft fly over us he would order us to look up as he barked, 'That's the real Royal Air Force and you might be part of it one day.' Then it was back to marching, saluting, about-turning and so on.

Any one of us would gladly have strangled Warrant Officer Tynan, but I was glad no one did. For it was only after I had left ITW that I realised what a great man he was. It was he who taught us discipline, he who turned young boys into young men, and he who made sure that we all had the grounding we were going to need so much in the future. He wasn't the sadist we thought. Just the opposite, in fact. He tried to follow the fortunes of we 'amateurs' who had been trained by him, and I received from him a congratulatory message when I was commissioned as a pilot officer and also when I was first awarded the Distinguished Flying Cross. That is the sort of man he was, and if he is still alive and reads this I would just like to say to him, 'Thank you for all you did for us.'

My first posting away from Cambridge was to Sywell, near Northampton, where I continued flying Tiger Moths. I had flown solo before the war and only those who have learned to fly will know the feeling when the instructor takes off his harness, gets out of the aircraft and says, 'You're on your own now.'

That is when near panic sets in. Your mouth goes dry, your hands clammy and you pray. But there is no finer moment than when you feel the wheels settle onto the ground – never mind the odd bounce – and you have done it. You have flown solo.

I wasn't to know it then but my short time at Sywell was to play a part in my post-war career.

From Sywell I went to Shawbury in Shropshire to do twin-engine training on Airspeed Oxfords, which I seem to remember had the gliding angle of a brick. But it could have been worse. I could have been posted onto Ansons, whose undercarriage had to be wound up and down manually instead of operated hydraulically. And you don't need two guesses who would do the manual labour – over 100 turns, if I remember aright – the pupil or the instructor.

Mind you, I did fly Ansons on one of my rest periods from an operational squadron. It was at Millom, just outside Barrow and my job was to fly the aircraft navigated by pupils just arrived from training in Canada. These navigators came to Millom with no experience of wartime conditions, and the first thing which hit them was the lack of lights on the ground. This put a high premium on their dead reckoning because to the north of the airfield was the menacing Black Coombe mountain, to the south was Barrow's balloon barrage. Mind you, we had the same sort of worry at Shawbury with the Wrekin too close for comfort.

My first operational posting was to 107 Squadron of No. 2 Group. We were stationed at Wattisham in Suffolk and equipped with Blenheims which had a crew of three, pilot, navigator and air gunner. According to the propaganda they could do 300 mph. My recollection is that 200 mph was the maximum, and that was with full throttle and nose down!

We were soon moved north on attachment to Leuchars in Scotland, and my first experience of a crash was at a neighbouring station, Crail. I wrote off one side of the undercarriage. No one was hurt, but the Station Commander came down to see what had happened. He rested his right hand on the pitot head underneath the nose of the aircraft and suddenly let out a scream of pain. In my haste to get out of the aircraft I had forgotten to switch off the pitot head heater and the burn across the Station Commander's hand did nothing for my popularity.

We later moved south again to Great Massingham, Norfolk, a satellite station of RAF West Raynham. It was from here that the squadron resumed its low level attacks on shipping and inland targets in Holland or France, but not before we had taken on the locals in a cricket match which we were bound to win because one of our pilots was Pilot Officer W. J. Edrich ... yes, Bill Edrich of that formidable Edrich-Compton partnership for England and Middlesex.

One day the squadron was called upon to make a low-level attack on the heavily fortified island of Heligoland. I remember we were briefed to abandon the operation if we came across any flak ships, which, as their name implies, were ships bristling with guns and which maintained excellent radio contact with the mainland to warn of any impending attack.

We flew at 50 feet across the North Sea in tight formation and a few miles from Heligoland met quite a number of flak ships, which opened fire. For a few seconds there were aircraft and flak bursts everywhere and I suddenly found myself flying at top speed towards a steep cliff.

I pulled back on the control column and managed to clear the cliff but the next second there was a tremendous explosion and the cockpit was full of acrid smoke. By the time enough of it had cleared to allow me to see we were almost across the island. Once over the sea, I turned left and hot-footed it towards home. It was only then that I noticed the damage to the front of the aircraft and that my navigator had half his head blown away.

I saw two other homeward-bound Blenheims and flew over to join them – there is safety in numbers – but one of them ditched in the sea. I seem to remember that the pilot's name was Ratcliffe. The other was piloted by Roy Ralston and navigated by Syd Clayton. Roy climbed to about 2,000 feet, circled the ditched aircraft and sent out a plain language radio message so that the German air-sea-rescue service could get a fix on the ditched aircraft and come out to rescue the crew. That was typical of Roy and Syd, whose bravery and teamwork became a legend in 2 Group.

I was now left to my own devices but managed to get home and land at West Raynham, our parent station, but there was nothing that could be done for my navigator, a New Zealander called 'Polly' Wilson. He had been killed instantly.

I don't think I ever knew Polly's real name. Come to think of it, my gunner was always known as 'Tich' Tales. He was later killed in action. It is surprising how many people were known only by their nicknames. Offhand, I can remember 'Tug' Wilson and 'Junior' Ruskell and the last navigator I had was an Australian called 'Pip' Piper. He would never reveal his real first name. He came from the beautiful West Australian city of Perth and every week got from home a copy of *The Perth Mirror*, a Saturday night newspaper which made our modern *Sunday Sport* seem like a parish magazine. One front page story was headlined '70 Marries 70 ... Divorce. She Wouldn't Sleep Without Pyjamas'. Tucked away at the bottom of an inside page was a two paragraph story about the Australian troops suffering heavy casualties in the Far East war zone!

From the end of 1942 the bomber offensive escalated, spearheaded by the Pathfinder Force, of which I was now a member. Mind you, we all laughed at the rivalry between Air Vice Marshal Don Bennett, who commanded No. 8 Group, Pathfinder Force, and Air Vice Marshal Ralph Cochrane, who led No. 5 Group.

We of 8 Group called 5 Group 'The Independent Air Force' but while the two commanders had different views on tactics, they would both have the same views about the modern historians who criticise the bombing offensive from the safety and comfort of the modern day.

The Mosquito aircraft which I was now flying, with just a navigator as crew, was used for just about every role in the aerial war and sometimes we were ordered to protect the heavy bombers by attacking the enemy night fighter stations. Many years after the war I was sent a copy of a magazine containing a letter from a former Luftwaffe night fighter pilot by the name of Emil Nonnenmacher. He was describing what it was like during a heavy raid on Nuremberg from 'the other side of the hill.' He wrote:

Some 20 aircraft were to scramble shortly before midnight. The bombers were approaching abeam Brussels. Four aircraft were already off. I was No. 5 when a Mossie (a friendly name for a Mosquito) dropped some medium bombs in front of my just rolling aircraft. Post-war investigations revealed that the Mossie concerned was ML938 with pilot Flight Lieutenant Wolstenholme and navigator Flying Officer Piper. I managed to cut the power and bring my aircraft to a halt. The bombs had perfectly hit the junction of two crossing runways. In the confusion I took, after a while, the chance via some taxiways to get off a few minutes after midnight, catching up with the bombers in the Nuremberg area and shooting down a Lancaster. All the rest of our Gruppe were delayed up to one hour and they totally missed the bombers. Only the first five aircraft were to see action and they shot down eight bombers. I would not hesitate to say that the conditions to bring down a bomber were so excellent as never before or thereafter. Thus at least this one Mossie was to prevent some of you bomber men from becoming an equal easy prey.

If the other 15 aircraft hadn't been held up from reaching the scene in time they would have added quite a few more to the total score (of RAF bombers) of that night.

After the successful D-Day operation there was a surplus of aircrew so many operational crews were allowed to go to non-operational duties. I was sent to RAF Cranwell for an interview for a posting as a Flying Training Command instructor, a job few people wanted. Our attitude was that if we had lived this long we didn't want to be killed by the stupid mistake of a pupil pilot. Remember, we had been green pilots once and knew just how stupid they can be!

We were all a bit wild the night before the interviews. There was a lot of drinking, singing and the playing of those time-honoured mess party games. The staff loved it but it was obvious the powers-that-be would not.

During the pep talk the following morning we were told that if we wanted to stay in aviation a tour in Training Command would be invaluable because we would be taught to fly properly and not in the irresponsible way we flew on operational squadrons. That clinched it for us. We were all from Pathfinder squadrons so we went back and reported that remark to our squadron commanders, who in turn reported to Group Headquarters. We got our blow in first and nothing was heard of our 'high spirits'.

Having just started in journalism before the war and being keen to pick up the pieces when war ended, I wanted to get into the RAF Public Relations department. I went to see Lord Willoughby de Broke, a doyen of the Jockey Club, who was Deputy Director of Public Relations (Service) or DDPR(S) in the initials so beloved of HM Services. He got me posted to No. 4 Group, a bomber group in Yorkshire with its headquarters in Heslington Hall, York. The Air Officer Commanding No. 4 Group was Gus Walker, a superb pilot, rugby player and referee who had lost one arm trying to rescue a pilot from a crashed aeroplane.

I was only a short time at 4 Group because the officer I was succeeding was being posted to the Far East but he failed the medical and it was decided to send me instead. Gus Walker agreed with my reasoning that after 100 operations I should be excused a Far East posting. In fact Gus and I became firm friends and remained so until his death a few years ago.

Just before I was due to leave for the east, Lord Willoughby asked me if I would like to join John Macadam, who was the chief RAF PRO with the 1st Allied Airborne Army. I jumped at the chance because John was one of the top sports writers in Fleet Street and I wanted to be a sports writer.

We got on famously from the start and our first big job together was the airborne crossing of the Rhine in March 1945. I had to look after, among others, Ed Murrow, the celebrated correspondent of CBS of America. At the final briefing, the DPR (yes, you've got it, the Director of Public Relations) assured us that the news of the operation would be released simultaneously in Paris and London, but Murrow bet him a fiver that Paris would break the story first. The DPR accepted the bet and concluded, 'I would like to wish you gentlemen the best of luck because as you fly east over enemy territory I will be flying west to a conference in the United States. But I'll be back to collect my money, Ed.'

He never did collect his money because the story was broken in Paris... by Ed Murrow's colleague! But Ed never collected the bet, either, for whereas all the correspondents came back safely, the DPR's aircraft went down somewhere in the Atlantic.

The Rhine Crossing was a complete success and the Allied forces rolled on to victory. On the day Churchill announced that tomorrow would be VE Day, I was in a car being driven to the Air Ministry. The West End was packed with people already celebrating and as we inched our way through Leicester Square a man reading a newspaper walked right in front of our car.

Our driver shouted at him, 'The news might be good, but don't get killed reading it.' By the time we reached Whitehall, more and more people had tried to kill themselves under the wheels of our car, happily unsuccessfully, and the mass of human bodies finally brought us to a halt.

Drastic measures were called for so we all put our hats on and then called to a senior-looking police officer, 'The war isn't over yet, you know. There's still Japan and we've got to get to an important conference at the Air Ministry.' It worked like magic. Two mounted policemen got in front of us and forged rather than forced a way through, telling the people that we had to get to an important conference at the Air Ministry. We were cheered all the way down Whitehall and finally reached the safety of the Air Ministry. And our important conference was a long one. It took place in the bar!

I had to get back to Earls Colne near Colchester quickly – a rather hairy task getting through the celebrating crowds – because I was due to fly to Oslo with a token force for the liberation of Norway. Sadly the weather let us down and only a few aircraft were able to land at Gardermoen airfield. Those of us who did manage to land had a wonderful reception from the Norwegians as we drove into Oslo, where we made our base in the Hotel Bristol.

Following us by sea was the then Crown Prince Olav, later to become King Olav, and his arrival was like Mafeking Night. It seemed the whole of Norway had turned out, let alone the whole of Oslo.

We were running a little short of goodies such as cigarettes, chocolate and decent drink – there was some brandy taken from the Germans but that was a real killer – so a colleague and I decided to visit the Royal Navy the next morning. About half a dozen ships had escorted the Crown Prince home and unbeknown to us it had been decided to allow civilians into the docks so that they could see them.

When we arrived we were met by a crowd of Cup Final proportions, but in those days a uniform meant priority so the two of us strode to the gangway of a minesweeper, the Bo'sun piped us aboard and we remembered to salute the moment we stepped aboard. We asked to see the radar officer – it was the first thing that came into our heads – and we were immediately shown into the tiny wardroom, where there were more pretty Norwegian girls than there were British naval officers!

The ships had stocked up for a long cruise but had only sailed from Edinburgh and were returning there immediately. This meant that the two of us staggered ashore with just about enough goodies to last us for weeks. Generous lot the Navy.

May 17th is Norway's National Day and May 17th 1945 was a day to remember for all time. There was a huge parade and in the evening a ball in the Hotel Bristol at which I suffered some embarrassment as a result of a bit of line-shooting. I was dancing with a very attractive Norwegian girl and she was interested in the various medal ribbons I wore. I explained that as she looked at them the most important medal was on the left, followed by the others in descending order of importance. When the music stopped, she pointed to my DFC ribbon then asked as she pointed to someone behind me, 'Is your medal more important than his?' I turned quickly to see who was trying to get into the act and saw an Army general. My sweet Norwegian girl was pointing straight at the ribbon of the Victoria Cross!

To his great credit, the general smiled and said, 'Of course it is, my dear,' and walked away. I thought no further explanation was necessary!

Those were heady, happy days in Norway, but there were also sobering days such as when I was taken to see the Grini concentration camp. Despite the fact that the Norwegians felt not enough had been done to help them when they were invaded, despite all their suffering they were so friendly towards us.

I learned that the RAF Exhibition, which had been such a success in Copenhagen, was going to move to Oslo so I suggested I should be the officer in charge. With a straight face I told the Air Ministry I could speak Norwegian so they gave me a list of exhibit captions to translate. These I immediately passed on to the Norwegian Office in London, where they were delighted to do the translations while I had a week's unofficial leave.

The Crown Prince opened the exhibition in one of Oslo's big stores, the Kristiana Glasmagasinet, and after a few days it was announced that the king was to pay a visit. Now the quislings, some of whom were still at large, threatened that if Quisling, the arch traitor, was put to death, the king would be assassinated. I laboured under no illusions as to where the buck would stop if such a thing should happen during the king's visit to us. Happily it didn't and King Haakon proved a friendly, knowledgeable gentleman on our tour of the exhibition. He didn't agree with the weather forecast we were showing in one display (who does?). 'I'm a seafaring man,' he told me, 'and you can take my word for it that the wind has got to change before the weather improves.' He was right.

We had two other royal visitors, Prince Harald, now Norway's king, and his sister. They had just returned from their wartime evacuation to Canada, and both spoke with distinct Canadian accents. What I found amusing was that I addressed them as 'Your Royal Highness' and their nanny kept ordering them to 'Say sir to the officer.'

One of our finest exhibits fascinated the young Prince Harald. It was a huge working model of a Lancaster built specially by A. V. Roe. Everything on it worked.

Acting on an impulse I said, 'Would Your Royal Highness like the model?' to which he replied, 'Oh, yes please' adding the 'sir' on a prompt from nanny. So I gave it to him.

I signalled the Air Ministry and told them what I had done towards cementing Anglo-Norwegian relationships and sat back waiting for the highest commendation for my excellent PR work. Instead I got a rocket of atomic proportions.

How was I to know that the model was the only one in existence and had only been loaned by A. V. Roe to the Air Ministry? Anyway, I am sure A. V. Roe were glad to know that I had found a good home for their excellent model. I wonder whether it is still there in Oslo's royal palace?

Soon after the closing of the exhibition in Oslo I was demobbed from the

RAF and in retrospect I can only say that the decision I made in 1938 to join the RAF was the right one because not only did I enjoy my time in the RAF but the RAF laid the foundation stone for my future career.

Remember my flying training at Sywell? The timekeeper there (the man who checked the aircraft on take-off and again on landing) was a journalist who had taken that outside job to recover from an illness. His name was Harold Mayes.

I next met him at an FA Cup semi-final when I was on demob leave. He was now the sports editor of the *Sunday Empire News* and he asked me to write a column on Northern league cricket for him. My first column was about a club that was a candidate for the title 'Oldest Cricket Club in the North'. At that time the BBC in the North Region was trying to find the oldest cricket club in the North. The BBC got into touch with me and the rest is history.

So thank you, Royal Air Force, and thank you, Harold Mayes.

29

WILLIAM WOOLLARD

The Time of My Life

I DON'T THINK it's being too imaginative to say that in a sense my flying career started when I was about twelve. I had always had an interest in planes but now, with a new bicycle for grammar school and rather more freedom I could do something about it. I used to pack a rucksack with a couple of sandwiches and a bottle of drink and cycle out to Elstree on a Saturday afternoon to watch the planes trundle out onto the little narrow strip of tarmac that stretched across the small grass field. The planes came very low across the fence, seemingly only a few feet over my head to climb and bank away over the trees.

My eyes were on the pilots sitting straight in the cockpit as they went over. This proximity to what were clearly very ordinary mortals, flying aeroplanes, confirmed my ambition. I would be a pilot.

Six years later I was at Hornchurch going through the three day ordeal of pilot selection. It wasn't the most auspicious of beginnings. I remember that I was pretty tense because I knew it was the first hurdle, but more importantly, I was suffering from a totally prostrating bout of 'flu. I could scarcely breathe. I spent the three days with a benzedrine inhaler more or less permanently stuck up one nostril to keep enough of the air passages open for survival. But nobody had warned me that these things can have powerful side effects. I managed to cope with most of the dexterity tests like sticking round pegs in round holes and keeping the pipper in the middle of the screen with rudder pedals and stick. But when it came to the written stuff I was as high as a kite. I remember pausing in the middle of one paper to consider a problem, only to return to consciousness you might say, what seemed to be hours later as the examiner collected the papers.

I was called in by the selection officer and told what I had known all along. I had made a pig's ear of the whole thing. I had failed. Pause. Then, without the trace of a smile...

'However we've decided to let you go on into flying training because of that scholarship of yours to Oxford... you can't be as daft as your papers suggest. Off you go.'

I've never been able to see one of those devices since without thinking of that moment.

*   *   *

That winter in Lincolnshire was one of the coldest I can remember. I was at Cranwell partly to be taught how to be an RAF officer, which was a process surrounded by unbelievable amounts of mumbo jumbo. But the prize was certainly worth it; getting my hands on a Tiger Moth.

It's easy to see why the Tiger has been called the finest trainer of all time; it's impossible to think of it without a surge of affection. And these first few hours flying it seemed as natural and as straightforward as riding à bicycle.

Bumping out across the grass field talking the checks through to the instructor: opening up to bounce and bounce, and then suddenly lifting off so that you could see the grass beneath you bent under the slipstream. We wore big heavy flying overalls and huge old fur-lined flying boots, worthy of a Lancaster crew on a 7 hour mission, and felt like real aviators.

I was lucky enough to go solo in a few hours and crowding round the noticeboard one day found my name on a scrap of paper listing half a dozen people who had been selected to continue their flying training alongside Canadian and French and Italian pilots under the aegis of NATO, in Western Canada.

Perhaps the most enduring single memory of Curry Field, Calgary, is of abundance. Flapjacks with maple syrup *and* peanut butter for breakfast; huge steaks and hash browns and lashings of ice cream for lunch. It was enough to turn the head of a chap accustomed to the rigours of rationing. And outside the hangars, a row of bright yellow North American Harvard trainers stretching almost as far as the eye could see.

The Harvard was a genuine dream machine. A yellow monster with a big roomy cockpit, a powerful throaty engine and that propeller whose tips go supersonic to create that immensely satisfying, shattering thunder. When we got on to night flying we used to zoom down to roar low over the heads of the canoodling couples in their cars at the open air cinemas. Who knows, we may even have caused the odd inadvertent ejaculation.

If the Harvard had a vice it was its unnerving desire to ground loop; that is to say to pirouette neatly on its undercarriage as the tail came down when you landed. A slight swerve, a squeal of brakes and round she would go in a swirl of prairie dust. If you were lucky you just dented a wing tip. If you weren't you wrote off the undercarriage.

On my first solo in a Harvard I had just turned onto finals after a fairly neat circuit when the aircraft in front of me did just that. Half way down the runway it swerved gently to the left and then with the speed of a cobra striking it flipped to the right and ended up lying legless in the dust pointing back up the runway. I was waved off and spent a nervous half hour or so while they cleaned up the mess. When I eventually came in to land I was so concerned about flicking to the right that I jammed on a bootful of left rudder and finished the run teetering neatly down the left hand edge of the runway, one wheel on the tarmac, the other in the grass. But I had avoided the dreaded groundloop. During the rest of my time on Harvards I had one or two hairy moments that left a fair bit of rubber on the runway but I never actually performed a full blown pirouette.

The Canadian instructors took the business of training a hand-picked bunch of European youth very seriously. 'Through these portals pass some of the best pilots in the world' was emblazoned over the mess door. The CFI's call sign was 'Tiger One.'

But I became totally addicted to the Harvard. After you had clocked up enough hours you could, if you wanted, miss lunch in the mess and sign yourself out for an hour's free flight. I would simply pack in a huge double breakfast and spend my lunchtimes flying off into the foothills of the Rockies just to the west; climbing and weaving up the valleys and skimming over the surface of the huge silent lakes. Or I would spend the hour polishing up the aerobatics. Canada is addicted to the right angle; all the section lines marking the limits of the property on the prairies are laid out north–south and east–west. So it was a perfect arena so to speak for clover leafs and figures of eight and all the other geometric figures that were all the rage then.

I obviously have something of a fanatical streak. I do exactly the same today for example on the ski slopes; working over and over at a slope of moguls until I have got them licked to my satisfaction. The point is that I had just been given an objective. We had been told that the top graduate would be offered a permanent commission in the RAF. I wanted that permanent commission, even if it meant giving up Oxford.

We stayed in Alberta for almost a year. We flew through the long hot summer when the sun beat down out of endlessly blue skies and mountainous cumulo-nimbus clouds towered to 30 or 40,000 feet. Hailstones as big as golf balls and ice all over the leading edge were a reality. We flew through the winter when the outside temperature stayed locked at 40 below and you landed between two high banks of snow built up by the snowploughs. You risked frost bite if the external check took more than a minute or so.

There is no doubt I had some of the finest days of my life at Curry Field, although it wasn't without tragedy. We lost no less than six students in accidents, three of them in certainly the worst aviation accident I have actually witnessed. A group of us were lined up at the holding point waiting for take-off. It was dusk and we were about to do a night navigation trip. The aircraft in front of me pulled out onto the button just as another Harvard sailed in over the threshold. One landed on the other and both aircraft exploded into flames. I just sat frozen in my cockpit, the tears streaming down my face.

Later on a close friend failed to recover from a spin, and there was a mid-air collision during formation flying, from which only one pilot bailed out. On reflection it seems an extraordinarily high proportion of deaths, but it was never allowed to interrupt the flying programme. The day after the spin-crash for example we were all up there going through spin recovery firmly convinced that the god who protects all pilots was sitting alongside us.

I did graduate at the top of the course but it was all for nought because even at the moment of getting the certificate of honour we were told that we weren't going to get our coveted 'wings'; nor were we going back to England. We were going off to a place called Portage La Prairie near Winnipeg to convert to jet aircraft. Jet aircraft! Several people were severely injured in the rush to pack up our kit.

The immensely desirable aeroplane that was to be delivered into our hands was the T-33 Silver Star, developed from America's first operational jet, the F-80 'Shooting Star'. It was an aircraft completely without vices and with its top speed of well over 550 mph and a ceiling in excess of 40,000 feet it was a revelation.

Flying out of Portage the sky was virtually clear of aircraft so we had an almost completely free rein. The low flying area for example was endless since there was nothing much there except lakes and muskeg swamp anyway. 500 mph at 10 feet over lakes and low hills is pretty exhilarating stuff. As indeed was slicing up through 20 or 30,000 feet to play around the tops of the massive cumulo-nimbus that used to build up over the prairies in the late afternoons.

With its big wing tanks this aircraft had a very useful range; well over 1,000 miles; so we flew off on long range nav trips mainly to places that had rather more stimulating night life than Portage. At least two of them stick in my mind. On one of them, I was scheduled to make it to Trenton in far away Ontario. I took off just before a huge electrical storm front swept in from the south and climbed up through about 40,000 feet of really threatening dense red cloud; red from all the dust that had been sucked up from the plains. Everything seemed to be functioning correctly enough so although I felt a certain disquiet in the face of this thick red stuff, I set course more or less due east and ploughed on. After a suitable interval I began to call up Trenton. No answer. Dead silence. I switched channels and made one or two more calls. Nothing. At last I summoned up enough courage to put out my first, and come to think of it, my last, mayday call.

After what seemed an immense gap of time back came a deep southern drawl;

'Aircraft calling mayday this is Sandy Point Air Base St Louis. Can we help.'
St Louis? Where the hell in Ontario was that?

It wasn't in Ontario, or for that matter in Canada. It was St Louis USA. It seemed that the electrical storm had played havoc with the instruments. I hadn't been flying due east at all, but more or less due south, deep into Missouri in fact. I spent a great evening recounting my story in the bar at Sandy Point before I returned to Portage the next day to get my arse kicked. But ever since I've wondered why some of those hot American pursuit ship pilots hadn't come up to intercept this unknown intruder wandering in from the north.

About a month later I was on another trip this time intentionally heading north towards Hudson Bay. The whole of northern Manitoba is a land of a thousand lakes; a glacial wasteland of rock and ice and snow. Absolutely no place for a forced landing. This time there were two of us on board and as we rounded our first turning point about 400 miles north of base, suddenly that comforting hum that tells you that the engine is still burning, died away. Absolute silence. And all those previously comforting instrument needles suddenly flicked unnervingly to the left. Definitely a flame out. I stuffed the nose down and scanned the mass of red lights flashing all over the panel. Which of all the things that could go wrong, had done so? Stuart in the back seat was yelling at me over the intercom but I was too busy trying to identify the problem, as we came down to 20,000 feet which was the approved re-light height. We were sitting on those marvellous Canadian survival packs that fit into the ejection seat and which contain everything from rabbit snares to chewing gum, but who wanted to make use of them in the middle of the Canadian Arctic?

Then Stuart's voice broke through to me... 'Fuel cock... pulled it off...'

Stuart, it seemed, had given his legs a stretch in the rear cockpit and as he pulled them back under his seat the calf pocket of his flying suit had pulled off the main fuel cock. Within seconds I had the motive force re-lit and we were climbing back up to 35,000 feet, while I reached into the furthest recesses of my vocabulary to tell him what I thought of him.

Three months later I was back in the UK at RAF Oakington in Cambridge-shire trying to find my way around the pocket-handkerchief English country-side, where no one it seems since the Romans had ever considered putting in a straight line. I would go out and do some simple aerobatics and get totally lost.

I converted to Vampire 5s which seemed almost a toy aeroplane, and the T 11 which was the somewhat bloated two-seat trainer version. Both were absolutely delightful aerobatic aircraft, particularly the 5 at about 20,000 feet, and about as agile as you could want. But both seemed a trifle tame after the T-33. A couple of days after my arrival the station commander himself, who was to a sprog pilot officer a somewhat remote being to say the least, strolled in to the crew room and asked to take me for a check flight.

'No problem.' We sauntered out the aircraft, chatting a little stiffly as one does to station commanders and took off.

We did a few aerobatics and a couple of instrument let-downs and a GCA and after about an hour or so I turned onto finals and brought the station commander in to land, fairly well pleased with myself; convinced that I had proven myself to be a pretty hot pursuit-ship pilot; only to round out far too high and, before I could recover, thump her down fit to bust the oleo legs. I heard his teeth come together with a terrifying snap as if he'd cracked some horribly expensive denture. We walked back to the crew room, chatting somewhat stiffly as one does with station commanders.

Landings I think are a bit like rugby tries... there are some that one never forgets. That particular one remains permanently in my personal archive.

As indeed does the whole of that summer. It was a truly great time. I had converted to Meteor 8s and I spent the summer at RAF Stradishall in the heart of greenest Suffolk, on a gunnery course. The towing aircraft was a superannuated Mosquito which I managed to scrounge the odd flight in, despite my utter disbelief that any body could get out of that tiny escape hatch in extremis. We spent the days off the East Coast banging 20mm cannon shells into, or perhaps I should say in the general direction of the target. Then we would sit and review the gun-camera film with the instructor to analyse where we were going wrong. I have to say I wasn't the hottest shot on the course. The Meteor was a very stable platform and you could if you got everything right more or less unload the shells from all four cannon into a helpless target. I never managed to do that. I would do the regular quarter attack and come sweeping past the flag with all guns blazing, to find that I had scored about six hits. However the instructor seemed to think that I had a hairline chance of survival in the event of WW3 breaking out so I was allowed to join a squadron.

By now it had become clear that letting the Oxford scholarship go was not a good idea so I joined 604 Squadron Royal Auxiliary Airforce with the intention of taking up the offer of a permanent commission as soon as I had graduated.

The squadron was housed in a World War 2 vintage hangar on the far side of the airfield at North Weald in Essex; an old Battle of Britain airfield which now sported 3,000 feet or so of metalled runway. I turned up on a still almost windless late summer's day, and made my way round the airfield. Nobody seemed to be about. I went into the crew room and slowly put my stuff away in a locker and then, with as much casualness and nonchalance as I could muster, I climbed into my flying overalls. Outside, in the sunshine, stood a row of infinitely accessible Meteor 8s. I'd made it. That long road from the kid at Elstree to my becoming a squadron pilot had been travelled.

The Meteor, I have to say, was a much maligned aeroplane. She deserved a much better press. The Mark 8s could do just under 600 mph; they had a very creditable rate of climb of about 6,500 feet a minute and they could give a very good account of themselves up to about 40,000 feet. The official ceiling was 45,000 feet, but that last few thousand was a bit of a stagger. Aerodynamically she was just about viceless, even asymmetric flight on one engine was utterly predictable. She wasn't by any stretch of the imagination a refined or sophisticated machine so you had to work really hard to get the best out of her; and she certainly ran out of steam at altitude. The difference between compressibility at around Mach .84 and stalling speed at that height wasn't great so you learned to handle her gently.

But she was a tough old buzzard able to absorb immense amounts of hard work; and she had to. We flew all the year round, and in most weathers. That would often mean carving your way up through 20 or 30,000 feet of cloud, tucked in as close as you could to your flight leader so that you didn't lose him in the gloom, before you broke out on top. I did more flying in clag within a few months of joining 604 than I had through two years of intensive training. Then after the sortie you would tuck in again to slide down through the grey stuff to do a close formation GCA. It was always a marvellous moment, as you came in on finals; flaps and undercarriage down, nose up, controls pretty mushy at 180 knots, still in cloud, to suddenly break out of the gloom at a few hundred feet and begin to pick up the approach markings to the runway. Indeed after all these years I still feel it as a passenger, that swift inner response as the aircraft breaks out of cloud on final approach.

In those days Stansted, only a few miles from North Weald, was beginning to attract a lot more traffic, and when we were on finals we passed very close to their circuit. Understandably comments were made about 'pairs of jet fighters, wheels and flaps down, cruising slowly past their downwind leg.' Until someone at North Weald saw fit to let it be known that when we were passing Stansted we usually had enough fuel on board for about five minutes of flight; that is to say one approach plus an overshoot. The comments abruptly died away.

Fuel wasn't really a problem with the Mark 8. She had a big ventral tank which didn't do a great deal for the rate of climb, but it did mean that you could get in a good long sortie. However there was never a lot of margin for error.

On one late afternoon sortie for example, in fact with a very close friend with whom I'd been through all my Canadian training, we were practising quarter attacks above cloud at about 20,000 feet. When the time came to go home his radio was found to be stuck on the remote channel we'd been using so I took over the lead and brought him down through the now very much thicker cloud bank. We broke out at a few hundred feet into the thickest snow storm I've been in this side of St Moritz.

'Snow,' I thought, 'where the hell has snow come from?'

But it's always the way. One small thing goes wrong, quickly followed by another, and before you know it you're facing a disaster. I couldn't see a thing. Fred, the number two, had his wing tip almost in my back pocket for fear of losing me; the radar and the RDF at North Weald were blacked out because of the snow clutter. And we had just five minutes' fuel left. The options seem to sort themselves out in milli-seconds; either climb and bang out, or try to pick your way back to base. It was far too cold to bang out, so we slid gently downwards, virtually glued together, while I peered through the snow for recognisable landmarks.

We eventually came to the runway at a terrible angle, about 45 degrees off. But nothing was going to make me go round again in that weather so we dropped everything that wasn't already dropped and just slid in. And then went off to the mess and had double helpings of jam toast. Sunday afternoon teas were always the best.

As it happens the only other occasion I can remember when flickering fuel needles impressed themselves upon my consciousness was also a Sunday afternoon, this time a brilliantly sunny one. The squadron commander,

Squadron Leader Tommy Turnbull DFC, had decided to put a twelve-plane formation up to polish our formation flying skills. We normally buzzed around the skies in pairs or in fours, spread out in the much more comfortable battle formation. Rarely, if ever, did we go up as a full squadron in close formation, so this was something of an event.

We all went out to our aircraft, did the checks and started up. The standard check, I ought to mention, to ensure that the big belly tank was full, was to give it a swift kick with the point of the toe, and register the dull thud that indicated fullness.

Anyway, we got airborne and joined up smoothly enough and set off cruising around East Anglia. The aircraft on the wings of the formation and at the back end would normally use rather more fuel than the rest simply because their pilots are working like stevedores trying to keep it tight. It wasn't long before I thought that Tommy must surely soon turn back to base. My fuel level wasn't dire, but I would have preferred to be closer to home. I kept quiet, thinking that one of the flight commanders would pipe up. They didn't. And then to my horror Tommy turned boldly out over the Wash as if he were going to strike out towards Holland. By this time I was down to 30.40.30. Every Meteor pilot will recognise those figures as the level at which it is prudent to rejoin the circuit. And we were over the North Sea!

With sinking heart I called up Blue Leader and told him that I couldn't play any more. I had to go home. After brief explanations I broke away from the formation and immediately switched off one engine and throttled back the other to maximum cruise. Then I set course for the nearest field which happened to be my old shooting ground, RAF Stradishall.

As I came to rest at the end of the runway the needles rested gently against the stops. I motored back the hood and let the cool air blow against my delicately moist forehead as I waited for the tractor to tow me in. The lesson of this episode I have since applied throughout my life. Always kick belly tanks twice!

The squadron motto somewhat freely translated was 'If you want peace prepare for war.' We certainly did a great deal of that. The Meteor, and for that matter the Hunter were of course both pre-missile aircraft. BVR attacks, that is to say, attacks carried out beyond visual range, weren't even a twinkle in the designer's eye. To knock a target down with 20mm cannon you have to get in close. The effective range is about 1,500 feet, which seems very close indeed when you're approaching the target at a couple of hundred miles an hour. So we all spent a lot of time in the air trying to get better at getting closer.

In low level 'rat and terrier' exercises we roared across the East Anglian countryside at tree top height being vectored on to low level intruders by ground control radar. For us of course it was hugely exciting; like playing touch rugby at 400 mph. But it must have been immensely annoying to the owners of livestock over whose premises we thundered. I have seen entire chicken farms explode in a sea of white as we passed overhead.

At high level it was PI's or Practice Interceptions; creaming along at 35 to 40,000 feet with ground control trying to put you in a position to make an instant attack. If you got it wrong at that altitude you rarely had a second chance. On one occasion I was out as a pair with a leader I hadn't flown with before so I wasn't sure how he would react. I picked up the target fairly early on at about 11 o'clock, about 5,000 feet beneath us and called it to him. I expected him to break easily to starboard and come in on a nicely positioned quarter attack. To my surprise he turned slightly towards them to put them on the nose, and then, as they passed directly beneath us, to my utter astonishment not to say horror, he rolled on his back and dived. Being the well-mannered wing man I followed him.

Well, needless to say we never saw the target again. If you roll and pull through at that height in a Meteor you can expect to use up about 20,000 feet. I had the throttles off and the dive brakes out and I blacked out momentarily as I pulled it out of the bottom of the dive. There was my erstwhile leader's aircraft, nicely set up about 1,000 feet away and below me, in a shallow dive. The only difference was that the cockpit canopy had gone and so had the pilot. I shadowed it down until it crashed into the sea, calling up the rescue services.

I learned later that he had banged out at about 18,000 feet. He landed in ten feet of water alongside Southend pier, inflated his dinghy and rowed ashore, none the worse for his escapade, until he faced the Court of Inquiry that is.

But I did manage to lose my leader again in rather less fraught circumstances. All the year's training came together in the shape of the annual Autumn Exercise when Fighter Command was called upon to retain command of the air over the UK in the face of determined and repeated air attacks from the Continent. Generals, we're told, always fight yesterday's battles. But who wouldn't revel in it? Real war games. Plenty of sweat but no blood and tears. And like all wars it was that classic mixture of long hours of boredom interspersed with short bursts of frantic activity.

We spent hours strapped to aeroplanes that were in turn strapped to electric starters, fuming over the fact that Control was scrambling every other aircraft on the block except us. And then the call would come to set the adrenaline coursing:

'Scramble Red Section. Course 130 degrees. Angels 25. Multiple targets.'

We would press the starter button and taxi straight off the trolley-acc and then open up down the runway. Really exhilarating stuff. This was what all that training was about.

I bet every pilot remembers just about every interception he has ever made, even years afterwards.

Mine were pretty inconsequential of course but on this occasion I was scrambled with Norman, Norman Tebbit that is, to intercept low level intruders over central London. The weather was terrible, the stratus was right down on the deck and the visibility was appalling. We flew straight south into London at about 500 feet in and out of low scud. Then suddenly, no more than 100 yards away sitting at three o'clock, a silver grey F-84 slid out of one bank of scud and into another. There were no friendly F-84's, this was the enemy. Without a second thought I slid sideways right on his tail and let go with the gun camera, utterly cock a hoop with my kill. But I had lost my leader, well and truly. There was no getting back together in that murk. When I eventually got back to base I was duly ticked off. But you know I can still see that huge tail pipe absolutely filling the gunsight.

When I look back on those years now I feel glad to have flown at a time when the regulations perhaps were less restrictive and the sheer exuberance and the elation were immense. You won't often catch pilots using those sorts of words, but there was real elation every time you lifted off and raised the gear and went into a tight climbing turn. Airborne again.

The marvellous quality of the squadron; perhaps every squadron, was this blend of intense professionalism; a constant desire to improve the way the job got done; and a sort of buccaneering spirit of adventure. It's a powerful and heady mixture, once tasted, never forgotten.

30

LORD ZUCKERMAN

S.Z. and the RAF

M Y CONNECTION with the RAF had anything but a conventional start. When World War II began I was a lecturer at Oxford, with my research focused mainly on problems that entailed experiments with monkeys. Some two weeks after war was declared, I was asked by Sir Reginald Stradling, the Director of the R & D Division of the Ministry of Home Security (the Government department that was responsible for civil defence) to help find out what basis in fact there was for a prevailing belief that the shock waves that pass through the ground when bombs explode beneath its surface could concuss people sheltering in nearby trenches. To help provide an answer an experiment was carried out on Salisbury Plain on 15th October 1939, in which monkeys were restrained against the wall of a concrete-lined shelter that was close to a bomb that was then detonated. None of the monkeys was at all affected, although the wall to which they were fixed had fractured.

The Spanish Civil War had also generated a belief that high-pressure shock-waves that had passed through the air could cause serious casualties hundreds of yards from an explosion. The consequence was that I soon found myself immersed in experimental work in what became known as 'wound ballistics'. When German air-raids began, first with desultory attacks, then with the night-time blitz on London, it became possible, with the help of rapidly-recruited field staff, to check my experimental findings against the actual circumstances in which people were being killed or wounded.

The application to strategic policy of the knowledge that we were gaining came about by chance. Criticisms were widespread at the time about the presumed ineffectiveness of the bombing attacks that the RAF was directing against German targets. Late one night in August of 1941, a talk that Lord Cherwell (Professor Lindemann, Churchill's personal adviser on matters technical, economic and strategic) and I were having about the matter ended with my suggesting that it would help settle the argument about the wisdom of diverting resources to the build-up of Bomber Command, were he to arrange for the Ministry of Home Security to undertake a survey of what the Germans had achieved from their bombing of Hull (then busy with shipping supplies to the USSR) and of Birmingham (a critical manufacturing centre) in relation to what it had cost them.

After the usual bureaucratic delays, Stradling appointed Desmond Bernal, a distinguished physicist who had joined his staff, and me to direct the survey, I to be responsible for its casualty and social aspects, and Bernal for the rest. I kept Cherwell informed about our progress, but he could not wait. On 30th March 1942, a week before our report was submitted, he sent Churchill a Minute declaring that while he did 'not wish to anticipate any results of the Birmingham–Hull survey', it was possible to calculate how many Germans would be 'dehoused' during the average operational lifetime of a British bomber on the basis of what we had already learnt about the number of dwellings demolished and people displaced per ton of German bombs dropped. He reckoned that most of the Reich's population would be either casualties or homeless if Bomber Command focused its attacks on some fifty-eight cities. The inevitable consequence would be that 'the spirit of the [German] people would be broken'.

In fact, our report specifically said that there had been no breakdown of morale in the two cities we had investigated. There was nothing wrong with Cherwell's sums, but there was no basis in our findings for what he assumed would be the outcome of the policy he was advocating. Unaware of this fact, it was not surprising that the War Cabinet endorsed his recommendations, and committed the Government to the build-up of Bomber Command for a policy of night-time 'area-bombing'. In reality Cherwell was making a virtue out of necessity. In those days our bombers did not possess either the navigational or bombing aids to permit of anything other than night-time area-bombing.

My second contact with the RAF came about a week after the submission of the Hull and Birmingham report when, jointly with Bernal, I was appointed a scientific adviser to Combined Operations Headquarters. Soon after our arrival, Admiral Mountbatten, its chief, issued an order that his two scientific advisers were to participate in his 'planning syndicates, each taking a different operation in turn'. Mainly because Bernal had become far too involved in technical matters where I had nothing to contribute, planning and field-work became my major occupation for the rest of the war.

After a slow start, it was arranged that I should take part in the planning of a proposed three-service assault on the Channel Island of Alderney. My job was to devise a bombing plan to 'silence' the German defences. No one could tell me precisely what this meant, and in the end my own arbitrary criterion that a gun-battery would be put out of action when on average one in three of its guns was knocked out was never challenged. The idea at the back of my mind was that the density of bombing that this would entail would be bound to cause sufficient collateral damage to render the other two guns useless. The weight of attack that would be needed to achieve this would have to be calculated on the basis of the concept of 'vulnerable area' that had emerged from our studies of the effects of German bombs. I was told that 250 bombers would be attacking during an hour and a quarter before the assault landings, and that on a realistic estimate the average distance that bombs would fall from a designated aiming point would be about 1,000 yards. I therefore made a series of probability calculations for average bombing errors of 1,000, 1,500, and even 2,000 yards. I also tried to see what the results might be when I superimposed over a map of the island scale-tracings of actual bomb plots as recorded from German attacks on British towns. My calculations showed that given a radial bombing error of 1,000 yards, one in five bombs aimed at the island would miss it, and that for one of 1,500 yards, the figure would be one in two. In the end, the assault, planned for May 1942, had to be abandoned because, as I understood it at the time, the Germans had got wind of our intentions. Whatever the reason, the work provided me with first-hand experience of what turned out to be a new kind of planning.

The third step in my association with the RAF was decisive. Bernal and I were despatched to the Middle East to see what lessons about Army/Air cooperation could be learnt from the presumed failure of the Desert Air Forces to turn Rommel's retreat after El Alamein into a rout. We did not manage to reach Cairo until the end of January 1943, and both Air Chief Marshal Sir Sholto Douglas, who had just taken over from Sir Arthur Tedder as C-in-C Middle East Air Forces, and Air Vice Marshal Hugh Pughe Lloyd, his Senior Air Staff Officer, famous for his leadership on Malta, saw to it that during the four days we spent in Cairo we were adequately briefed by RAF and Army officers, before being sent on to Tripoli which the British 8th Army had just captured.

After we had spent a couple of days reconnoitring the town and harbour, Bernal was summoned to Canada to discuss Mountbatten's highly con-troversial project to build a vast aircraft carrier out of fortified ice, leaving me to carry out the various enquiries for which the two of us had been sent out. By good chance, however, I had asked an 8th Army major soon after we landed at Tripoli how to make contact with a Brigadier Walker to whom I had a letter of introduction. Obviously suspicious – we could not have been more oddly dressed – he questioned us closely, and then asked whether I was related to the Zuckerman who published papers in the *Journal of Physiology*. When I had satisfied him that I was the person he had in mind, and he had given us his name – 'Sandy' Thomson – he asked whether he could join us in whatever it was we proposed doing. He was a medical officer who had been in the Middle East for nearly two years, and had been trained to deal with gas casualties, but he had come to the view that chemical weapons were not going to be used. The next morning he turned up at our billet with a staff car, and remained with me to the end of what turned out to be my first tour in the Mediterranean Theatre. With Bernal gone, I would have been helpless without him.

My main idea was to produce a report in which I compared what could be learnt from civic records and by way of a survey of the ground about the effects of the air bombardment to which Tripoli and its port had been subjected for some two years, with what had been deduced at the time from photocover and secret intelligence. It was the first opportunity of the war to make such a study. There was also much to be learnt about the effectiveness of our own and American bombs – US bombers had also attacked Tripoli – as compared with those used by the Germans in their raids on the UK. I also wanted to learn about the relative effectiveness of different types of bombs and fusing which were being used in attacks on personnel, tanks and armoured vehicles, a job that called for excursions into the desert in the wake of the army.

Thomson was a quick learner. We worked flat out, and the fact that my mission was sponsored from on high, and that I had already learnt a fair amount about bombs and fragmenting weapons both from experimental work and from field-work on air-raid casualties, meant that we were given all manner of help. I was soon treated as some kind of expert, and my views were taken seriously when, for example, I questioned whether bigger bombs were better than an equivalent aircraft load of smaller weapons in attacks on troops in the open. Air transport was immediately laid on when I wanted to make a rapid survey of the damage that Tobruk had suffered, and to spend a few days in Cairo in order to obtain intelligence and sortie data.

In Cairo Air Vice Marshal Lloyd was particularly impressed by what I had already learnt. He was about to leave Sholto Douglas's staff, having been appointed head of the Mediterranean Coastal Command in the reshuffle of the control of all Allied Mediterranean air forces which had been agreed at the Roosevelt–Churchill Casablanca summit that had just taken place. Sholto Douglas asked me to prepare a preliminary report for him before I left Cairo, and Lloyd arranged to pick me up in Tripoli on his way to Algiers, where he wanted me to meet Tedder, now Deputy Supreme Commander to Eisenhower, and Tooey Spaatz, the US general who had been appointed C-in-C of the Western Mediterranean Air Forces. All worked according to plan. When back in Tripoli I continued with the enquiries that I had started, and laid out a programme of work for Thomson to pursue after I had gone, the results of which I needed for the reports that I proposed writing on my return to Combined Ops.

The four days that I then spent in Algiers were taken up in what became a continuous series of meetings with Tedder, Spaatz, and their staff officers. I left for London with a general warning that I would soon be wanted back!

And that is what happened. There was barely time to catch up with the work of my Wound Ballistics Unit in Oxford and to complete reports about what I had learnt on my Mediterranean trip before Mountbatten received a signal asking for my return. Mindful of the air plans that I had produced for the aborted assault on Alderney, Air Marshal James Robb, who had been Mountbatten's air deputy in Combined Ops, and was now deputy to Spaatz, had proposed that I be made responsible for the part the air was to play in the plan to capture Pantelleria (Mussolini's Mediterranean island fortress), an essential preliminary to the invasion of Sicily. This time I was given the honorary rank of group captain, although as an indication of my true status as a civilian, I insisted on wearing a felt hat over field uniform (my salary was still being paid by Oxford University!).

The Pantelleria operation was a success. After little more than a week of bombing, with daily photocover assessments of the results of each day's attacks on the targets which my plan designated, the garrison commander put up the white flag an hour or so before our troops landed. With a scratch team of a few helpers, I was on the island the following day to plan a detailed ground survey of the destruction caused by our bombing. My particular concern was to see whether my estimates of the density of strikes necessary to cause critical damage at a precise point were sound or not.

Pantelleria was captured on 11th June. My final report on the effects of the air bombardment was completed in the middle of July, and a month later the invasion of Sicily was launched. In the intervening period the main rail centres in southern Italy and Sicily became prime targets for air attack. Apart from the bombing of airfields, previous raids on Sicilian and southern Italian targets had not followed a coherent plan, although they certainly helped to keep the enemy guessing about the likely sites of our landings. The railway plan was my response to Tedder's asking me what I thought should be a coherent bombing objective. As I saw it, the enemy depended on the rail system for major military traffic, and I had learnt that lines and small bridges could not be dealt with by the 'precision bombing' that was possible at the time, whereas rail centres were not only big enough targets, but that every bomb dropped on them counted, with the consequence that the marshalling of rolling-stock, the signalling systems, and the repair of locomotives would inevitably be disrupted.

Little more than ten days after they had landed in Sicily, General Patton's forces had captured Palermo, where Tedder immediately arranged for me to set up an HQ, together with rapidly assigned staff, in order to survey what had been achieved in nearly three years of bombing, with particular emphasis on the effects of the more recent attacks on rail centres. Sandy Thomson and a Corporal Barney Campion (hijacked by me for the Pantelleria operation) were the only members of my scratch team who had any experience of what I wanted done, but after a couple of weeks of hard work I was ready to return to Tunis to tell Tedder that a rapid survey of the Sicilian railway records pointed to the clear conclusion that the more our bombing attacks had been concentrated on rail centres where the movement of trains was marshalled and regulated, and which were responsible for the maintenance of rolling-stock, the greater had been the return in terms of the dislocation of military traffic.

Having cross-examined me closely, Tedder was not only persuaded to this view, but agreed that I should return to the UK to get Stradling to release the staff I needed to form a Bombing Survey Unit to work in Sicily. Mountbatten was about to leave Combined Ops to become Supreme Commander South East Asia, where he wanted me to join his staff – an invitation I did not take up. But he also arranged for me to meet Air Chief Marshal Sir Trafford Leigh-Mallory, who had been selected as C-in-C of the Allied Expeditionary Forces for the projected invasion of Europe, and who wanted me to join him as scientific adviser on planning as soon as I completed the work I was doing for Tedder.

By mid-October I was back in Palermo, and with a survey staff numbering about seventy, began a detailed study of the effects that bombing had had on Palermo town and harbour, on shipping, on airfields and, most important, on the enemy's movements. The Sicilian authorities provided me with some twenty railway clerks to help in the analysis of their records. Determining the vulnerability of rolling-stock, of railway lines and bridges, and of other installations called not only for accurate field-surveys and the statistical analysis of masses of figures, but also a study of bomb craters to make sure that we knew what weapons had caused what damage. I reported to Tedder as frequently as appropriate, and he flew over to Palermo to see how the work was being carried out, for it had soon become clear that the Sicilian and southern Italian railway system had been all but paralysed by attacks on only six railway centres. In mid-December he sent an aircraft to fly me to Tunis to meet the CAS, Sir Charles Portal, who had stopped on his way back to the UK from the Teheran summit Conference. At dinner that night the conversation focused on what I had learnt, and on the desirability of putting the lessons to use in the preparatory phase for the projected invasion of France. I was told confidentially about Eisenhower's appointment as Supreme Commander for the operation, and of Tedder's posting as Deputy Supreme Commander, and warned to be ready to leave for the UK by the end of the month.

By working all hours during the following two weeks, I just managed to complete my two major reports, the one on the railway system and the other on Palermo and its harbour.

On New Year's Day of 1944 I was therefore able to report to Portal and Leigh-Mallory. Portal straightaway asked me to spend the following night with the C-in-C of Bomber Command, Sir Arthur Harris, at his house outside High Wycombe, in order to tell him what lessons drawn from the Mediterranean Theatre might help in deciding on his Command's part in the projected invasion. He did not want to know.

The Army/AEAF plan that I was shown on my first day back in London included a requirement that the railways should be 'cut' at some twenty points in an arc about fifty to sixty miles from the area of the proposed assault – all this to be done about the time of the landings. I pointed out that the idea was hazardous, not just because it was dependent on good weather and extreme bombing accuracy, but also because it took little time to repair straightforward line cuts. After I also pointed out that the most economical way to dislocate a railway system was through the destruction of its nodal points, a new plan was drawn up to bomb the main rail-centres of north-western Europe, extending back into Germany, with the consequence that not only military but also economic traffic would be disrupted. Such a policy called for a longer period of bombing, and for the full support of RAF Bomber Command and the US Strategic Air Forces. After a short period during which this plan seemed to have found favour, all manner of objection was raised. Harris was determined that the area-bombing of German cities should not be interrupted (he also claimed that the average bombing accuracy of his command would not permit of the density of strikes needed to destroy rail centres). For his part, Spaatz submitted as a strategic alternative the destruction of the Reich's synthetic oil plants. Most important, neither leader was prepared to be placed under Leigh-Mallory's command.

On 25th March Portal convened a large meeting to settle the matter, with Eisenhower and Tedder present. In summing up, Portal, with Eisenhower concurring, gave his view that there was no suitable alternative to the 'railway plan'. Attacks on rail centres therefore had to be given first priority. This decision was immediately endorsed by the Combined Chiefs of Staff. Control of all the air forces passed to Eisenhower, with Tedder as his executive air-deputy. Spaatz accepted the decision more gracefully than did Harris.

A week later a new obstacle emerged. Churchill was totally opposed to the interruption of Harris's programme of area-bombing attacks, and began a series of meetings of the Cabinet's Defence Committee (they started at about 10 p.m. and ended in the early hours of the next morning), focusing his attack on the railway plan mainly on the possible numbers of French who would be killed when their railway centres were bombed. I accompanied Portal and Tedder to three of the five meetings. On 7th May, after the fifth, Churchill sent a message to Roosevelt to express his continued opposition, and to ask him to intervene. Instead, the President replied saying that he was unprepared 'to impose any restriction' on what had been agreed by the military commanders on whom responsibility for the success of the invasion rested. This time Churchill backed down.

Tedder had made it plain to me that had the decision gone the other way, he would have had to resign. Not until I read Eisenhower's personal papers years later did I discover that he also saw resignation as the alternative to the rejection of his demand to have the strategic air forces obey his command. Maybe Roosevelt knew. I cannot imagine what would have happened had it become necessary to change the top levels of command for an invasion that was planned to take place little more than two months later.

This is not the place to go into detail about the results of the offensive against the European rail network. It is enough to say that before D-Day the railways of north-west France were virtually paralysed, and that the further into Germany the rail-centre offensive had been pushed, the more extensive and immediate was the resultant chaos, not only in military traffic but also in the movement of coal and other essential goods. In the end, Harris himself was to say that it was the disruption of the German railway network that was the most critical effect of his area-bombing of German cities. Had he known it, not only was the average bombing accuracy of RAF Bomber Command considerably better than he had said it was, but the plan had been coloured by so much prejudice that Intelligence staff either twisted the Ultra information that they were receiving about the effects of the breakdown of rail-traffic, or, as is emphasised in the latest historical analysis, ignored it altogether. Alas, events do not evolve rationally in wartime.

At the end of the war, I was appointed scientific director of the British Bombing Survey Unit, with Air Marshal Sir Claude Pelly as its executive head. We took two years to analyse the effects of the bombing of Germany, and I still regret that Tedder, to whom as CAS our reports were submitted, restricted their circulation mainly, I imagine, because they endorsed what the corresponding US survey had reported about the indecisive consequences of Bomber Command's area attacks. No doubt the day will come when historians will consult the British reports as much as they now exclusively do the American (which were immediately declassified) and in which Bomber Command's central policy of night-time area-bombing of cities was judged as having failed in its purpose, at the same time as undue weight as a war-winning policy was placed on the bombing of the Reich's synthetic oil plants – regardless of the fact that these were dependent for coal, their raw material, on the rail network.

The winding-up of the BBSU in 1947 marked the end of my unconventional wartime connection with the RAF. When in 1960 I was appointed Chief Scientific Adviser to the Secretary of State for Defence, I once again became concerned in the affairs of the Service. Since, however, the Secretary of State was the overlord of all three services, my association had to be at arm's length, a fact which happily did not affect the close RAF friendships I had already made, and the new ones I was to make.

GLOSSARY

AC1 and AC2	Aircraftman 1st/2nd Class
Ack-ack (AA)	Anti-aircraft fire
ACRC	Air Crew Reception Centre
Adastral House	Housed part of the Air Ministry
ADF	Aircraft Delivery Flight
AEF	Allied Expeditionary Force
AG	Air Gunner
AI	Airborne Interception Radar
AID	Aeronautical Inspection Department
Alan Cobham's Flying Circus	Air displays organised in the 1930s by Alan Cobham, the famous record-breaking pilot and pioneer
AOA	Air Officer Administration
ASV	Air to Surface Vessel (radar)
ATA	Air Transport Auxiliary
BEA	British European Airways
BCHQ	Bomber Command Headquarters
BOAC	British Overseas Airways Corporation
CAS	Chief of the Air Staff
CFI	Chief Flying Instructor
CIA	Channel Islands Airways
CO	Commanding Officer
DAF	Desert Air Force
DCAS	Deputy Chief of the Air Staff
DDPR	Deputy Director of Public Relations
DFC	Distinguished Flying Cross
DFM	Distinguished Flying Medal
DSC	Distinguished Service Cross
DSO	Distinguished Service Order
DZ	Dropping Zone
E & R FTS	Elementary and Reserve Flying Training School
FEAF	Far East Air Force
FO	Flying Officer
FRS	Fellow of the Royal Society
FTS	Flying Training School
GCA	Ground Control Approach
Gee	Radio aid to navigation
GR	General Reconnaissance
Guinea Pig Club	Formed at East Grinstead Hospital by badly burned pilots attended by the famous plastic surgeon Dr Archibald McIndoe
H_2S	Radar navigation and bombing aid

HE	High Explosive
IFF	Identification Friend or Foe
IFTS	Initial Flying Training School
ITW	Initial Training Wing
Kites	RAF slang for aircraft
LAC	Leading Aircraftman
Mae West	RAF slang for lifejacket, after the well endowed film star
MAP	Ministry of Aircraft Production
MARU	Mobile Air Reporting Unit
MC	Military Cross
Me109	Messerschmitt 109, more correctly termed the Bf109
Metox	ASV transmissions detector/receiver used by German U-Boats
NAAFI	Naval, Army and Air Force Institutes
NCO	Non-Commissioned Officer
Oboe	Navigational bombing system
OC	Officer Commanding
OCTU	Officer Cadet Training Unit
OM	Order of Merit
OTC	Officers' Training Corps
OTU	Operational Training Unit
PO	Pilot Officer
POL	Petrol, Oil and Lubricants
POW	Prisoner of War
PSP	Pierced Steel Planking (used for temporary runways)
R & D	Research and Development
R/T	Radio Telephony
RAF Regiment	Primarily airfield defence troops
RAFVR	Royal Air Force Volunteer Reserve
RAFO	Reserve of Air Force Officers
RDF	Radio Direction Finding
RFC	Royal Flying Corps, forerunner of the RAF
RNAS	Royal Naval Air Service/Royal Naval Air Station
RNC	Royal Naval College
SAC	Senior Aircraftman
SAS	Special Air Service
SASO	Senior Air Staff Officer
Serrate AI	Airborne Radar designed to pick up German AI.
SEAC	South East Asia Command
SFTS	Service Flying Training School
SL	Squadron leader
Sprog	Slang for new recruit
TAF	Tactical Air Force (eg 2nd TAF 3rd TAF etc)
UAS	University Air Squadron
Ultra	Code-name given to information from deciphered German signals
USAF/USAAF	United States Air Force/US Army Air Forces
V–1	Vergeltungswaffe (reprisal weapon) 1, German flying bombs, known as doodlebugs or buzz bombs, loosed on Britain from June 1944.
V–2	Vergeltungswaffe 2, the German rocket, the first of which fell on Britain in September 1944.
VC	Victoria Cross, Britain's highest award for valour.
W/AG or WOP/AG	Wireless operator/air gunner
WAAF	Women's Auxiliary Air Force and its serving personnel

252

WID	Works Inspection Department
Wilton, Robb	Popular wartime comedian, known for his monologues beginning 'the day war broke out...'
'Window'	Code-name for strips of foil dropped from Allied bombing aircraft to confuse enemy radar
WRAF	Women's Royal Air Force and its serving personnel